THE SKULL OF ALUM BHEG

KIM A. WAGNER

The Skull of Alum Bheg

The Life and Death of a Rebel of 1857

HURST & COMPANY, LONDON

First published in English in the United Kingdom in 2017 by
C. Hurst & Co. (Publishers) Ltd.,
41 Great Russell Street, London, WC1B 3PL
© Kim A. Wagner, 2017
All rights reserved.

The right of Kim A. Wagner to be identified as the author of
this publication is asserted by him in accordance with the
Copyright, Designs and Patents Act, 1988.

A Cataloguing-in-Publication data record for this book
is available from the British Library.

ISBN: 9781849048705

This book is printed using paper from registered sustainable
and managed sources.

www.hurstpublishers.com

Printed and bound in Great Britain by Bell and Bain Ltd, Glasgow

This book is dedicated to the memory of a certain Merlot-drinking reference-*munshi*–I will always carry you with me.

CONTENTS

LIST OF MAPS AND IMAGES

Maps

Map 1: India. ('India—showing the Field of the Church of Scotland in the Panjab', John F. W. Youngson, *Forty Years of the Panjab Mission of the Church of Scotland, 1855–1895*, Edinburgh: R. & R. Clark, 1896)

Map 2: Sialkot and the part of Punjab bordering onto Kashmir—the battle of Trimmu Ghat took place where the road crosses the Ravi River, between Shakargarh and Awankha, near 32.18 latitude and 75.33 longitude. ('India Mission of American Church', Andrew Gordon, *Our India Mission: A Thirty Years' History of the India Mission of the United Presbyterian Church of North America*, Philadelphia: Andrew Gordon, 1886)

Map 3: City and cantonment of Sialkot in 1857. ('Sialkot and vicinity to illustrate the Sepoy Mutiny of 1857', in Andrew Gordon, *Our India Mission: A Thirty Years' History of the India Mission of the United Presbyterian Church of North America*, Philadelphia: Andrew Gordon, 1886)

Map 4: Battle of Trimmu Ghat ('Sketch of Operations at Trimmoo Ghat, 16th July 1857', G. Bourchier, *Eight Month's Campaign Against the Bengal Sepoy Army, During the Mutiny of 1857*, London: Smith, Elder and Co., 1858)

LIST OF MAPS AND IMAGES

List of Images

Image 1: The skull of Alum Bheg. (Author's photo)

Image 2: Newspaper report about the discovery of the skull in The Lord Clyde pub in 1963. (Author's collection)

Image 3: The note found with Alum Bheg's skull. (Author's photo)

Image 4: The church and bungalows of a quintessential cantonment station in mid-nineteenth century British India ('Our Station', G.F. Atkinson, *Curry and Rice," on Forty Plates; or, The Ingredients of Social Life at "Our Station" in India*, London: Day & Son, 1860)

Image 5: A late nineteenth-century view of Sialkot city taken from the fort. ('Sialkot city, view from the fort in the city', Youngson, *Forty Years*)

Image 6: The artillery barracks in Sialkot cantonment, late nineteenth century (Author's collection)

Image 7: Sudder Bazaar, Sialkot, late nineteenth century (Author's collection)

Image 8: Reverend Thomas Hunter (Youngson, *Forty Years*)

Image 9: Jane Scott Hunter (Youngson, *Forty Years*)

Image 10: Dr James Graham (Courtesy of National Army Museum, Chelsea, London)

Image 11: Reverend Andrew Gordon (Gordon, *Our India Mission*)

Image 12: New recruits for a *sepoy* regiment in the Bengal Army. (Anon., *Narrative of the Indian Revolt: From Its Outbreak to the Capture of Lucknow by Sir Colin Campbell*, London: George Vickers, 1858)

Image 13: *Sepoys* practising with the Enfield rifle. ('Sepoys at rifle practice', G.F. Atkinson, *The Campaign in India, 1857–58: From Drawings Made During the Eventful Period of the Great Mutiny*, London: Day & Son, 1859)

Image 14: The *khalasi* at Dum-Dum telling a high-caste *sepoy* about the offensive grease on the cartridges. (Author's collection)

Image 15: The circulation of chapattis before the outbreak in May 1857. (*The Leisure Hour*, 1858)

Image 16: A proclamation prophesising the imminent end of British rule in India (W.H.G. Kingston, *The Young Rajah*, London: T. Nelson and Sons, 1876)

LIST OF MAPS AND IMAGES

GLOSSARY

ayah	Indian nanny
bania	trader or moneylender
barkandaze	matchlock man or armed guard
batta	extra pay for military service outside British territories
bazaar	market
bhang	food or drink to which cannabis has been added
Bhumihar	agricultural Brahmin, often employed as *sepoys*
Brahmin	high-caste Hindu, often employed as *sepoys*
Chamar	caste of tanners, untouchable
charas	hashish
charpoy	light Indian bedstead
chauki	police post
chaukidar	police officer or watchman
chauprassi	police officer or messenger
cote	bell-of-arms, small structure where muskets were kept
dak	official mail
darogha	police or prison officer
dhoti	cloth worn by sepoys instead of trousers when out of uniform
fakir	Muslim ascetic or mendicant
ganja	cannabis
ghat	landing place
Gujar	pastoralist caste, often described as 'predatory' during the Indian Uprising
havildar	sergeant

GLOSSARY

jemadar	lieutenant
kaffir	infidel
khalasi	low-caste worker
khansama	house-steward or cook
khitmutgar	servant
kotwali	police station
lathi	staff or metal-studded stick
lota	brass drinking vessel used by high-caste Hindus
Mehtar	caste of sweepers and scavengers
munshi	clerk or learned man
naik	corporal
nullah	ravine or creek
panchayat	council or meeting
perwanah	official proclamation or letter
Purbiya	literally: easterner, refers to *sepoys* from Awadh and Bihar
Rajput	high-status Hindu warrior or cultivator
ryot	peasant
salaam	formal greeting
sati	widow-burning
sepoy	private infantry soldier—sometimes spelt *sipahi*
serai	resting place or shelter for travellers
sowar	cavalry trooper
subadar	captain
syce	groom or grass-cutter
'Thug'	highway robber and bandit-retainer
'Thuggee'	the phenomenon or practice of 'Thugs'
tulwar	curved Indian sword
yogi	Hindu ascetic or mendicant
zamindar	landholder or petty ruler

A NOTE ON SPELLING

Colonial spelling was invariably inconsistent and Sialkot, for instance, might thus appear both as Sealkote and Seealkot. While I recognise the colonial connotations of nineteenth-century transliteration, I have retained the original spelling in quotes to avoid confusion and to stay as close to the primary material as possible. Throughout this book I refer to the events of 1857–8 as the Indian Uprising. I use 'Mutiny' to refer to the manner in which the British conceived and commemorated these events.

PROLOGUE

THE SKULL IN THE PUB

In 1963, the new owner of The Lord Clyde, a pub in the eastern English coastal town of Walmer in Kent, discovered a human skull stowed away under some disused crates and boxes in a small lumber room in the back of the building. The skull was missing its lower jaw, the few remaining teeth were loose, and it had the deep sepia hue of old age. Inserted in the eye-socket was a neatly folded slip of old paper, a handwritten note that briefly outlined the skull's history:

> 'Skull of Havildar "*Alum Bheg*," 46th Regt. Bengal N. Infantry who was *blown away from a gun*, amongst several others of his Regt. He was a principal leader in the mutiny of 1857 & of a most ruffianly disposition. He took possession (at the head of a small party) of the road leading to the fort, to which place all the Europeans were hurrying for safety. His party surprised and killed Dr. Graham shooting him in his buggy by the side of his daughter. His next victim was the Rev. Mr. Hunter, a missionary, who was flying with his wife and daughters in the same direction. He murdered Mr Hunter, and his wife and daughters after being brutally treated were butchered by the road side.
>
> 'Alum Bheg was about 32 years of age; 5 feet 7 ½ inches high and by no means an ill looking native.
>
> The skull was brought home by Captain (AR) Costello (late Capt. 7th Drag. Guards), who was on duty when Alum Bheg was executed.'

In the exuberant handwriting typical of the late nineteenth century, the note purposefully seeks to breathe life into the inanimate skull. The sparse text conjures up the image of Alum Bheg, the alleged perpetrator of such horrible deeds, by describing his age, his height, his personality ('ruffianly disposition'), and his appearance (not 'ill looking'). Apart from his exotic name, the qualifying descriptor of his being a 'native' further emphasises his racial otherness. The text is in many ways closed and self-referential and the reader is presumed to already know and appreciate its context. There is, for instance, no indication as to why Alum Bheg would have murdered these people, apart from his innate 'ruffianly' character. Yet the allusions to the 'Bengal Native Infantry' and 'mutiny', would have rendered any such explanations superfluous within a British Victorian context.

As a 'principal leader' of the Indian Uprising of 1857, Alum Bheg is thus immediately identifiable as a deceitful conspirator, in the mould perhaps of well-known Indian rebels like Nana Sahib or the Rani of Jhansi. The description of the ambush and callous murders of innocent Europeans fleeing for their lives corresponds to the dramatic imagery associated with the event that the British referred to simply as the 'Mutiny'. The allusion to the 'brutal treatment' of the women is respectably vague but nevertheless hints at a sexual attack, thus drawing upon one of the most potent tropes of the British colonial imagination. Within the British Empire, rebellion was synonymous with the subversion of racial hierarchies and the inevitable rape and murder of white woman by dark-skinned men. The details of Alum Bheg's alleged crimes account for much of the brief note but are prefaced by the description of his execution and the brutal technique deployed: being blown from a cannon. The text describes the threat to British rule in India, but the skull itself testifies to the defeat of that threat. It thus establishes the skull as both a relic of Indian savagery and as a trophy of colonial retribution. The skull of Alum Bheg is the ultimate proof of colonial power.

The brief note accompanying the skull was the only clue to its origin, and nobody at the time knew how it ended up in The Lord Clyde to be discovered more than a century after Alum Bheg's execution. The 'nerve-shattering discovery' was duly reported in the local press in 1963, including photographs of the new owners of the pub proudly posing with the grisly trophy. The skull was subsequently put on display at The Lord Clyde as a mascot, and when the owners died it was finally passed on to their relatives, who kept it hidden away in a cupboard.

* * *

In 2014, as I was sitting in my office in Mile End in London, writing about colonial executions, I received an email from the couple who had come into possession of the skull. They did not feel comfortable with the 'thing' in their house, and yet did not know what to do with it. Having tried and failed to find anything out about Alum Bheg on the internet, they came upon my name as a historian with an interest in the Indian Uprising. My curiosity was obviously piqued, but I also did not really know what to make of the story. After further correspondence, we agreed that I would come and collect the skull in order to conduct further research, and, if possible, verify its provenance. It was clear from the outset that the skull belonged neither in their attic, nor in my office, and we agreed that the final aim of my research should be to prepare for Alum Bheg to be repatriated to India, if at all possible. And so it was that I found myself standing at a small train-station in Essex, on a wet November day, with a human skull in my bag. Not just any skull, but one directly linked to a part of history that I write about and that I teach my students every year.

It should be no secret that I felt an immediate urge to recover something of the life-story of the man who once looked out through those eye-sockets and chewed with those teeth—the man who in so many ways inhabited the skull as 'the palace of the soul' (to use Byron's words). Alum Bheg never imagined that, more than a century and a half after his death, the remains of his head would still be around, and furthermore be probed and prodded by perfect strangers thousands of miles from where he died. There is indeed a sense of intrusion in handling the skull of an individual who never consented to such an intimate touch, not to mention that Hamletesque realisation of one's mortality, that someday this could be myself (it also doesn't help that I am Danish).

To be the custodian, however temporarily, of the remains of another human being is a serious responsibility. I am keenly aware that I am only the latest in a long line of people who have held the skull of Alum Bheg and that it is for me to break the cycle of humiliation and ignominy that he has suffered. Both the manner of his execution, and the subsequent collecting of his head as a trophy, were acts of physical and symbolic violence intended to dehumanise Alum Bheg. In this book, I set out to restore some of the humanity and dignity that has been denied him by telling the story of his life and death during one of the most dramatic episodes in the history of British India. Very few people ever really knew that his skull existed: it was never exhibited in a museum, it is not described in the history books, and there are no descendants clamouring for its return. But returned he should be, and with this book I hope to have prepared the ground for Alum Bheg to finally find some peace, albeit 160 years late.

ACKNOWLEDGEMENTS

First of all, I would like to thank Dee and John for the serendipitous foresight they had in contacting me about the skull in their attic in autumn 2014. They subsequently trusted me to look after Alum Bheg, and none of this could have happened without them.

Writing this book has been an intense yet also fun process. I sent the proposal to Michael Dwyer at Hurst on 11 December 2016, proposing a 2018 publication-date. Michael immediately countered with an offer of publication if I could deliver the manuscript in seven months. Two days later I had the contract in hand and somehow I managed to finish on time. Thanks to Michael for seeing the potential in this project. Thanks also to Jon de Peyer and the rest of the staff at Hurst, and Ranjana Sengupta at Penguin India, who have been amazing to work with. Two anonymous readers cleared the way for the US imprint, and I appreciate their generous feedback which was based on only a few rough chapter drafts. Research for this book has been generously supported by the Marie Skłodowska-Curie Global Fellowship Programme.

During the short but hectic period I have worked on Alum Bheg's skull, I have collected many debts of gratitude. I owe much to my friends and colleagues including, in no particular order: Sarah Longair, Clare Anderson, Doug Peers, Steven Wilkinson, Vijay Pinch, Michael Vann, Saul Dubow, Erica Wald, Jon Wilson, Will Jackson, Crispin Bates, Kama Mclean, Harald Fisher-Tiné, Michael Mann, Gautam Chakravarty, William Gould, Matt Shutzer, Chris Cowell, Sarah Morton, Katherine Schofield and William Dalrymple, as well as Stephen Casper and everybody else at the 'Phrenology,

ACKNOWLEDGEMENTS

Anthropometry, and Craniology' workshop at Clarkson University in 2015.

I am very fortunate to have close friends who work within the same subject area, broadly speaking, and with whom I have been able to share and refine my ideas over the years—a heartfelt thanks to Mark Condos, Gavin Rand, Gajendra Singh, John 'Balu' Pincince, Ricardo Roque and Derek Elliot (thanks also for the company during research-trips, the illegally downloaded pdf's, the post-panel drinks, the laughing-fits and the smoked salmon. Sincere apologies to anyone we annoyed or offended along the way). Mark had the dubious honour of reading and editing the first and very rough draft of the manuscript, and he did a beautiful job turning my inchoate ramblings into readable prose—any remaining Danishisms are no fault of his. Hopefully I will be able to return the favour, Bandar-ji!

I am much indebted to fellow head-hunter Jeremiah Garsha for sharing his work and thoughts—he read the completed manuscript in just a few days and made numerous insightful suggestions. I cannot say I am not envious of his project on Mkwawa's head and I look forward to much more 'skulduggery' in the future. Thanks also to Gajendra for so proficiently, and patiently, helping translate the odd Hindi and Urdu words and sentences I would throw at him at all hours of the day. Jacob Smith helped me out with additional research in London and I have relied heavily on his excellent thesis on the hunt for Nana Sahib and the aftermath of the Indian Uprising.

Dane Kennedy hosted me at George Washington University and has been a generous and amazing interlocutor during my time in the US. Dane is living proof that it is possible to be a nice person, and all-round good-guy, despite the corrupting influence of power in Washington, DC. I would also like to express my gratitude to Ammar Ali Jan, Tabby Spence and the Jan family who made my stay in Lahore truly memorable. In Sialkot, I was extremely fortunate to have Shaloom and Solomon Naeem as my guides. They, and their family, went above and beyond what can reasonably be expected from perfect strangers and helped me get the most out of my visit.

I am grateful to Heather Bonney at the Natural History Museum, London, for taking the time to examine Alum Bheg's skull and for providing me with enough scientific certainty to let me pursue this

ACKNOWLEDGEMENTS

research with some degree of confidence. Another debt is owed to Frances Larson, author of the highly recommendable *Severed: A History of Heads Lost and Heads Found*, which has been a great source of inspiration. On a similar note, Simon Harrison's *Dark Trophies: Hunting and the Enemy Body in Modern War* was also extremely useful as I was working on the manuscript—readers who want to know more on this grisly subject are strongly encouraged to consult their books.

Many thanks to the editorial board of *Past & Present* for permission to use material from my article 'Calculated to Strike Terror: The Amritsar Massacre and the Spectacle of Colonial Violence'. Thanks also to the staff at the Gelman Library, George Washington University, the National Archives of India in Delhi, and the Asian & African Studies Reading Room and Map Collections in the British Library. I could furthermore not have written this book from a small town in rural Maryland without hathitrust.com, archive.org or any of the nineteenth-century newspaper databases.

The environment in which one works while writing is crucial to the creative process and I would like to express my deep-felt appreciation to the following musicians who have, unknowingly, provided the soundtrack for my work over the past many years: Eluvium (Matthew Cooper), 36 (Dennis Huddleston), Thom Brennan, William Basinski, Stray Ghost (Anthony Saggers), Rafael Anton Irisarri, and the late Lucette Bourdin. Also thanks to the distilleries of Islay.

I owe an apology to Ada and Max, and further away, to Sigrid and Gustav, for having been so absentminded while writing this book—and thanks to Netflix for stepping in when I should have been parenting. Thanks also to Elaine and Pop-Pop for letting us stay with them in Maryland. Finally, I cannot begin to express my love and gratitude to my beautiful wife Julie, who may be my harshest critic, but who has been a patient and constant source of support—tak, min elskede!

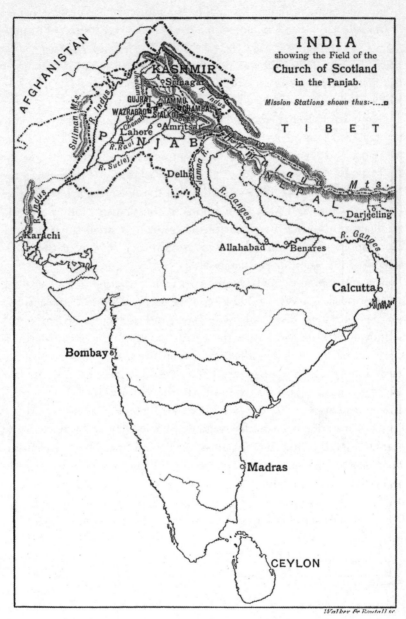

INDIA
showing the Field of the
Church of Scotland
in the Panjab.

Mission Stations shown thus:-....◻

AFGHANISTAN

KASHMIR
Srinagar
R. Indus
Jhelum
R. Indus
Suliman Mts.
R. Indus
GUJRAT
WAZIRABAD
JAMMU
CHAMBA
Lahore
SIALKOT
Chenab R.
R. Ravi
Amritsar
PANJAB
R. Sutlej
R. Indus
Delhi
Jamna R.
TIBET
Himalaya Mts.
NEPAL
Darjeeling
Karachi
R. Ganges
Allahabad
Benares
R. Ganges
Calcutta
Bombay
Madras
CEYLON

Walker & Boutall sc

Map 1

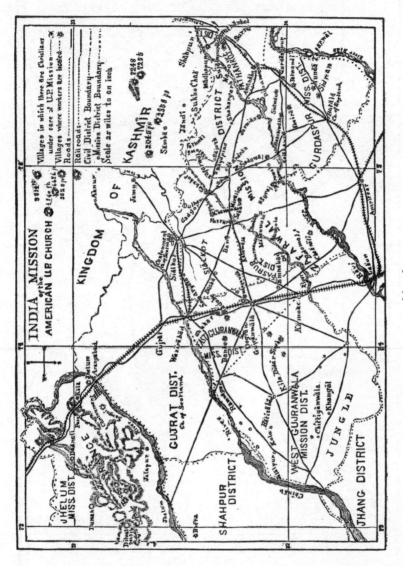

Map 2

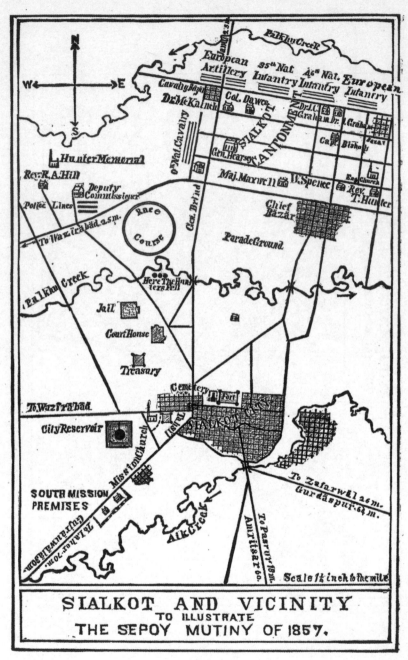

Map 3

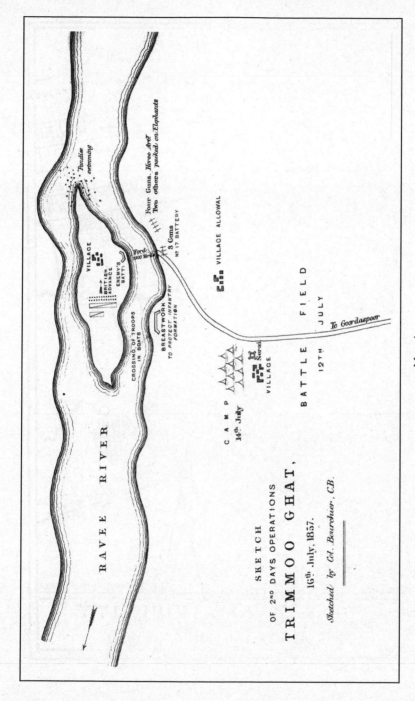

RAVEE RIVER

Troubles outcoming

Four Guns, Horse Artillery
Two others packed on Elephants

VILLAGE

BRITISH ADVANCE

ENEMY'S BATTY.

Ford 1000 Yards

3 Guns
No 17 BATTERY

VILLAGE ALLOWAL

CROSSING OF TROOPS IN BOATS

BREASTWORK
TO PROTECT INFANTRY
FORMATION

To Goordaspoor

CAMP
14th July

Seraï

VILLAGE

BATTLE FIELD

12TH JULY

SKETCH
OF 2ND DAYS OPERATIONS

TRIMMOO GHAT,
16th July, 1857.

Sketched by Col. Bourchier, CB.

Map 4

INTRODUCTION

'And then I made a brusque movement, and one of the remaining posts of that vanished fence leaped up in the field of my glass. You remember I told you I had been struck at the distance by certain attempts at ornamentation, rather remarkable in the ruinous aspect of the place. Now I had suddenly a nearer view, and its first result was to make me throw my head back as if before a blow. Then I went carefully from post to post with my glass, and I saw my mistake. These round knobs were not ornamental but symbolic; they were expressive and puzzling, striking and disturbing—food for thought and also for the vultures if there had been any looking down from the sky; but at all events for such ants as were industrious enough to ascend the pole. They would have been even more impressive, those heads on the stakes, if their faces had not been turned to the house. Only one, the first I had made out, was facing my way. I was not so shocked as you may think. The start back I had given was really nothing but a movement of surprise. I had expected to see a knob of wood there, you know. I returned deliberately to the first I had seen—and there it was, black, dried, sunken, with closed eyelids,—a head that seemed to sleep at the top of that pole, and, with the shrunken dry lips showing a narrow white line of the teeth, was smiling too, smiling continuously at some endless and jocose dream of that eternal slumber.'

'I had no idea of the conditions, he said: these heads were the heads of rebels. I shocked him excessively by laughing. Rebels! What would be the next definition I was to hear? There had been enemies, criminals, workers—and these were—rebels. Those rebellious heads looked very subdued to me on their sticks.'

Joseph Conrad, *Heart of Darkness* (1899)[1]

1

When today we encounter human skulls, it is usually within the context of a natural history museum or perhaps a medical collection, or even an ethnographic display. Such skulls rarely retain the name of the individual to whom they belonged, but are anonymised and referred to by a catalogue number, which renders them ethically more palatable. A skull in the doctor's office might affectionately be referred to by a name, but it is really meant to represent humankind and supposed to show what a generic human cranium looks like. The anatomy students also do not need to know who the person they are dissecting was, nor how he, or she, died. Trying to determine racial categories in the past, the anthropometrist similarly did not care for individuality, but on the contrary sought to identify the broadest possible categories based on statistics of measurements. This sanitised presentation of skulls hides the sad and sordid past of the individuals whose remains ended up on the dissection table or in the display cabinet. The collection of human body parts indisputably entails some degree of violence, whether it was the posthumous dissection of the unclaimed corpses of criminals and the poor two centuries ago, the emptying of graves in far-away places a century ago, or the decapitation of a donated corpse today. And even when that violence is explicit in the exhibit, as is the case, for instance, of the *tsantsas* or shrunken heads displayed at the Pitt Rivers Museum in Oxford, neither the name of the individual, nor the exact circumstances under which they died, are considered significant.[2]

A trophy-skull like that of Alum Bheg is different. Where a scientist's collecting of a skull is not supposed to be about violence, that of a trophy-skull is irrevocably linked to a narrative of violence. The trophy in that sense becomes meaningful by highlighting the circumstances of its taking—as opposed to scientific museum specimens, whose presentation in glass cabinets deliberately obscures any trace of the human being and the circumstances of their death. Without a story, it ceases to be a trophy. While provenance is obviously important for all human remains, in order for them to be considered of value, in the case of a trophy, this is the only thing that really matters. On their own, both the skull and the note are meaningless, and would probably have been discarded. To use the words of one of my colleagues, Alum Bheg exists only as a 'composition of actual bone and historical narrative'.[3] The note is accordingly central to the 'making' of the skull of Alum Bheg, and, in that sense, this book is as much about the note as it is about the skull.

Taking the meagre information contained in the note—little more than 150 words in total—as my starting point, I have sought to sketch out a biography of the skull. My ambition was to uncover as much as possible of Alum Bheg's journey, in life and in death, from trusted ally of the East India Company in the nineteenth century to forgotten war-trophy in a pub in Kent a century later. The first things I had to do was to confirm that the skull itself matched the story. If, for instance, it turned out to be that of a 90-year-old woman, then that would have been the end of it—there would have been no book to write. Analysis of the skull carried out by Dr Heather Bonney of the Natural History Museum, London, suggested that the age was consistent with a mid-nineteenth century date, that it was definitely from a male who was probably in his mid-30s, and who was likely of Asian ancestry.[4] There was no sign of violence, which one would not necessarily expect to find in the case of execution by cannon, where the cause of death is blast trauma to the torso. There were, furthermore, no signs of cut marks from a tool, which would indicate that the head was defleshed either by being boiled or simply by being left exposed to insects. While the examination did not provide as much certainty as I had perhaps hoped for, there was nothing about the skull that was incompatible with the story of its provenance and I decided to proceed with the research.[5]

It did not take long to discover that the 46th Bengal Infantry Regiment—BNI for short—mutinied on 9 July 1857 at the military cantonment station of Sialkot in what is today Pakistan. Despite the considerable historiography devoted to the Indian Uprising, the outbreak at Sialkot has not attracted any real attention, from either British or Indian scholars, and is only mentioned in the most cursory fashion, if at all.[6] To the extent that the outbreak at Sialkot is described, it is usually in reference to the Europeans who were killed, which included Dr Graham and Thomas and Jane Hunter and their child—the very victims described in the note.[7] The basic facts were thus easily confirmed, though that alone did not provide enough material on which to base a book.

My biggest challenge was that I never found Alum Bheg's name in any of the original documents, reports, letters or memoirs from the period. I searched long and hard in archives and libraries, in the UK and in India, and even had friends and colleagues look for me. I scoured online newspaper databases without success and neither trial records and official reports of executions, nor regimental lists of recruits, have survived for this period. The only names of Indian soldiers serving in the 46th BNI at Sialkot in 1857 that have been kept for posterity, are those of three non-commissioned officers (NCOs) who remained loyal to the British, and Alum Bheg was evidently not one of them.[8] The most that can be said on the basis of Alum Bheg's name, properly trans-literated as Alim Beg, is that he was probably a Sunni Muslim from northern India. The 46th BNI had originally been raised at Cawnpore, in what is today Uttar Pradesh, and it seems likely that Alum Bheg and most of the men of his regiment came from that particular region within the traditional recruitment area of the Bengal Army.[9]

As I continued the research, I turned my attention to Captain Costello, described in the note as being present at the execution of Alum Bheg, and also the person who allegedly brought the skull back to Britain. Costello was easy to identify and although there was not an awful lot to go on, I was able to establish some sort of biographic outline. Arthur Robert George Costello was born in 1832 to a major landholding family in County Mayo, Ireland. Although the fortunes of the Costellos were on the wane, and the family plagued by numerous creditors, Arthur was able to purchase a commission as a cornet in the illustrious cavalry regiment, the 7th Dragoon Guards, in 1851.[10] He had never seen action by the time he purchased his captaincy in June 1857 and later that year the 7th was deployed to India. By the time Costello landed in Karachi in January 1858, most of the actual fighting was already over, and the regiment was subsequently posted to Sialkot. Much as they had back in Britain, Costello and the 7th Dragoons spent most of their time with parades and drill exercises.[11] By August 1858, Costello had apparently had enough and retired from his commission.[12] He boarded the P&O steamer *Ganges* on 9 October 1858, and reached Southampton little more than a month later.[13] The following summer, Costello formally left the 7th Dragoon Guards, but retained the infor-mal title of 'Captain' for the rest of his life.[14] He built a large house in the style of a Scottish manor at his ancestral seat of Edmondstown in 1864, but in doing so incurred serious debts. By the 1880s he was forced to sell most of his extensive landholdings to the tenants.[15] Costello had married in 1862, but never had any children, and when he died in 1891, his gravestone stated that he was 'last Dynast and Baron De Angulo'.[16] None of the historical records relating to Costello makes mention of a skull in his possession, nor would he seem to have had any connection with The Lord Clyde in Walmer.

The timeline was somewhat troubling. Costello and his regiment only arrived in India at the very tail-end of the conflict, long after the outbreak at Sialkot, and Costello himself left the subcontinent after just ten months. The method of executing rebels by blowing them from cannon was used extensively during the suppression of the Uprising, but mainly during the feverish summer months at the height of the fighting in 1857. Three discrete discoveries made during my research nevertheless confirmed the accuracy of the note left in Alum Bheg's skull and spurred me on to write this book.

While searching nineteenth-century newspapers online for any mention of Sialkot (sometimes also spelled Sealkote), I came across one article in *The Morning Post* of 4 September 1858. It reproduced an eye-witness account of an execution that had taken place at Sialkot on 10 July 1858, when three Indian soldiers of the 46th BNI were blown from guns.[17] The 7th Dragoon Guards were listed among the regiments present at the execution. I searched in vain for more detailed accounts of the 7th Dragoon Guards, and of their time in India, and on a whim I emailed the archive of the Royal Dragoon Guards Museum, which allows you to submit a query related to an individual, usually a great grandfather who served in one of the world wars, for a fee of £15. I soon received a reply informing me that very little material existed from the nineteenth century, but the archive just happened to have a diary from an officer who was stationed with Costello at Sialkot in 1858 and who mentioned him in several places. The diary had been transcribed and was sent to me as an electronic document. The entry for 10 July 1858 was brief but significant: 'Witnessed the execution of the three Sepoys, they were blown into a thousand pieces in the most expeditious manner'.[18] There was, in other words, little doubt that Costello had in fact been present at the execution of mutineers from the 46th BNI, and it also seemed highly likely that that this was indeed Alum Bheg's execution that was being referred to. Following the initial outbreak in July 1857, Alum Bheg would accordingly appear to have evaded capture for almost a year. The final discovery, which to me really seemed to clinch the matter, was a brief notice, accompanied by a photograph, that I came across entirely by accident during yet another online newspaper search. Under the headline 'A Ghastly Memento—A Protest', the illustrated newspaper *The Sphere* in 1911 reported on a remarkable exhibit in London:

> This ghastly memento of the Indian Mutiny has, we are informed, just been placed in the museum of the Royal United Service Institution at Whitehall. It is a skull of a sepoy of the 49th Regiment of Bengal Infantry who was blown from the guns in 1858 with eighteen others. The skull has been converted into a cigar box as we see. The Indian Mutiny is a thing of the past. While we may be able to understand all the savagery of the terrible time—the cruelty of the natives and the cruel retribution which followed—is it not an outrage that a memento of our retribution, which in these days would not be tolerated for a moment, should be placed on exhibition in a great public institution? We hope that a question will be asked in Parliament and that the War Office or the India Office, whichever has the power to act, will order the immediate removal or destruction of the relic.[19]

Although the report and the RUSI catalogue both refer to the 49th BNI, that is evidently a misprint, and the skull most likely came from one of the eighteen *sepoys* of 46th BNI whose execution in September 1858 was also described in the Dragoon Guards diary.[20] It is unclear who originally acquired this particular skull, but the fact that another war-trophy from Sialkot existed, in many ways so similar to that of Alum Bheg, removed any doubts I may have had about the accuracy of the note. What I had was in fact the skull of Alum Bheg, and it was furthermore not the only trophy taken from executions at Sialkot during the aftermath of the Uprising.

The narrative arc of the book came together when I found the letters of Alum Bheg's alleged victims. The correspondence between Dr Graham and various family members, which are held in the Public Record Office of Northern Ireland, have actually been published, as have the letters from Thomas Hunter to his church back in Scotland.[21] Surprisingly, the letters and memoirs of the American Presbyterian missionary, Andrew Gordon, also turned out to be crucial in piecing this story together.[22] Gordon lived in Sialkot before and after the outbreak, he knew both Dr Graham and the Hunters personally, and he was, as incredible as it may sound, also present at the execution of Alum Bheg.[23] The final written words of the people Alum Bheg was supposed to have killed, and eyewitness accounts of Alum Bheg's own final moments, offered me a glimpse of several life-stories that were intimately connected, and whose historical entanglement was captured in the note and the skull. This book is accordingly not just about Alum Bheg, but also about the experience of ordinary people, from across the world, whose lives were so dramatically transformed, or simply cut short, by the maelstrom of fear, panic, and violence of the Indian Uprising. The story of the outbreak at Sialkot and its aftermath has never really been told but I hope to show that there is some value in looking beyond the well-trodden paths of the big events, and beyond the famous men and women who we are told shaped these events.

This book was written not just against the grain, but also against the scarcity of evidence.[24] Where the classics of microhistory have been able to rely on extensive trial records or detailed pamphlets and memoirs, I have had to trace an outline of Alum Bheg against his archival absence (but in his physical presence).[25] In trying to piece together an account that was not exclusively dependent on British material, I have relied extensively on the letters, petitions, proclamations and statements made by Indian rebels, *sepoys* and others before and after the outbreak of May 1857. I have also drawn from the later published accounts by Indians who worked within the British colonial administration, including those of Sayyid Ahmed Khan and Shaik Hedayut Ali.[26] The attentive reader will notice that I do not rely on the so-called biography of Sita Ram, *From Sepoy to Subedar*, first published in 1873, which has for generations been cited whenever historians of British India required an 'authentic' *sepoy* perspective. Sita Ram, however, is clearly a literary construct and an example of colonial ventriloquism in the style of Meadows Taylor's loquacious 'Thug', Ameer Ali, from *Confessions of a Thug*.[27]

This fragmentary evidence obviously has to be used with great care and the usual caveats concerning issues of translation and the power dynamics inherent to the colonial archive must be kept in mind.[28] I make no claims to have recovered the authentic voices of Indian rebels of 1857, but this book is characterised by a commitment to reflect the multiplicity of experiences and the ambiguity of historical events.[29] Rather than a biography in the conventional sense, my reconstruction of the life and death of Alum Bheg is thus more a collective study of Indian *sepoys* and their common characteristics, what scholars would call a subaltern prosopography.[30] Readers familiar with the historiography of the Indian Uprising will recognise in my account and analysis how much I owe to the work of Rudrangshu Mukherjee, Tapti Roy, Eric Stokes and even Ranajit Guha.[31] I have studiously tried to steer clear of the worst clichés and avoid yoking Alum Bheg to a political agenda that would have been completely foreign to him. The story of Alum Bheg is also the story of thousands of Indian soldiers in British service whose names have been lost to history, and whose existence was recorded only as a number when they deserted, were executed, or killed on the battlefield. Consequently, there are no heroes in this book, only victims.

This book is in many ways about violence and death—as a story about the Uprising of 1857, and about colonial practices within the British Empire, it could hardly be any different. Yet before the 'post-colonially melancholic' choke on their tea (claret, or whatever else), I wish to point out that I did not write this book to show that British rule in India, or the Empire more generally, was 'bad'—nor that it was 'good' either. This book is, in other words, not a critique of the Empire, which would be about as meaningful as yelling at the television (though that never stopped my father). My agenda, to the extent that I have one, is merely to suggest that those to whom the red blotches on the world map represents nothing more than the spread of progress and liberalism to the eternal glory of Britannia might want to look more closely.[32] By the same token, those who believe that the actions of indigenous people and subalterns are invariably noble, and that their violence is inherently legitimate, might also want to reflect on this again.

In my view, the biggest stumbling-block to constructive debates about the history and legacies of the Empire today is the overwhelming reliance on the notion of the so-called 'balance-sheet of Empire'. The idea that the complexities of the past can be so easily reduced to a moral binary, of either 'good' or 'bad', is both analytically inept and intellectually parochial. Simply countering Niall Ferguson or Andrew

Robert's anachronistic and unashamedly Whiggish celebrations of the Empire with a litany of colonial massacres, as Richard Gott does, lead us exactly nowhere—and leaves the past as opaque as ever.[33] Shashi Tharoor's more recent book on the iniquities of the Raj similarly fall woefully short of making a meaningful, let alone empirically accurate, intervention.[34] Tharoor's subtitle, 'What the British Did to India', ignores the fact that the Empire-project was never uncontested among the British themselves and that it was always riven with internal contradictions and inconsistencies. More importantly, this narrative deprives Indians of any agency whatsoever, making the colonised the passive victims of history and mere foils to other peoples' actions. Mindless empire-bashing is as tedious as jingoistic empire-nostalgia and while it might make for good politics, which is indeed what it is, it makes for poor history. And I am sufficiently naïve to still believe that a critical and more nuanced understanding of the past is required if we truly want to address the enduring legacies of the Empire and of imperialism that are still with us today.

My particular take on the events of the Indian Uprising will not appeal to everyone, and for those who prefer their Raj Nostalgia or Indian nationalist mythology unchallenged, there are literally hundreds of books that will provide reassuring and politically edifying narratives. This book is not one of them.

1

THE HOT WIND OF AN INDIAN MAY

In the late afternoon of 13 May 1857, a rider galloped across the plains of Punjab, leaving a trail of dust in his wake. Although the worst part of the day was over, the dry heat still lingered like the waft from an open oven. By the middle of May, the onset of the hot season could no longer be denied, let alone ignored: 'the wheat and barley-fields reaped close to the bare clay, exposed their surface to the sun's perpendicular rays; hot air quivered over the plain, and the atmosphere was all ablaze.'[1] Whipping the horse to keep up its desperate pace, the rider passed by the small villages of clay-coloured huts scattered along the road, not even stopping at the *dak chaukis*, or post-stations and travellers' bungalows, that were located at stage intervals. The rider carried an urgent message destined for Sialkot, a military cantonment station at the foothills of the Himalayas. Travellers approaching Sialkot would marvel at 'the grand and glorious wall of the Himalaya mountains, on which the sky seemed to lean [...] The mountains are far away, but between them and the eye there is a wide flat plain.'[2] Even miles from the base of the mountain-range, 'there is nothing to hide the entire range, except here and there clouds in the horizon; and even these are pierced by the summits, and serve only to add variety to the magnificent view.'[3] By the time the rider reached Sialkot, night had fallen, 'changing the touch of the air, drawing a low, even haze, like a gossamer veil of blue, across the face of the country, and brining out, keen and distinct, the smell of wood-smoke and cattle and the good scent of wheaten cakes cooked on ashes.'[4]

Though little more than seventy miles from Lahore, the centre of the British colonial administration in Punjab, Sialkot was an isolated station. Located twenty-five miles off the Grand Trunk road that connected Lahore to Peshawar and the North-West Frontier, it marked the end of the line, and the border with the independent states of Jammu and Kashmir were just a few miles to the north-east. By 1857, the station was not yet connected by telegraph, the proud measure of imperial 'progress'. Telegrams from Lahore would be wired to Jhelum, sixty miles to the north, written out and then physically carried by messenger south again to Gujrat and Wazirabad, and only then onwards to Sialkot.[5] In the aftermath of the Second Anglo-Sikh War (1848–49), the British had established a military cantonment in this northern outpost of their Indian territories and by 1857 Sialkot looked virtually identical to any number of such colonial stations throughout the East India Company territories: a British cantonment with military barracks and expansive bungalows, built along wide, ruler-straight roads and then, quite separate, the old 'native' town with its medieval lay-out and crooked, narrow lanes. Seen from the air, the impression was roughly that of a large rectangle balancing precariously above an egg.

The 'native' city, with its bazaars and local temples and shrines, was clustered around a small fort that commanded the intersection of the main roads. Built on a mound formed by the debris of an older settlement, the fort of Sirdar Teja Singh was the highest point in the area and from its round bastions one could survey the entire town and surrounding countryside.[6] To the south, roads forked off towards Gujranwala and Lahore, and Amritsar, and to Gurdaspur, respectively. Due west, the road would take you to Wazirabad and then either south to Lahore, or north towards Jhelum and eventually Peshawar. Immediate to the north of the fort, four roads opened up in fan-shape to connect the town with the cantonment and civil lines on the other side of the Palkun Nullah, or creek. On the western side, two roads led north, past the courthouse, the treasury, and the jail, to the scattered bungalows and police barracks of the civil lines. Due north, two roads led straight up to the cantonment, the eastern-most passing through the extensive Sudder Bazaar, or market, that served the troops, before entering the well-ordered lines of the military station. The centre-point of the station was undoubtedly the imposing Holy Trinity Cathedral Church, built in the ubiquitous Victorian style found all over India, and which had only just been completed in January 1857. Next to it stood the Catholic Church of St James. Just outside the cantonment, there was also a small French convent of the order of Jesus and Mary, as well as the mission of the American Presbyterians south of the old city, adjacent to the road to Gujranwala.[7]

With a garrison of almost 4,000 British and Indian troops, Sialkot was a busy station in 1857. There were three full infantry regiments. The Queen's 52nd Oxfordshire Regiment consisted exclusively of British troops, while the 35th and 46th Bengal Native Infantry (BNI) regiments were composed of Indian soldiers, or *sepoys*, commanded by British officers. Additionally, there was an Indian cavalry regiment, the 9th Bengal Light Cavalry (BLC), and two artillery batteries, one British, one Indian.[8] When the officials of the civil administration, priests and doctors, as well as wives and children, were included, Sialkot had a permanent European population of several hundred. The number of *sahibs* and *memsahibs* was nevertheless dwarfed by the local population, who in the old city and immediate environs alone numbered as many as 20,000.[9] To this should be added the thousands of camp-followers and denizens of the cantonment bazaar, as well as the innumerable clerks and servants associated with the British establishment at Sialkot in one capacity or another. While the Indian population in the old city was local to Punjab, composed mainly of Muslims and Sikhs, most of the Indians in British service were Hindus from the Gangetic plain who had arrived along with the British forces and administration after the defeat of Ranjit Singh's Sikh kingdom in 1849.

It was past midnight when the rider, a British officer, could finally deliver his message to Deputy Commissioner Henry Monckton, the highest-ranking civil official in Sialkot and Chief Magistrate of the district.[10] Monckton had just prepared his application for sick-leave, having 'long been ailing', but the message compelled him to remain in his post, regardless of his health. Most of the population, English and Indian, was by this time sound asleep, and yet it did not take long for the news to seep out. A British officer of the 52nd recalled being woken up by the bugle sound of the rouse or 'short reveille', and stumbling out of bed just a few hours later in the early morning of 14 May:

13

'the moon was shining brightly and I looked at my watch, it was just three or about one hour and a half before the usual time. Immediately after the rouse, the bugle sounded for orders; I rather wondered what was wanted so early in the morning, but in a few minutes down came one of my corporals, and I heard him ask for me. I called out to him, to know what he wanted, when he answered, the regiment parades in ten minutes with ball ammunition. I jumped out of bed and dressed as quickly as I could, and then galloped off to the parade, where the men were falling in.'[11]

Half-awake British troops were then issued forty rounds of ammunition, in addition to the usual twenty they carried, and were left waiting while an officer rode down to the lines of the Indian troops. Soon after, he returned, informing the men that they were no longer needed, but had to remain alert and prepared to turn out at any moment when the bugle was sounded. They were then dismissed. Afterwards, they discovered that the 35th Native Infantry had suddenly, without orders, turned out at 2.30am, fully armed. Their officers nevertheless managed to get them to return to their lines and nothing further occurred. As a precautionary measure, the British officers moved the guns of the native battery into the barracks of the British troops, and a company of the 52nd was sent down to protect the guns in the artillery barracks. Control of the guns was of paramount importance to ensure the safety of the British in the station.[12]

* * *

Early next morning, 14 May, Alum Bheg was awoken by the reveille. Despite the disturbance of the night, his day began the same as most days when his regiment, the 46th Bengal Native Infantry (BNI), was not on campaign. As a *havildar*, or sergeant, he was responsible for a small detachment of *sepoys*, spending the day on guard-duty or occupied as instructor in the school of musketry. According to the account of an Indian clerk in a Bengal Army regiment, the daily routine of a *sepoy* was gruelling:

'He had to wake up very early every morning when the bugle was sounded and had to get ready very fast while drums were being beaten. As soon as the bugle was sounded a second time, the sepoy had to rush out to the field for their parades in full uniform with guns in their hands. Parades though not held every morning, were regular in winter days, barring Sundays and Thursdays. They were serious affairs, rigorous and exhausting for the sepoys equipped with their full kits, and sometimes even caused physical injuries to them. Another duty of the sepoys was guarding various important areas of the camp both during the day and night—the armoury, the mess of the sahibs, the treasury, the market area of the regiment, the perimeter of the camp etc. Every soldier had to be on guard duty for eight hours a day. The guard duty involved two hours at a stretch for every soldier, followed by a change of guard and a four-hour rest for the previous sepoy. The guard duty was very serious business as the slightest slackness resulted in very harsh punishment. In addition to this, the sepoys also had to work as orderlies (carriers of letters and as peons) for higher officials of the regiment. In this way, 200 to 250 sepoys functioned as guards and orderlies every day. The rest of the sepoys participated in the parades.'[13]

For Muslims such as Alum Bheg, who made up around 20 percent of the largely Hindu regiments, this was particularly arduous service since May was the month of *Ramadan*. The Muslim *sepoys* would not be eating anything during the day, and thus had precious little time to feast after sunset and before the 4am morning parade.

The *sepoys'* uniform consisted of the ubiquitous heavy red coat with deep-green facings, the design of which had changed little since the days of Waterloo, with long white trousers of a distinctly European pattern. The ornate but impractical black leather chako cap, modelled after the British stovepipe pattern, had by this time gone out of use and was only worn occasionally for special parades. Instead Alum Bheg and the *sepoys* wore a Kilmarnock cap with a white cover, bearing the regimental number in front; on their feet, they wore sandals or locally-made shoes. Their weapon was a slightly updated version of the smooth-bore Brown Bess, known as the Pattern 1842, where the flint-lock mechanism had been replaced by a percussion cap system. Completing their equipment, a white belt and cross-strap held their bayonet, a bag for cartridges and a small pouch for firing caps. Alum Bheg's uniform differed from that of his subordinates by a red sash worn around the waist, a braided cord or *aguilette* hanging from his shoulder, and the three stripes on his shoulders indicating his rank. When on guard-duty, he might also carry a pace stick rather than a musket.[14]

In 1857, the 46th was commanded by Brevet Colonel G. Farquharson, who, assisted by eleven other British officers, was in charge of the 994 Indian officers and private soldiers.[15] These were organised into ten companies, each company consisting of a *subedar* (captain) and a *jemadar* (lieutenant), as well as Indian NCOs, namely six *havildars* (sergeants), and six *naiks* (corporals), eighty *sepoys* (privates), in addition to a trumpeter and a drummer.[16] The battle-honours of 46th BNI, also known as 'Marrerroo Ke Becan Paltan', included Assam, Punjab, Chillianwalla, and Gujrat—the latter two revealing that Alum Bheg and his regiment had played a key role in helping the British conquer the region less than a decade earlier.[17]

At Sialkot, Alum Bheg and the other *sepoys* were referred to as *Hindustanis*, or people inhabiting the region between the Ganges and the Jamuna River—the so-called Indo-Gangetic Plain. Further south, however, at places like Meerut and Delhi, they were referred to as *Purbiyas*, or 'Easterners', as most of the soldiers recruited by the British hailed from the region of Awadh and Bihar. Infantry regiments were usually composed of roughly 80 percent Hindus and 20 percent Sikhs and Muslims, while the drummers and buglers were Christian converts or of Eurasian background. Cavalry regiments on the other hand tended to be almost exclusively made up of Muslims.[18] The famous officer, William H. Sleeman, described something of the bond that existed between men like Alum Bheg and their families and their villages back home:

> 'Three-fourths of the recruits for our Bengal Native Infantry are drawn from the Rajpoot peasantry of the kingdom of Oude, on the left of the Ganges, where their affections have been linked to the soil for a long series of generations. The good feelings of the families from which they are drawn, continue through the whole period of their service, to exercise a salutary influence over their conduct as men and as soldiers. Though they never take their families with them, they visit them on furlough every two or three years; and always return to them when the Surgeon considers a change of air necessary to their recovery from sickness. Their family circles are always present to their imaginations…'[19]

As a *havildar*, Alum Bheg received a pay of 14 rupees per month, double that of ordinary *sepoys*, and this had been the rate for more than half a century, even as the prices of commodities increased over time.[20] After 16 and 20 years' service, *sepoys* would receive an extra bonus of one or two rupees per month, which according to one Indian officer, made a big difference: 'A prudent sepoy lives upon two, or at utmost three rupees a month in seasons of moderate plenty; and sends all the rest to his family. A great number of the sipahees of our regiment live upon the increase of two rupees, and send all their former seven to their families.'[21] A substantial part of their salaries were indeed sent back to the *sepoys'* villages, as Sleeman explained:

> 'They never take their wives or children with them to their regiments, or to the places where their regiments are stationed. They leave them with their fathers or elder brothers, and enjoy their society only when they return on furlough. Three-fourths of their incomes are sent home to provide for their comfort and subsistence, and to embellish that home in which they hope to spend the *winter* of their days.'[22]

The close link to a particular region and the ties between the *sepoys* and the villages, was an outcome of the unique recruitment practices of the Bengal Army as they had developed over the past century. As the East India Company became increasingly involved in politics during the second half of the eighteenth century, the nature of British rule in India gradually assumed all the trappings of a sovereign power.[23] The Company was thus transformed from primarily a trading venture to a colonial state in its own right, which by 1818 derived most of its income from land revenue rather than trade. In order to maintain and expand its territorial possessions, the Company depended on local Indian soldiers led and trained by British officers along European military principles. At the time, however, the British were still an emerging power and had to compete with both Indian and European rivals, who were also offering similar service to local soldiers. Before the advent of the 'civilising' impulse, much of the Company's legitimacy as a state power was, in fact, derived through the continuation of pre-colonial practices, which included the establishment of an army of high-caste Hindu *sepoys*. Out of sheer necessity, the Company in Bengal thus tapped into the military labour market of northern India and relied on existing networks of patronage and caste-ties to recruit peasant regiments directly from the *zamindars* or landholders of Awadh and Bihar.[24] Accommodating high-caste usages and practices within its regiments was an effective means by which the East India Company could become an attractive and legitimate military employer in India during this period. The Company thus managed to establish a loyal base of recruitment by employing the rhetoric of high-caste status as well as the promise of regular pay and pension. The British recruited directly from the villages of Awadh and Bihar, and when *sepoys* returned from furlough, they would bring younger family members back to their regiment as prospective recruits. This dynamic reinforced the links between the regiment and the village and meant that parts of the Bengal Army functioned as a sort of extended kinship network. The end-result was a uniquely homogeneous body of *sepoys* in the Bengal Army, composed mainly of high-caste Brahmins, Bhumihars, and Rajputs.[25]

The religious identity and social status of Alum Bheg and his fellow *sepoys*, however, did not simply pre-date colonial rule or reflect Indian traditions that were then merely adopted within the Bengal Army—the social status of the *sepoys* was itself a product of service within that army. A number of the religious and social identities linked to military service, the status of which was taken more or less for granted by 1857, had actually only emerged during the preceding century and were thus 'invented' traditions rather than timeless castes.[26] The decline of the Mughal Empire had caused significant political and social tur- moil, but it had also enabled groups such as the Rajputs and Bhumihars, or so-called agricultural Brahmins, of eastern Uttar Pradesh and Bihar, to establish a high-caste status through military service. This entailed a combination of the warrior ideal with the ritual purity and social privi- lege of Brahmins, and the observance of strict dietary rules associated with priestly Hinduism.[27] At the same time, the indigenous military labour market was becoming increasingly constricted as the British, with the help of the *sepoys* expanded their sphere of influence. By 1818, the Company had established an effective monopoly of power on the subcontinent, having defeated or pacified most rival Indian states that would otherwise have provided employment for thousands of Indian troops. The Bengal Army, which constituted the military force through- out the newly ceded and conquered territories in north India, provided the perfect frame within which the reinvented high-caste military tra- ditions of the Bhumihars and Rajputs could be formally institution- alised. It presented the *sepoys* with the opportunity to improve and secure their new-found status and by endorsing and encouraging the high-caste status of the *sepoys*, the British were better able to control their troops and ensure continued support from the local landowners in the regions that supplied recruits.

In order to bolster the high-status profile of its army, the British allowed the observance of the dietary and ritual requirements of

Hindus, and encouraged their religious festivals; at times, the regimental colours were incorporated in the religious ceremonies of the *sepoys* and worshipped as idols. What has been described as 'military Hinduism' and 'barracks Islam' thus emerged as a distinct socio-religious ethos and ritual practices within the framework of the military cantonments of British India.[28] Although he was Muslim, and probably Sunni, Alum Bheg's religious beliefs would thus have been an eclectic mix of popular beliefs. Muslim *sepoys* would patronise local Sufi *pirs*, or teachers, whose shrines, of which there were several at Sialkot, became the sites of social interaction between Indian soldiers—*sepoys* congregate at these shrines to discuss matters of importance, or to exchange gossip and smoke. Crucially, Hindus would frequent such shrines as well, while at other times, local Muslims might participate in ostensibly Hindu festivals. The syncretic nature of popular religious beliefs shared by the wider population, and the unique culture encouraged within the Bengal Army, meant that there was more that tied Hindu and Muslim *sepoys* together than that which divided them. Ultimately, serving in the Company's army bestowed high status upon the *sepoys* and although Alum Bheg was a Muslim among a majority of Hindus, all the *sepoys* of the regiments in the Bengal Army can be regarded almost as a caste unto themselves, irrespective of creed. The Bengal Army became the space within which a unique military identity was both encouraged and actively cultivated, and service in the Company's army became one of the most significant means by which the *sepoys* could assert their high status. Alum Bheg and his comrades were thus always more than just peasants in uniforms. Though they retained strong ties to their families and villages, links that were remade and revived during furlough and through the informal recruitment networks, their particular military ethos, status and religious identity was something that could only exist within the Bengal Army.[29]

The living arrangements within the space of the cantonment also set the *sepoys* apart as a community.[30] Unlike British troops of the time, the *sepoys* did not live in barracks or eat in mess, but maintained their own quarters where they also prepared their own food. When Alum Bheg was off duty, he retired to his hut just north of the Sialkot cantonment, where he would discard the hot and uncomfortable uniform in favour of loose *dhotis* and a light cotton shirt. In their huts, built by themselves out of their own salary, the *sepoys* could spend their free time talking and smoking with one another, with very little oversight. Although many British officers prided themselves of the close links the maintained with their *sepoys*, in true paternalist fashion, they were effectively excluded from the off-duty lives of their men. Lieutenant Edward Martineau, at the school of musketry at Ambala, acknowledged that:

'We make a grand mistake in supposing that because we dress, arm and drill Hindustani soldiers as Europeans, they become one bit European in their feelings and ideas. I see them on parade for say two hours daily, but what do I know of them for the other 22?

What do they talk about in their lines...?'[31]

* * *

What Alum Bheg and the *sepoys* at Sialkot talked about in their lines was what most soldiers talk about when they think their superiors cannot hear them: they give voice to grievances over the conditions of their service. Mutiny was in fact endemic in the East India Company army, and was indeed a part of the traditional terms of employment which the *sepoys*, to some extent, still assumed to be in place. The century following 1757 was accordingly one of continuous negotiations between the British and their Indian troops, caused, in part, by the incommensurability of British notions of a standing army and Indian terms of military service. It was, for instance, often claimed that Hindus would lose their caste if they crossed the '*kala pani*' or black water: that is, if they crossed the ocean.[32] This apparent taboo actually reflected more practical concerns: Most of the *sepoys* of the Bengal Army, whether Hindu or Muslim, came from a peasant background, in landlocked regions, and had little or no experience of the sea. They were most likely averse to risking their lives on the ocean and engaging in service far from home. Overseas service could entail years of being away from their families, to whom they were much attached. When parents died, their sons were supposed to tend to their funeral and perform certain rituals, and this added another disincentive for the *sepoys* to leave the shores of their ancestral home. Water from the sacred Ganges river (or one of its tributaries) was also a prerequisite for various purification rituals among north Indian Hindus, including the absolution of sins at the time of death, and being unable to access Ganges

water therefore posed a real problem. High-caste Hindus would furthermore not eat any food that had been prepared by or been in physical contact with a person of a lower caste; they certainly could not
share pots or drinking vessels, or eat in a communal mess. Onboard a
ship it would be virtually impossible for high-caste *sepoys* to observe
their daily rituals and dietary purity, such as cooking their own food
and eating by themselves, and provisions were likely to be handled by
any number of people.[33]

Considering the history and extent of Indian seafaring and trade in
the Indian ocean region the fear of *kala pani* was not actually a rigid
taboo, and it was certainly limited to upper castes.[34] On several occasions, high-caste *sepoys* had actually proved willing to overlook the
restrictions when volunteering for service overseas and those who did
were paid an extra allowance, known as *batta*, which assisted them in
overcoming these fears—and alleviated the financial burden of undergoing purification if they were subsequently ostracised by their families.[35] At other times, however, *sepoys* might refuse to travel by sea if
they had simply been ordered to do so; yet by couching their objections in terms of caste prohibition, the *sepoys* had an effective bargaining
tool to negotiate with a British military administration eager to avoid
any confrontation on religious grounds. The idea of *kala pani* thus
became firmly entrenched as a traditional caste-taboo, and confirmed
to the British that their Hindu *sepoys* were enslaved to superstition and
the prejudice of caste. Over time, however, this notable exemption to
service became a key source of contention in the recurrent conflicts
between the British command and the Indian soldiers.

In 1824, several regiments of the Bengal Army were assembled at
Barrackpore, waiting to be marched to Rangoon as part of the British
campaign in Burma.[36] In order to avoid crossing the Bay of Bengal,
which was the faster route, the regiments were to be marched on foot
to Rangoon via Chittagong. Unfortunately, the British had failed to
arrange for a sufficient number of bullocks to carry the *sepoys'* personal
possessions, which weighed 10.5 kg per man in addition to their equipment, and they were ordered to carry these themselves or leave them
behind. The outraged *sepoys*, however, refused to leave until the trans-
port for their possessions had been provided or their extra allowance
increased, so that they could arrange carriage themselves. Swearing an

21

oath on Ganges water, the holy *tulsi* plant, and the Koran, the *sepoys* committed themselves to protest what they considered a breach of contract on part of their officers.[37] It was furthermore rumoured that once they had reached Chittagong, they would be forced to board ships and sail to Rangoon after all. At one point the *sepoys* armed themselves in the lines at Barrackpore, and when they refused to lay down their weapons and comply with the orders of their officers, the British opened fire on them with artillery. Several hundred were killed immediately or subsequently hunted down and executed. It later emerged that peer pressure and threats had ensured assured solidarity amongst the Hindu and Muslim *sepoys*. According to a Muslim soldier, 'those *sepoys* who were Hindus objected to go on board ship and told the Mohammedan *sepoys* that if they went to the Colonel they would kill them, consequently we did not go but endeavoured to please them.'[38] The crucial fact that the British were trying to organise an overland march, and not ship the *sepoys*, appeared to have been lost on them.

One outcome of the Barrackpore mutiny, was a lasting fear amongst the *sepoys* of the Bengal Army of being disarmed by British troops and having the artillery turned against them. Considering the British slaughter of hundreds of *sepoys* in 1824, this was perhaps not an illogical fear, yet amongst the *sepoys* it turned into a recurring nightmare and became something of a *bête noire*. Another result of the events at Barrackpore was that the dominance of high-caste Hindus came to be seen as the root cause of discontent within the Bengal Army.[39] The maintenance of a high-caste army, which had retained much of the mentality of mercenaries, was thus considered incompatible with the requirements of an efficient and modern military force required to serve the empire.[40] In 1834, a General Order was accordingly passed to allow for the recruitment of a wider range of Hindu and Muslim groups in order to break the high-caste monopoly of the Bengal Army.[41] General enlistment constituted an open challenge to the social exclusivity maintained by the high-caste *sepoys;* if low-status groups could enlist alongside the Rajputs, Bhumihars, and Brahmins, service in the Company's army no longer constituted a guarantee of high status. It directly undermined the identity and ritual purity of the *sepoys*, and furthermore challenged the guaranteed networks that had ensured employment within these communities. A new General Enlistment

Order, passed in 1856, explicitly decreed that new recruits would have to serve wherever they were ordered, including overseas.[42]

While this applied only to new recruits, it obviously caused concern among all the *sepoys*, as it seemed to suggest that they might all in time be deployed regardless of the original terms of their enlistment. 'When the old Sepoys heard of this order,' the Indian police officer Shaik Hedayut Ali noted,

> 'they were much frightened and displeased; they said, "Up to this day those who went to Afghanistan have not been re-admitted to their caste; how are we to know where the English may not force us to go: they will be ordering us next to go to London." As I have said above, any new order issued by the Government is looked upon with much suspicion by the Native Army, and is much canvassed in every Regiment.'[43]

The days of special treatment, when the British had to ask for volunteers for their overseas campaigns, were definitively over.

There were also more conventional issues over promotion that occupied the *sepoys*, and British commentators identified the reliance on seniority to determine promotion as a major problem within the Bengal Army: it provided no incentive to younger soldiers while senior Indian officers were as a rule too old to be effective by the time they were promoted. When explaining to Sleeman the new practice of promoting younger men, one Muslim officer nevertheless provided a very different view:

> 'We all feel for them, and are always sorry to see an old soldier passed over, unless he has been guilty of any manifest crime, or neglect of duty. He has always some relations among the native officers, who know his family, for we all try to get our relations into the same regiment with ourselves, when they are eligible. They know what that the family will suffer, when they learn that he has no longer any hopes of rising in the service, and has become miserable. Supercessions [*sic*] create distress and bad feelings throughout a regiment, even when the best men are promoted, which cannot always be the case; for the greatest favourites are not always the best men. Many of our old European officers, like yourself, are absent on staff or civil employments; and the command of companies very often devolves upon very young subalterns, who know little or nothing of the character of their men. They recommend the men whom they have found most active and intelligent, and believe to be the best; but their opportunities of learning the characters of the men have been few. They

have seen and observed the young, active and forward; but they often know nothing of the steady, unobtrusive old soldier, who has done his duty ably in all situations without placing himself prominently forward in any. The commanding officers seldom remain long with the same regiment; and, consequently, seldom know enough of the men to be able to judge of the justice of the selections for promotion.'[44]

The *sepoys* had a very strong sense of what was fair and just, based on a set of moral principles that they perceived to be embedded within the terms of their contract. Changes to the rules of promotion, that seemed entirely logical to the British, might thus be perceived as gross infringements of the traditional terms of their service by the *sepoys*. According to the Muslim officer, Indian troops 'all feel that the *good old rule of right*, (*huk*) as long as a man dies his duty well, can no longer be relied upon.'[45]

Low pay was another chronic issue for the *sepoys* of the Bengal Army, and especially those like Alum Bheg who were stationed far away from their homeland. For service outside the British territories, *sepoys* received *batta* in order to cover the increased cost of foodstuffs while in the field, but also as an incentive for the men who would be separated from their homes for longer periods. Once the campaign was over, however, the *batta* ceased to be paid and for those *sepoys* permanently posted in recently occupied territories this caused bitter resentment.[46] Minor mutinies had broken out over the issue of *batta* after the conquest of Sindh in 1843, and again became a cause for contention following the annexation of Punjab in 1849. Due to their close links, the *sepoys* in different regiments were able to organise their protests, and 'delegates from several corps went about from station to station, and letters were exchanged between those at a distance.'[47] At the time, the British feared that the newly defeated Sikhs might join forces with the mutinous *sepoys*, and at Delhi, officers found 'unmistakable signs of a confederation of many regiments determined not to serve in the Punjab except on the higher pay'.[48] Five ringleaders of the mutiny in one regiment were subsequently sentenced to transportation for life, and the 66th Bengal Native Infantry, which had tried to seize the fort at Amritsar in 1850, was disbanded and its name struck from the army list.[49] Time and again, the *sepoys* and the Company clashed over issues such as pay, as the *sepoys* insisted on the traditional prerogative of soldiers to seek better terms of service. Some events, however, were beyond their reach.

For men like Alum Bheg, their close ties to their villages also created tension in terms of loyalty. When the British annexed Awadh in 1856, effectively usurping the control of the *sepoys'* homeland, it had a far greater impact on their troops than the British ever realised. The British dispossessed the King of Awadh on the pretext of his alleged despotic misrule, and the takeover caused immense disruption in the region.[50] The police officer, Shaik Hedayut Ali, explained the sense of betrayal experienced by the *sepoys* over what they perceived as an illegitimate annexation: 'They were all of opinion that the Government had acted unjustly in annexing the country of Oude, and they all sympathised with the king and his Sirdars.'[51] The *sepoys*, Hedayut continued, 'were all indignant at the king of Oude being dispossessed of his kingdom, and talked openly amongst themselves as to the little faith that could be placed in the English after their treatment of the king, who himself and his progenitors had been so faithful to them.'[52] Part of the *sepoys'* objection thus appears to have been that the British had proven themselves to be duplicitous in their dealings with the King of Awadh, and the moral legitimacy of their rule thus undermined. It did not help that the entire army of the King, some 50,000 men, were disbanded, again bringing into question the long-term political strategy of the British in India. 'Oude was the birthplace of the Purbeah race,' according to Mainodin Hassan Khan, an Indian police officer well acquainted with the *sepoys*,

'and these feelings of dissatisfaction affected the whole Purbeah race in the service of the British Government. To the native mind the act of annexation was one of gross injustice, and provoked a universal desire for resistance. The King, and all those connected with him, although bowing to the hand of fate, became henceforward the bitter enemies of the English.'[53]

As a sign of things to come, the annexation had in 1856 prompted *sepoys* of the 34th BNI to send letters to their brothers in other regiments of the Bengal Army:

'These letters reminded every regiment of the ancient dynasties of Hindustan; pointed out that the annexation of Oude had been followed by the disbandment of the Oude army, for the second time since the connection of the English with Oude; and showed that their place was being filled by the enlistment of Punjabis and Sikhs, and the formation of a Punjab army. The very bread had been torn out of the mouths of men who knew no other profession than that of the sword. The letters went on to say that further annexations might be expected, with little or no use for the native army. Thus was it pressed upon the Sepoys that they must rebel to reseat the ancient kings on their thrones, and drive the trespassers away. The welfare of the soldier caste required this; the honour of their chiefs was at stake.'[54]

By thus tying together the annexation of Awadh with the General Enlistment, the letter pointed to a concerted effort on part of the British to undermine the very livelihood of the *sepoys*, and by extension the well-being of their families. Resisting British reforms within the army was thus presented as a matter of duty upon which the *izzat*, or honour, of the *sepoys* ultimately depended. What the British were doing in India more generally, and the changes that were taking place within the Bengal Army more specifically, were in other words perceived as part of the same existential threat. British officers at the time had but a vague sense of the range of issues that concerned their Indian troops—and rarely any real understanding of the nature of their grievances. When Shaik Hedayut described the widespread resentment of the *sepoys*, he added that:

> 'Don't let any English gentlemen think that the above is not true because they were not acquainted with it at the time: a native of Hindoostan seldom opens his mind to his officer; he only says what he thinks would please his Officer. The Sepoys reserve their real opinion until they return to their lines and to their comrades.'[55]

* * *

While Alum Bheg and his men would head back to their huts after a long day of parades and guard-duty, the British population of Sialkot took shelter in their bungalows, which they tried in vain to insulate against the punishing heat:

> 'thatched shades had been erected over our doors to break the glare; *khaskhas* mats had been placed in the doorways, with water at hand for sprinkling; windows had been darkened, *pan'khas* swung up, and arrangements made in general for keeping the heat out, and maintaining a cool temperature within; and to avoid all needless exposure, the programme

for out-door work had been shifted to the cooler hours of the morning and evening...'[56]

Dr James Graham, the Superintending Surgeon at Sialkot, and his daughter Sarah were making the final preparations for their upcoming trip to the hills—the annual ritual for so many Anglo-Indian families to escape the warm weather of the plains.[57] The Grahams were one of those extensive Protestant Irish families with close links to India and they were well-acquainted with the Lawrences—John Lawrence was then Chief Commissioner of Punjab and his younger brother Richard Lawrence, Captain of Police at Lahore. As the senior member of the family, Dr Graham was much concerned with the future of the family, and preoccupied with arranging marriages and manoeuvring relatives into good positions within the Company administration. Dr Graham had no less than three sons serving in the Bengal army, as well as his nephew, also named James Graham, who was an officer in the 14th BNI. Dr Graham had made substantive investments in the stocks of the Delhi Bank and although Sarah's mother had passed away, father and daughter 'lived in splendid style', according to one Sialkot resident, 'like a prince upon his three thousand rupees a month.'[58] The Graham residence, 'the finest in the whole station', was located just behind the barracks of the European infantry and the 46th BNI lines on the very northern side of the cantonment.'[59] In a letter to his nephew James at Landour, Graham wrote excitedly of the hill-station north-east of Jammu that he and Sarah had decided upon:

'It is by far the finest site for a convalescent depot of any yet discovered in India. At the top of this mountain you have level ground extending sixteen miles, no thick bush jungle, no thick forest, but wooded like a nobleman's park. It is from eight to nine thousand feet high with a beautiful puka fountain which pours out water throughout the year...'[60]

Their departure was planned for 16 May to 'escape the hot winds, the furnace heat of which you know I dislike.'[61]

Others, however, were prepared to brave the weather and stay in Sialkot during the hot season. Just a few bungalows down the road, right next to the church, Reverend Thomas Hunter and his wife Jane were doubling down on their arduous schedule of missionary work.[62] Hunter had been ordained just two years before with the explicit purpose of establishing the Church of Scotland Punjab mission. Punjab had only just been opened up by the British conquest, and for missionaries so concerned with carving out their own kingdom in which to spread their particular interpretation of the gospel, this made the region particularly attractive. Thomas had married Jane Scott, a devout Sunday school teacher, the very same day he was ordained and a month later they had set out for India. Photographs taken of the couple before they left Scotland show Thomas to be stern-looking, with rimless glasses and a puritan beard, while Jane appeared quite mirthless and dressed all in black. After arriving in India, Thomas Hunter decided upon Sialkot as the site of the mission, writing to his church back in Scotland:

> 'Permit me with the utmost respect and *diffidence* to give a sketch of a plan of operations we have often dwelt upon as likely, under the blessing of Almighty God, to further the cause of Christ in the Panjab. Of course the conversion of souls, not the education of the young, is the Church's design in sending her ministers to India. The time was when education was the only means open to our Church, and with praiseworthy zeal have we lavished large sums in preparing—simply preparing—ground for the reception of good seed, for educated men do listen to, and reason on, Bible truth. But now the Government comes forward, and offers to take the work off our hands. Is not this a call to redouble our exertions in teaching and preaching Christ crucified? And how? If you still propose entrusting me with the Church's work in the Panjab, I should humbly propose that no educational institution be formed, but that I should be as one of the natives, never resting until I have thoroughly mastered the language and customs of the country, and also labouring, in season and out of season, to proclaim the great salvation, directly, faithfully, fearlessly [...] I am perfectly willing to go alone, and commence the work. If health be granted me, you will always have one labourer in possession of this highly interesting field; if the Lord be pleased to lay me aside, and also my truly missionary wife, still, even this will not be such a loss, as if an institution were depending for life on one. [...] I should not write so strongly did I not see and feel the importance of very early embracing an opportunity thus presented us for preaching and teaching nothing but the doctrine of the Cross.'[63]

The eager missionary accordingly proposed to embark on a mission of pure preaching, leaving aside the education of Indians, which was the usual strategy favoured by missionaries as a gateway to conversion. In the same letter, Thomas Hunter had also pointed out that Sialkot 'is a station for European troops, and thus perfectly safe.'[64]

The couple arrived at Sialkot with their new-born son in December 1856 following an arduous three-month journey of more than 1,700 miles from Bombay, during which they had been much plagued by sickness.[65] They brought along a Muslim convert, Mohamet Ismael, to help in their work, but found to their consternation that Sialkot was not the virgin soil they had imagined it to be. Apart from the cantonment church and the Catholic chapel, the American Presbyterian Church had just built a mission just south of the old city, while French lay-nuns had recently established a convent on the western outskirts of the cantonment. The Hunters had been beaten to the draw and, considering its size, Sialkot was by the beginning of 1857 practically overrun by zealous Christians. This is not to say that Hunter's rivals had had much success. The American mission had been struggling from the outset and apart from a small school for non-Christian boys, their orphanage had just three children, with two Indian catechists in training. After two years, they had made not a single convert in spite of a vigorous, if somewhat amateurish, programme of preaching at markets and fairs in Sialkot and the surrounding villages. The American missionaries were notably poor and only survived by the charity of British officials and other clergymen when the meagre financial support from the home church in far-away America failed to arrive.[66] The head of the mission, Andrew Gordon, was nevertheless worried about his 'turf' when the Hunters arrived and set up camp, noting grumpily that when the newcomers 'set out for this field with the design of opening in it a new mission, they seem not to have been aware that it was already efficiently occupied, whilst other needy and inviting fields lay before them.'[67] Gordon, however, managed to overcome his initial misgivings of the Hunters and the two groups of missionaries eventually established a friendly relationship and divided up their respective areas of proselytising. With the American mission south of the city, Thomas and his wife moved into a house in the cantonment to the north, between the church and the Sudder Bazaar.[68] 'Instead of proving an objection', Hunter sought to convince his church back home, the presence of the American missionaries 'is likely to be a great advantage. We can heartily co-operate, and enjoy the results of their Christian as well as missionary experience. They are also about three miles away on the farther side of town; so they cannot interfere with our operations.'[69]

With the field of operations established, Thomas Hunter now had to face the reality of his project. The formerly ambitious Reverend Hunter had to explain to his church how the actual situation differed from what he envisaged:

> 'I had hoped to lay before you our plan of operations: it is not matured; let, me therefore, beg a little time. The *end*, the conversion of souls, is indelibly impressed; the *means* for the accomplishments of the glorious object have not yet come fully before me. This is a time when, we hope, prayers will ascend by us and for us, that the Lord Jehovah would manifest His own glory.'[70]

Thomas and Jane Hunter thus found themselves settled at Sialkot with much to prove to their congregation back home. Thomas had to go back on his disavowal of teaching, as a means to proselytise, and soon established two small vernacular schools, one for boys and one for girls. Additionally, they held a Sunday service in Hindi for an audience consisting mainly of their own servants, as well as services for the British officers and troops at the station.[71] These activities occupied all their time, and despite the fact that they had a nine-month-old son, a trip to the cooler climate of the hills in the summer was a luxury they could ill afford. Neither could their friends in the American mission who lived on a shoestring budget. Andrew Gordon had originally chosen Sialkot because of its reputedly mild climate, yet the summer heat still proved unbearable to a native of Allegheny, North Carolina:

> 'As when the chilling blast of December from the frigid north sweeps down upon the United States, driving pulverised snow through every key-hole and crevice, imperilling the life of every one who ventures out, so the hot wind of an Indian May or June, surcharged with double-refined dust, penetrates our dwellings, withers and scorches those who expose themselves, and sets all our foreign blood simmering.'[72]

In the morning of 14 May, after the arrival of the messenger, and the nights' turmoil in the cantonment, things were still quiet south of the city. By 9am, however, Gordon and his little congregation, which included his wife Rebecca, his sister and two other American missionaries and their families, were interrupted by a trooper in uniform, riding a fleet horse, who rushed up to the bungalow with an urgent message from the Deputy Commissioner:

'My Dear Mr. Gordon:—Please suspend your preaching for a season—
especially do not allow your native preachers to go about. Have you heard
that *Delhi has been taken by the mutineers, and the European population massacred?* This reached me last night by express. The *Dak* [post] is cut off, and
the electric telegraph broken. Please do not mention this to any native.

Yours sincerely, H. Monckton'[73]

The American missionaries did not dare to leave their compound
and stayed inside all day—none of the adults had any appetite as they
sat down for lunch and only the children ate, blissfully unaware of the
fears that wracked their parents. A few hours later, Gordon received
another letter brought by special messenger, this time from an acquaintance in Lahore and with more details of what had occurred in the
south. The news confirmed their worst fears:

'I am sorry to tell you that the bridge of boats at Delhi was captured by
150 mutineers from the 3rd Light Cavalry at Meerut. The 54th native infantry was ordered out against them, but refused to obey, and joined the
mutineers; and their officers, I hear, are killed. Col. Ripley commanding
the 54th, is mentioned as killed. The whole of the native population of
Delhi have risen; and I fancy by this time every Christian in Delhi is murdered. The Commissioner, Mr. Fraser, Captain Douglass commanding the
palace guards, Mr. Beresford of the Delhi bank, and others were murdered
when the telegraph message was sent, and they expected to share the same
fate. The magazine had fallen into the hands of the mutineers. The native
troops at Lahore have all been disarmed. This is sad news.'[74]

At Delhi, the two assistants at the telegraph office had been frantically messaging their colleagues in Ambala, as the situation grew
increasingly worse. Their final message sent during the afternoon of the
11th, before they had to flee for their lives, had been rather terse:
'Several officers killed and wounded. City is in a state of considerable
excitement. Troops sent down, but nothing known yet. Information
will be forwarded.'[75] That message hardly conveyed the true extent of
the disaster that had befallen the British at Delhi, but since then, more
details had emerged and the news that reached Gordon and the others
at Sialkot on 14 May sent them into a state of panic. Gordon's little
son, Silas, was sick with fever at the time and Dr Graham had explicitly
forbidden that he be exposed to the sun, which meant that fleeing was
out of the question. Where exactly they would have fled to, was an

altogether different question. Their situation seemed desperate as Gordon later recalled:

'Between us and the nearest sea-board town, with fourteen hundred miles of staging as the fastest mode of travelling, a thousand deaths intervened. Successful disguise was exceedingly difficult. We could easily change our costume and complexion, if that were all; but to walk and talk, eat and drink without betraying ourselves, would perhaps be impossible; nor could we conceal ourselves in a dark hole and lie dormant, as some animals do in order to escape observation. Yet we all instinctively set about bundling up a few necessary articles ready to be snatched and carried with us whithersoever a sudden emergency might impel us.'[76]

Prompted by Monckton's warning not to mention the news to any Indians, Gordon and the missionaries began looking at their servants and the locals outside the compound with a new-found suspicion bordering on paranoia, 'for it was impossible to know who could be trusted.'[77] In India, even poor Europeans lived surrounded by 'native' servants who attended to the most intimate aspects of daily life: Indian *ayahs* looked after the white children, a local watchman guarded the entry to the house, a local cook prepared the food. The notion that local servants, or slaves, should turn on their masters was one of the oldest fears in colonial societies—and it was a fear that materialised along racial lines, as each and every Indian suddenly became a potential threat. The acute sense of vulnerability and uncertainty was given full expression in Gordon's description of the missionaries' fears as they huddled together within their bungalow on that long, hot afternoon:

'"Do they know what we know?" we whispered anxiously one to another. Our very appearance must reveal to them that something appalling is apprehended. Surely they cannot fail to see anxious forebodings written in our very faces. Hark! Have our Sepoys risen? Is that the sound of arms, or only fireworks of some wedding party? Who are these native troopers galloping at such unusual speed?—Oh! These dark visaged Moslems and pagans of solemn mien—how sullenly they seem to move about! How deceitful and treacherous we know them to be! If they have heard it, why should they feign absolute ignorance? Their silence is ominous! They would sell our heads for a penny apiece; and every one of them looks as if he might be an assassin waiting his opportunity.'[78]

Finally, after eight hours of tense waiting, Gordon, another American missionary and one of the Indian converts ventured outside to gather news and perhaps get a sense of what they should do next. In the marginally cooler afternoon, they made their way through the city, up to the house of District Commissioner Monckton in the civil lines. At Monckton's house, they found the Commissioner seated at dinner along with two guests, Captain C.A. McMahon, the assistant commissioner, and Reverend W. Boyle, the chaplain of the station. Much like the American missionaries, the trio had little appetite, and were,

> 'not eating, but endeavouring to go through the form, for the purpose of keeping up appearances before the Indian servants. Muhammadan waiters in snow-white costume, girded about the waist with redundant girdles, were standing behind their masters, as solemn as elders[79], ever and anon gliding out and in as noiselessly, on their bare feet, as if they had been so many black-faced ghosts; and all direct allusion, in their hearing, to impending danger was studiously avoided.'[80]

Despite the absurdity of the situation, Monckton managed to convey to the Gordon and the others that he was as much in the dark as they were and had no advise or reassurance to offer. Monckton was not even sure whether the Indian policemen under his command, who were quartered near the house, were to be relied upon and 'instead of being any longer a source of confidence and strength, had become a source of weakness and danger.'[81] As the missionaries were leaving, still fearful and none the wiser, Reverend Boyle, visibly excited and constantly looking over his shoulders lest someone should listen, walked them to the door and implored Brother Scott, the Indian convert: 'Now, Scott, is the time for you. You are a native, and you know the natives. If you can obtain information for the Government you will be well rewarded.'[82] Boyle's wild-eyed plea to Scott belied the notion that the British truly knew the land, and during times of crisis, it was 'native' informants who came to be relied on. The fact that Scott was a Christian, meant that he was exempted from the suspicion that attached itself to all other Indians at the time.

Gordon and the two others then drove over to Colonel Dawes, commanding the European artillery, and who was also in charge of the school of musketry. Although the old officers was rather more composed than the civilian authorities had been, 'Still he felt it necessary to converse in a quiet tone, occasionally dropping a sentence in the middle, or finishing it enigmatically when he saw natives approaching, because, as he remarked, many of them know enough English to catch a word here and a word there, and make out the subject of our conversation.'[83] Dawes advised the missionaries to move into a nearby bungalow, whose owner had gone to the hills, rather than to risk remaining at the isolated compound south of the city where help would be difficult to get should the need arise. The result was that Gordon, his family and the four other missionary families, altogether some thirty-two people, moved up to the empty house right at the edge of the cantonment. The missionaries were now as far from the city as they could be, but in dangerous proximity to the *sepoys'* lines. 'As soon as our mission band had taken refuge in this place of comparative safety,' Gordon noted, 'a rumour spread throughout the Cantonment that the Sepoys purposed to mutiny that very night, and murder all the English. In case they should mutiny, we were instructed to escape if possible to the barracks [*of the British troops*] one hundred and fifty yards north of the house.'[84] Once installed, the missionaries organised themselves into two groups: one was to keep watch from the flat roof of the house, while the other group was engaged in praying throughout the night. Gordon himself felt safer sitting on the ground outside the house in the dark, hoping that in the event of a disturbance, he might be mistaken for an Indian: 'Our white faces, European dress and houses are our great danger.'[85] In any event, nothing happened and all the Europeans— including Andrew Gordon, Dr Graham, his daughter Sarah, and Thomas and Jane Hunter with their small son—could breathe a sigh of relief as darkness descended over Sialkot on 14 May 1857. This was the day that news of the outbreak of what became known as the Indian Uprising reached this far corner of the British Empire.

* * *

The elaborate charade kept up by the missionaries and the entire British establishment at Sialkot that day—keeping calm and carrying on—had been an exercise in futility that was entirely wasted on the local troops. Alum Bheg and the *sepoys*, as well as most of the local population at Sialkot, already knew about the outbreak at Meerut and the fall of Delhi and they had known almost as soon as the British did. It only took an hour and a half from when the messenger reached Monckton in the Civil Lines and to the time the *sepoys* of the 35th responded to the news and turned out in panic. In light of the night's disturbance, the cause of which was never explicitly referred to, the British officers of the 46th probed the loyalty of the *sepoys* during the morning parade on 14 May; the *sepoys* all declared that they were 'in no way dissatisfied, but would give their lives for the British flag.'[86] Whatever loyalty Alum Bheg and the rest of his regiment outwardly expressed that morning, they were deeply unsettled by the news of the outbreak and they too were putting on a brave front. A contemporary Indian account described how the news was received amongst the *sepoys*:

> 'When the news of the outbreak became known, the irritation of the sepoys increased. The whole army felt that their confidence in Government was at an end, that Government was only waiting for an opportunity to punish them all, and hence it was that their confidence in what their officers did and said was scattered to the winds. They used to say, "Government says this and that just at present, but when all is quiet again it will not do what it says it will do."'[87]

The outbreak signalled a catastrophic breakdown in the relationship between the British and their closest allies, and it affected every single *sepoy* across northern India. But it was a crisis that had been a long time coming and in faraway Delhi, the local police officer, Mainodin Hassan Khan, noted that 'When the rebellion had begun, the full force and significance of all that had preceded it became apparent, and men understood what it meant.'[88] If the news of the mutinies at Meerut and Delhi burst upon the inhabitants at Sialkot 'like a desolating cyclone', as Andrew Gordon put it, the clouds had been gathering for some time.[89]

2

A RELIGIOUS QUESTION FROM WHICH AROSE
OUR DREAD

In January 1857, schools of musketry were established at the major depots of the Bengal Army cantonments of Dum Dum, Ambala and Sialkot, in order to train *sepoys* in the use of the Enfield Pattern 1853 Rifled Musket.[1] This new firearm would replace the old smoothbore Brown Bess, which apart from the replacement of a flintlock with a percussion cap, had changed little since the days of the Napoleonic Wars. From each regiment stationed across northern India, a British officer, an Indian officer, and five NCOs and privates, would undergo instruction at the depot within their division.[2] At Sialkot, the grandiose-sounding Punjab School of Musketry was to train a total of 1300 men from no less than twenty-two regiments within the divisions of Peshawar and Lahore. In the words of one local newspaper, the training would enable the detachments 'to carry with them, on their return to the regiments, the germs of a thorough knowledge in the art of killing their enemies with precision.'[3] Indian NCOs of the 46th BNI, including *havildars* like Alum Bheg, served as drill instructors at the school in Sialkot and thus acquired an intimate knowledge of the drill and procedures involved in the use and maintenance of the Enfield rifle.[4]

The ammunition for the Brown Bess musket, which Alum Bheg and other *sepoys* in the Company's service had been using for decades, consisted of a paper cartridge containing a pre-measured amount of pow-

37

der and one round ball. When loading the musket, the paper cartridge had to be torn open at one end with the teeth and the powder poured into the barrel. The torn paper cartridge with the round ball would then be rammed down the barrel. The hammer was cocked, a percussion cap was placed on the nipple of the lock, and when the trigger was pulled the hammer would strike the cap which then ignited the gunpowder and fired the musket. The paper cartridge was required to prevent the ball and powder from simply rolling out of the barrel and also made the process of loading more efficient.

By the mid-nineteenth century, however, technological developments had made the smoothbore all but obsolete and most European armies were introducing rifles.[5] The percussion lock and muzzle-loading system remained unchanged, but the barrel of the Enfield was rifled with three grooves which would spin the bullet around an axis, dramatically increasing its range and accuracy. The shape of the bullet itself was also changed, and the Enfield fired a conical Minié-type 0.577 calibre bullet instead of the round ball of the 0.75 calibre Brown Bess. Whereas the old musket had an effective range of no more than 150–200 yards, the lighter and more accurate Minié bullet was considered more accurate at longer distance. There was, however, one more difference between the arms: to ease the process of ramming down the bullet and to make a tight fit once it was loaded, one end of the paper cartridge for the Enfield was coated in animal grease or some other kind of lubricant. When loading the Enfield, *sepoys* would now have to hold the greased end of the paper cartridge, where the bullet was, while tearing the other end open with the teeth. After the powder had been poured down the barrel, the cartridge would then be rammed down, greased end first.[6] And so Alum Bheg, and countless other *sepoys*, hundreds of miles apart, were all going through the very same motions as part of the drill to learn to handle their new firearm. 'The school of musketry at Sealkote', a newspaper report stated, 'is working along in great style; both officers and men, royal and native, evincing the greatest alacrity and desire to obtain all information they can possibly gain upon the subject which has drawn them together.'[7]

The fact that *sepoys* from so many different regiments were gathered in Sialkot for instruction, enabled a lively communication between the soldiers of the Bengal Army, spread out across northern India. Gossip and stories were exchanged—on the parade ground, in the depot and barracks, in the bazaar or the men's huts, and letters sent and received between cantonments as far apart as Calcutta and Peshawar. Soon rumours began to circulate of a disturbing incident that had happened at Dum Dum, involving a *khalasi*, or low-caste labourer, and a high-caste *sepoy*. An Indian account of the story, described in a letter sent from Amritsar to Peshawar, and probably very similar to the version that would have reached Alum Bheg, read as follows:

> Near Calcutta, five coss [about 14 miles] distant from it, there is a place called Achanuk [Barrackpore]. There is a Government cantonment at that place. At that place a Hindostanee[8] was drawing water out of a well. A 'Chumar'[9] came in and asked the Hindostanee to give him water to drink. The Hindostanee told him that he had better go to some other place to drink water.
>
> 'How,' said the Hindostanee, 'can I give you water to drink? You are a "Chumar."'
>
> Upon this words were exchanged between them. The Chumar said: 'You do not give me water to drink and affect to be so religious; and the fat of the cow and pig which I prepare with my own hands you will bite off with your teeth.'
>
> These and similar words having been exchanged between them, they came to blows. The other people, who had heard the talk about the 'fat,' rescued the 'Chumar,' and made inquiries from him in a conciliatory manner.
>
> Then two men went along with him to that place [The place where cartridges were said to be made], which was a little removed from the cantonment. There they saw with their own eyes about fifty or sixty Chumars working and putting on the fat of both animals on the cartridges. They returned from thence homewards, and described all to the Soubahdars[10] and other officers.[11]

For an untouchable to address a high-caste *sepoy* with such a request was in the first place a gross breach of social protocol; what was even worse was the implication of his revelation. As the Enfield cartridges had to be torn open with the teeth, it seemed as if the *sepoys* would be required to touch with their mouth, and thus possibly ingest, a mixture of pig's and cow's fat, which would be extremely offensive and ritually defiling to both Hindus and Muslims. The story of the *khalasi* at Dum Dum not only revealed the odious composition of the grease, but also illustrated how, as a consequence of biting the cartridge, high-castes would have to share water with untouchables. The threat posed by the greased cartridges was, in other words, one that erased all distinction between high and low, pure and impure. As the story of the cartridges circulated throughout northern India, *sepoys* undergoing instruction at the schools of musketry complained to their officers that their comrades would refuse to eat with them when they returned to their respective regiments. At Dum Dum, a British officer sought to allay their fears, assuring them that the grease was made up with sheep fat and wax, which were, given the context, both inoffensive substances. The *sepoys* replied: 'It may be so, but our friends will not believe it; let us obtain the ingredients from the bazaar and make it up ourselves; we shall know what is used, and be able to assure our fellow-soldiers and others that there is nothing in it prohibited by our caste'[12] The fear was accordingly as much about being ostracised as it was about the actual composition of the grease. Within weeks of the first appearance of the rumours, the British military authorities responded to the *sepoys'* concerns by stopping production of the pre-greased cartridges on 27 January 1857; in the future, cartridges were to be distributed ungreased and the *sepoys* could themselves purchase materials and apply the lubricant themselves.[13] This change in procedure was broadcast to all the regiments of the Bengal Army, and the British assumed that the issue had been put to rest.

The truth of the greased cartridges was that the British themselves could not say for sure whether or not fat from pigs and cows had been used. When Governor-General Charles Canning later stated that the *sepoys'* fears were 'well founded', he was not in possession of any decisive information, one way or the other. According to the Inspector-General of Ordnance, Colonel A. Abbott, 'No extraordinary precaution appears to have been taken to insure the absence of any objectionable fat.'[14] The *sepoys'* fears were accordingly well-founded in the sense that the British authorities could not guarantee that the grease on the Enfield cartridges was not contaminated. Yet the focus on the composition of the grease distracts from the fact that, contrary to the story of the *khalasi* and the *Hindostanee*, no *sepoy* had actually seen the greased cartridges, let alone handled them. The only troops in India equipped with the Enfield rifle in 1857, and who were therefore using greased cartridges, was the British 60th Regiment stationed at Meerut.

The greased cartridges that were being manufactured at Dum Dum, were either for the 60th or for the future use of the regiments of the Bengal Army, and that process came to an end in January. The only place where *sepoys* used Enfield rifles were at the schools of musketry at Dum Dum, Ambala and Sialkot and they had up until January only used ungreased blank cartridges since the purpose for the initial stages of the instruction was merely to practice the process of loading and firing. Not a single greased cartridge for the Enfield was ever distributed to *sepoys* anywhere during 1857.[15] Yet this mattered little as the story of the *khalasi* was told and retold throughout the cantonments of northern India. When troops at Barrackpore were shown the paper from which they were to make their own cartridges, they noted that it was different from the usual paper to which they were accustomed, and voiced their suspicion that 'there was something in it.' Frustrated by the stubbornness of the *sepoys*, the British officers held an inquiry and questioned their men on the matter:

'Question: Did you make any objections to the materials of which those cartridges were composed?

Answer: I felt some suspicion in regard to the paper, if it might not affect my caste.

Question: What reason have you to suppose that there is anything in the paper which would injure your caste?

Answer: Because it is a new description of paper with which the cartridges are made up, and which I have not seen before.

Question: Have you ever seen or heard from any one that the paper is composed of anything which is objectionable to your caste?

Answer: I heard a report that there was some fat in the paper; it was a bazar report.'[16]

When asked whether he would bite the cartridges, after having been satisfied that it was not greased, another *sepoy* replied that 'I could not do it, as the other men would object to it.'[17] Peer pressure thus played a significant role and since the *sepoys* did not actually know what the greased cartridges looked like, they implicitly distrusted any material used for ammunition. Testimony from a later inquiry provides a brief glimpse of how the *sepoys* would discuss the matter amongst themselves. One Jemadar Sewbuccus Sing, of the 70th BNI stationed at

Barrackpore, described an exchange that had taken place in his hut between him and a couple of other Indian officers, while they 'had a smoke and a chat':

'I and Isuree Sing, Havildar, Light Company, were talking together in my hut regarding furlough. [*Jemadar Salickram Sing then arrived*] After the usual salutations, I asked him to sit down; he then said: "Now tell me; I want only your opinion now, and I place great hope (*tawakku*)[18] in you." He said—"Tell us what is the state of your mind about it." I said: "About what?" He said: "About biting the cartridges." I replied: "I will bite cartridges if I get the order, and will obey whatever I get; I don't care if any one should say that I have lost my caste by biting them. I will still obey the Government, from whom I get my livelihooed." He said: "I will not bite them; I will cut them with my sword." Subadar Ram Kissen was passing my door at the time, so Salickram got up and joined him. Issuree Sing and I were left alone.'[19]

In his testimony, Sewbuccus made sure to present himself in the best possible light as a loyal officer, but what is truly noteworthy is the fact that months after the military authorities had stopped making greased cartridges, the *sepoys* still talked about them as if they were the real issue. Whatever the British had done to alleviate the fears of their men, they had not succeeded in conveying the fact that no greased cartridges would be distributed. To individual *sepoys*, it was furthermore difficult to ascertain the facts of the matter, let alone discern between the different stories circulating. Initially, the rumours did not create much of a stir at Sialkot but elsewhere things were getting increasingly out of hand and the news that reached Alum Bheg and his men in this isolated corner of the world were ever more worrisome.

Around the time that the rumours of the greased cartridges gained credence, cases of arson had become an almost nightly occurrence in and around the cantonment of Barrackpore and later also at Ambala. The buildings set on fire were in some instances merely store-houses or empty bungalows, but in other cases they revealed a measure of intent. When the telegraph office at Raniganj, a few hundred miles north-east of Barrackpore, was fired at the end of January, the attack struck at the very nerves of the British communication-system. According to Mainodin, the *sepoys* who carried out the attack 'calculated that the burning of a telegraph office would immediately be communicated along the line from Calcutta to the Punjab.'[20] Just as the British would read out orders during morning parade, and inform *sepoys* of news concerning other regiments, the *sepoys* too were 'communicating' throughout the Bengal Army, and not just by letters. Arson attacks, sometimes targeting the huts and bungalows of unpopular officers, were both an act of protest by exasperated *sepoys* and a way to send a message to other regiments that these stations were actively resisting what was generally considered an assault on their honour and status. Throughout 1857, the actions of the *sepoys* were shaped by the fear of being ostracised—by their brothers in other regiments, and by their families back home. When the Indian troops complained to, and negotiated with, their British officers during these tense months, there was always this imagined audience shaping the way men like Alum Bheg acted.

At the end of February, the *sepoys* of the 19th BNI at Berhampore, refused to accept percussion caps for their muskets in preparation for firing practice the following morning.[21] The station commander consequently arranged for both artillery and cavalry to be present the next day, to ensure that things did not get out of control; the artillery consisted of British personnel while the cavalry were recruited outside Awadh and thus considered reliable. News of these precautions, however, reached the *sepoys* during the night and they immediately broke into the *kotes*, or bells-of-arms, and armed themselves. Following a tense stand-off that lasted several hours, the *sepoys* eventually laid down their muskets, while the British officers agreed to retire along with the artillery and cavalry. The parade was held the following morning and went off without any problems, but the incident revealed just how fraught the situation was: this was the first open act of defiance by *sepoys* of the Bengal Army in 1857. A later petition written by the men of the 19th BNI gives some insight to how the *sepoys* experienced the whole issue of the cartridges:

'...on the 26th of this month we received orders, on the following day to fire fifteen rounds of blanks cartridges per man. At four o'clock in the afternoon the cartridges were received at the bells-of-arms and inspected by us. We perceived them to be of two kinds, and sort appeared to be different from that formerly served out. Hence we doubted whether these might not be the cartridges which had arrived from Calcutta, as we had made none ourselves, and were convinced that they were greased. On this account, and through religious scruples, we refused to take the caps. At half-past seven o'clock the colonel accompanied by the adjutant came upon the parade, and very angrily gave orders to us, saying: "If you will not take these cartridges, I will take you to Burma, where, through hardship, you will all die. These cartridges are those left behind by the 7th Regiment, Native Infantry, and I will serve them out to-morrow morning by the hands of the officers commanding companies." He gave this order so angrily that we were convinced that the cartridges were greased, otherwise he would not have spoken so. The same night, about a quarter to eleven, shouts of various kinds were heard; some said there is a fire, others that they were surrounded by the Europeans; some said that the guns had arrived, others that the cavalry had appeared. In the midst of this row the alarm sounded on a drum, then from fear of our lives the greater number seized their arms from the kotes. Between twelve and one o'clock, the 11th Regiment, Irregular Cavalry, and the guns with torches arrived on the parade with the commanding officer, which still more confirmed our suspicions of the cartridges being greased, inasmuch as the commanding officer appeared to be about to carry his threats into execution by force. We had been hearing of this sort of thing for the last two months or more, and here appeared to be the realisation of it.'[22]

The confrontation at Berhampore stemmed from the mutual distrust between the *sepoys* and their officers—the soldiers were increasingly convinced that their officers were deliberately, and insidiously, trying to undermine their ritual purity, while the British simply considered the *sepoys* to be guilty of gross insubordination. The finer details of general orders furthermore got lost in translation, especially when officers lost their head and berated the men. In this case, the *sepoys'* fears became self-fulfilling as their panic during the night had brought about the very thing they had feared would happen: namely, British artillery being deployed. The British response to the incident at Berhampore was prompt and Lord Canning, the governor-general, ordered that the 19th BNI be marched to Barrackpore to be disbanded in the presence of British regiments: 'Mutiny so open and defiant cannot be excused by any sensitiveness of religion or caste, by fear of coercion, or by the seduction and deception of others.'[23] The British had by this point convinced themselves that the *sepoys* were being manipulated by 'designing persons' such as dispossessed Indian rulers or disgruntled Hindus opposed to British rule on the grounds of superstition. There was no evidence for the existence of such conspiracies, but to many of the British officers it was inconceivable that the *sepoys* should be genuinely alarmed by the rumours of the greased cartridges.

Things were, however, only about to get worse. Two days before the 19th BNI was due to arrive, a *sepoy* of the 34th BNI at Barrackpore named Mangal Pandey attacked two British officers and seriously wounded them.[24] Pandey might have been under the influence of *bhang*, a strong cannabis concoction, but his panic was triggered by the arrival of a small detachment of British troops. Wearing his uniform jacket, forage cap, and *dhoti*, Mangal Pandey ran to the parade ground with his rifle and a sword in hand, calling out to his comrades: 'Come out, you *bhainchutetes*, the Europeans are here. From biting these cartridges, we shall become infidels. Get ready, turn out all of you.'[25] None of the *sepoys* of the 34th joined him, but then none of them came to the aid of their officers either. After a desperate struggle, Mangal Pandey was eventually disarmed and later sentenced to death. On 8 April 1857, the British carried out the first execution of a *sepoy* for to open mutiny. The execution took place at Barrackpore in front of all the *sepoys* of the 34th, as well as a sizable contingent of British troops as a precaution. An eyewitness-account was later published in the newspapers:

> 'At about a quarter to 6 a.m. Mungul Pundy was brought on the ground in a cart with the mehters who had been procured to execute the sentence, escorted by a party of the Body Guard and HM 53rd Regiment. The cart was at once drawn up under the gallows, and the rope adjusted round the criminal's neck, when the cart was drawn away and the man left hanging. He appeared to suffer a good deal judging from the apparently convulsive throes. The General then addressed the Native Regiments, when they were marched up to the front of the gallows to see the man hanging and afterwards returned to their lines. The man, it seems, had previously refused to make any disclosures, which it was expected might have been elicited, so there remained no alternative but to carry out the sentence.
>
> We are told that the spectacle had a most disheartening effect upon the *sepoy* regiments upon the ground. The 34th were completely cowed ...'[26]

After yet another inquiry into the state of the Bengal Army, the 34th was also ordered to be disbanded and within the space of just a few months, the British had thus dismantled two entire regiments of *sepoys*. These developments were disseminated all over India, and made a deep impression on troops elsewhere, as Ahmed Khan noted:

> 'When the regiment at Barrackpore was disbanded and the general order announcing the same was read out to each regiment, the deepest grief

was felt throughout the army. They thought that the refusal to bite the cartridges, the biting of which would have destroyed their caste, was no crime at all; that the men of the disbanded regiment were not in the least to blame, and that their disbandment was an act utterly devoid of justice on the part of the Government. The whole army deeply regretted ever having had anything to do with Government. They felt that they had shed their blood in its cause and conquered many countries for it, that in return it wished to take away their caste and had dismissed those who had justly stood out for their rights. There was, however, no open rebellion just then, as they had only been disbanded and had not been treated with greater severity; but partly from feeling certain that the cartridges were mixed with fat, partly from grief at seeing their comrades disbanded at Barrackpore, and still more by reason of their pride, arrogance, and vanity, the whole army was determined, come what might, not to bite the cartridges.'[27]

Although an illicit correspondence between *sepoys* from different regiments had been going on since the beginning of the year, the disbandment of the 19th and 34th BNI gave new impetus to the mobilisation of solidarity within the Bengal Army. At Cawnpore, disbanded men of the 19th BNI were heard telling locals that 'we shall quarrel with Government presently; for new cartridges prepared with cows' and pigs' fat are going to be served out, and the *sepoys* refuse to receive them.'[28] According to Hedayut, the men of the 19th BNI stated, 'We have lost our bread, but have held fast to our religion. The Government wanted us to bite the cartridges, and thus lose our caste, but we would not do it.'[29] By disbanding the *sepoys* of the Berhampore and Barrackpore garrisons, the British had, contrary to their intent, only managed to stoke resentment against the colonial state amongst its most trusted, and most needed, allies. At the time of their disbandment, further evidence of the seditious activities of the 34th BNI also came to light. A *sepoy* of the 37th BNI, who was on leave at Benares, took a letter, supposedly from an Indian officer of the 34th BNI, to the Raja of Rewa offering the support of 2,000 men if the Raja would rise against the English.[30] The Raja, however, seized the *sepoy* and sent him to the army station at Nagode where the hapless conspirator pretended to be mad. The officer of the 34th BNI was promptly arrested at Barrackpore, and it was reported in the newspapers that the Government 'has made a discovery of some papers belonging to the *subedar*-major of the 34th

NI. They consist of a correspondence with, it is said, all or nearly all the *sepoy* regiments in Bengal, and the contents disclose a general conspiracy to rise at an appointed time, and murder all the Europeans.'[31]

With the disbanded *sepoys* as the prime movers, networks of resistance to the perceived threat of the greased cartridges were being established and coordinated across the cantonments of northern India. 'By degrees it became known in native society which regiments were disaffected,' according to Mainodin, 'and it began to be inculcated as a creed that every Purbeah must withdraw his friendship from the foreigner; must ignore his authority, and overthrow his rule. Although these sentiments had become national, the methods to be employed in carrying them into action were but indistinctly known...'[32] Initially limited to the *sepoys* stationed in the vicinity of Calcutta, the disaffection had now spread far and wide, from Bengal to Punjab. At Sialkot, the Indian troops were somewhat shielded from the worst of the unrest, since the cantonment was essentially a border-post at the end of a road leading nowhere. There were numbers of *sepoys* attending the school of musketry, but unlike stations such as Ambala or Meerut, further down-country, there was no constant traffic of sepoys and camp-followers passing through. In March, however, the trouble reached Alum Bheg and the other *sepoys* at Sialkot in the form of one of the letters from the 34th, which brought home the seriousness of the situation in no uncertain terms. According to a contemporary British account:

> 'A paper was found in the lines occupied by the sepoys attached to the musketry depôt, calling on them to resist the attempt to break their caste by compelling them to use a bullet greased with cow's and pig's fat, so that Mussulman and Hindoo should be alike dishonoured, and telling them to act like their "bhaies" at Barrackpore, and refuse to handle or bite the cartridge. The author of the notice remained undiscovered, and it was unknown whether he belonged to the Depôt or to one of the Regiments in cantonments.'[33]

The wording of this letter, invoking the brotherhood between the *Purbiya sepoys*, was similar to that which reached dozens of other regiments posted elsewhere, and the central message was the same: 'If you should receive these cartridges, intermarriage, and eating and drinking in common, shall cease between yourselves and us.'[34] Matters had by then reached a point that the British had completely suspended the drill at the schools of musketry and the letter thus had no immediate effect at Sialkot. At the depot at Ambala, however, the unrest was keenly felt.

Captain Edward Martineau, of the 10th BNI at Fatehgarh, was one of the officers attached to the Ambala depot as Instructor of Musketry, and maintained a close relationship with the *sepoys*. Just as had been the case at Sialkot, rumours about greased cartridges, and news of the later disbandment of the 19th and 34th, had reached Ambala without causing much of a stir. In March, however, one of the *sepoys* came to Martineau with a letter from his brother, who was stationed at Cawnpore, and asked the officer to explain it to him. The letter consisted of the usual greetings and news of family matters, but ended on a curious note of caution: 'But oh brother! Have you eaten any of that flour? Some of it has arrived here, & I have not cooked in consequence for two days, look out for it at Umballa.'[35] Martineau was as puzzled as the *sepoy* and asked him to go back to the lines and make enquiries among his comrades about the peculiar warning. A few days later, the *sepoy* returned and told Martineau of a new rumour current amongst the Indian troops at the depot: ground bones were said to have been mixed in flour and all the flour from the Government depots for the supply of troops on the march was so adulterated.'[36] This bizarre story was circulating in other parts of northern India as well, in various versions involving different foodstuffs and pollutants:

> 'It was said that the officers of the British government, under command from the Company and the Queen, had mixed ground bones with flour and the salt sold in the Bazaars; that they had adulterated all the ghi with animal fat; that bones had been burnt with the common sugar of the country; and that not only bone-dust flour, but the flesh of cows and pigs, had been thrown into the wells to pollute the drinking water of the people. Of this great imaginary scheme of contamination the matter of the greased cartridges was but a part, especially addressed to one part of the community. All classes, it was believed, were to be defiled at the same time; and the story ran that the "bara sahibs," or great English lords, had commanded all princes, nobles, landholders, merchants, and cultivators of the land, to feed together upon English bread.'[37]

Even more puzzling, was the circulation of *chapattis*, small unleavened bread, which were passed from village to village by local watchmen throughout the Indian countryside. Nobody, apparently, knew where they had come from or what they meant. The *chapattis* never reached as far north as Ambala, or Sialkot, but they were talked about everywhere and Martineau again turned to the *sepoys*:

'I asked them what they understood in reference to them, and by whom they supposed that they were circulated; they described them to me as being in size and shape like ship biscuits, and believed them to have been distributed by order of Government through the medium of their servants for the purpose of intimating to the people of Hindoostan that they should all be compelled to eat the same food, and that was considered as a token that they should likewise be compelled to embrace one faith, or, as they termed it, "One food and one faith."'[38]

There was in other words a clear pattern to the rumours and peculiar stories current amongst both *sepoys* and the local population—all of which shared the common theme of a British conspiracy to deliberately undermine the purity of their religious identities. Martineau suspected that these stories had been deliberately spread to unite both Hindus and Muslims against the British, but was unsure who might be behind them. Shortly afterwards, the arrival at Ambala of the commander-in-chief, Major-General Anson, again brought the cartridge issue to the fore. Anson's escort was made up of a detachment of the 36th BNI, and two Indian officers from the same regiment, who were at Ambala for instructions at the depot, went down to the camp to greet their comrades on 19 March.[39] What should have been a friendly reunion did not turn out as expected. As one British officer described it:

'What was their amazement at finding themselves taunted with having become Christians, and that by a subahdar, a native commissioned officer of their corps! They had looked for the wonted greeting, "Ram! Ram!" after a separation of some weeks, but instead of this were branded as outcastes; the *lotah* and *hookah*, the water-vessel and the pipe, those love-tokens of Hindoo brother-hood, were withheld from them; they had touched the greased cartridge, and become impure.'[40]

Thus rebuffed by men of their own regiment, the two NCOs went to Martineau and despairingly told him what had just happened. According to Martineau, one of the two 'blubbered like a child in my room for an hour because his brethren in the corps had refused to eat with him.'[41] It is worth bearing in mind that the *sepoys* at the schools of musketry had not in fact handled greased cartridges at any point, yet undergoing the instruction in and of itself made them outcastes in the eyes of their brothers. During his subsequent enquiries, Martineau made a number of extremely worrying discoveries about the state of the *sepoy* army. According to Martineau, the *sepoys* at Ambala generally believed that the cartridges for the Enfield had been smeared with cow's and pig's fat to destroy their religion, and that 'in fact, the weapon itself is nothing more or less than a Government missionary [sic] to convert the whole army to Christianity.'[42] Martineau was also told that there were *panchayats*, or councils, in all the Indian regiments across the subcontinent, which were communicating on the matter of the cartridges. Furthermore, 'the army at large has come to the determination to regard as outcasts, and to expel from all communication any men who at any of the depots use the cartridges at all.'[43] The recent events at Ambala convinced Martineau of its truth and the *sepoys* with whom he talked certainly believed that all Indian regiments 'from Calcutta to Peshawar' were colluding, and the officer noted that the *sepoys* at the school were no longer in contact with their respective regiments; when they wrote letters, they received no reply.[44]

Using Martineau as a mediator, the *sepoys* undergoing training at the Ambala depot subsequently petitioned Major-General Anson to consider the 'social consequences of military obedience for themselves'.[45] In Martineau's own opinion these men were all loyal but 'prone to fits of religious panic that no rational explanation or measures could allay. He had been unable to discover what was behind the present unrest, 'but I am disposed to regard the greased cartridges ... more as a medium than the original cause of this widespread feeling of distrust that is spreading dissatisfaction to our rule, and tending to alienate the fidelity of our native army.'[46] Martineau proved to be a remarkably astute observer, a rare quality amongst the British at the time, and his assessment was entirely correct. Although the greased cartridges became the trigger for the outbreak in the Bengal Army, the fact was that the *sepoys'* fears stemmed from much bigger issues.

* * *

Contrary to popular belief, the East India Company did not pursue an official policy of Christian evangelising, even if many officials privately supported such efforts.[47] Missionaries were only reluctantly allowed to operate in India after 1813, and foreign churches, such as Andrew Gordon's American Presbyterians, only after 1833. It was feared, and with some reason, that the activities of missionaries might provoke unrest amongst the local population and increase resentment against the colonial state at a more general level. The British authorities were particularly worried that proselytising might alienate their Indian troops, and a *sepoy* who converted to Christianity in 1819 was promptly removed from his regiment, while some Company officials actually blamed the mutiny at Barrackpore in 1824 on the presence of missionaries in the area. It also caused some embarrassment to the Army when it emerged in 1857 that the British commander of the 34th BNI had been preaching to the *sepoys*. When called upon to explain himself, Colonel Wheler stated that for the past twenty years he had 'been in the habit of speaking to the natives of all classes, *sepoys* and other, making no distinction, since there is no respect for persons with God, on the subject of our religion, in the highways, cities, bazaars and villages (not in the lines and regimental bazaars).'[48] Wheler was subsequently declared unfit to command a regiment.

While the actual number of Indians converted during the first half of the nineteenth century was negligible, the underhanded methods used by some missionaries, including the conversion of orphans they adopted, led to considerable resentment. Missionary schooling as a deliberate tool for proselytising, such as that undertaken by Thomas Hunter at Sialkot, was also becoming more common, and conversion as a means of upward mobility for lower castes implicitly challenged the existing social order. If the numbers of missionaries were small, considering the size of the subcontinent, they nevertheless made their presence felt. At Sialkot, Gordon described how his small outfit operated in the bazaars, and how their efforts were received by the local population:

> 'Sometimes we have had very attentive audiences—the people, apparently, at least, listening with much interest. At other time we have met with a great deal of boisterous opposition—the people hooting after us, and manifesting all the contempt they were capable of, even proceeding so far as to inform us that if they had the power they would kill us. The most of this opposition proceeds from Mohammedans. These deluded followers of the false prophet are most malignant in their opposition to the meek

51

and lowly Jesus. The Hindu, with his subtle notions about the transmigration of souls and absorption into the Deity, is equally averse to the gospel in heart, but not by any means so ready to destroy its advocates.'[49]

The anger expressed against Gordon and the others, however, was not simply a reflection of an innate animosity against Christianity, as much as it was a response to what the missionaries were preaching. If Hunter and Gordon's letters are anything to go by, the content of their sermons was not exactly aimed at engaging their local audience in a respectful manner. Thomas Hunter described his work at Sialkot in stark terms, claiming it was nothing less than a struggle between the forces of good and evil:

'Every day impresses me more deeply with the importance of this undertaking which the Church has put in my hands. At the very outset we are met by difficulties of no mean character. It is not too much to say that our way seems to be hedged up with thorns. There are such obstacles to the preaching and teaching of Christ crucified as the people of Scotland cannot have much idea of. Verily "Satan's seat" appears to be in this place. Sialkot is a stronghold in which his followers stand garrisoned. Every point is defended—every motion of the Gospel messenger is watched—every effort on his part they try to counteract. Oh! for the wisdom of serpents and the harmlessness of doves.'[50]

Gordon was hardly less conciliatory when he described the conditions that prevailed in Punjab: 'The deepest ignorance, the foulest pollution, the grossest superstition, and the darkest crimes are committed and defended all around us.'[51] According to Ahmed Khan, the very approach taken by Christian missionaries was extremely provocative:

'The missionaries moreover introduced a new system of preaching. They took to printing and circulating controversial tracts, in the shape of questions and answers. Men of a different faith were spoken of in a most offensive and irritating way. In Hindustan these things have always been managed very differently. Every man in this country preaches and explains his views in his own Mosque, or his own house. If any one wishes to listen to him, he can go to the Mosque, or house, and hear what he has to say. But the Missionaries' plan was exactly the opposite. They used to attend the places of public resort, markets for instance, and fairs, where men of different creeds collected together, and used to begin preaching to them. It was only from fear of the authorities that no one bid them be off about their business. In some districts the Missionaries were actually attended by

Policemen from the station. And then the Missionaries did not confine themselves to explaining the doctrines of their books. In violent and unmeasured language they attacked the followers and the holy places of other creeds: annoying, and insulting beyond expression, the feelings of those who listened to them. In this way too the seeds of discontent were sown deep in the hearts of the people.'[52]

Although the East India Company and its administration had no plans to convert the Indian population, cases such as those of Colonel Wheler made it near impossible for Indians to discern the subtle distinction between personal conviction and official policy. At Sialkot, the distinction would indeed have been hard for Alum Bheg to make: The Holy Trinity Church in the cantonment had been built using the stones of a dismantled local fortress, while the roof was made in part from the metal of the weapons surrendered by the Sikh army in 1849—symbolically suggestive of a strong link between the British conquest of Punjab and the establishment of a Christian community.[53] Poorly-translated fire and brimstone sermons, shouted by the likes of Thomas Hunter or Andrew Gordon in the busiest part of the bazaar, might thus only too easily be heard as if they were Government proclamations. According to Hedayut Ali, missionaries would challenge local religious leaders and ask them:

'why they shut up their women, that they ought to let them out like women of other countries, told them that they ought not to circumcise their children or give them the Janeo,[54] or marry them until they were 18 years of age, and that none of the above forms should be carried out without the permission of the Magistrate of the District. These questions and remarks caused great fear in the minds of both the Mahomedans and the Hindoos; they said amongst themselves, if the Government insists upon our acting up to these orders, what next shall we not be compelled to do against our customs and religion? [...] The Missionaries of the Mofussil also spoke to the same effect to the Villagers, so that all, more or less, became alarmed for their religion, and displeased with the Government, for they thought the Missionaries dare not give such orders without the consent of the Government.'[55]

British commentators at the time regarded Indian opposition to social reforms as evidence of the superstition and prejudice of their subjects, which ultimately legitimised colonial rule. Yet people did not simply object to such reforms because they contravened their religious scriptures and traditions, but rather because they reflected the intrusion into everyday life of a foreign government. The abolition of *sati* in 1829, for instance, did not directly affect many Indians—it was an extremely rare practice with fewer than a thousand cases being recorded in Bengal between 1815 and 1829.[56] With the passing of the Widow Remarriage Act in 1856, the British nevertheless appeared to continue the same policy by allowing Hindu women to remarry after the death of their husbands. Women were also expected to leave purdah to receive treatment at newly established hospitals, while girls were being encouraged to attend school. As Ahmed Khan noted: 'There was at the same time great deal of talk in Hindustan about female education. Men believed it to be the wish of Government, that girls should attend, and be taught at these Schools, and leave off the habit of sitting veiled. Anything more obnoxious than this to the feelings of the Hindustanees cannot be conceived.'[57] British reforms accordingly provoked resentment because they directly interfered with some of the most intimate aspects of social life, touching on the key tenets of marriage and a woman's role in society. For the ordinary Indian, it was virtually impossible to discern between the civilising and the proselytising zeal of the British, if indeed such a distinction existed. The cumulative effect of social reforms led Indian observers to believe that the British had no compulsions about intervening in people's lives in profound ways, and would go to any lengths to secure their aims. Amongst the *sepoys*, and within the Indian population more generally, Ahmed Khan explained, British rule increasingly became synonymous with Christian rule:

'There is not the smallest doubt that all men whether ignorant or well-informed, whether high or low, felt a firm conviction that the English Government was bent on interfering with their religion and with their old established customs. They believed that Government intended to force the Christian Religion and foreign customs upon Hindu and Mussulman alike.'[58]

This placed *sepoys* such as Alum Bheg in a precarious position within Indian colonial society, a precariousness also reflected in their unique living arrangements, which were outside the cantonment proper but also apart from the local population. To serve in the East India Company army carried the risk of pollution by association—the suspicion that European military drill and equipment somehow carried with it the taint of the religion of the British. The British of course controlled almost every single aspect of the *sepoys'* lives, including what food they consumed, which had to be purchased from the Sudder Bazaar, and the uniform they wore. Under these circumstances, even the smallest changes were regarded with suspicion. According to Hedayut, people were used to 'wear the same clothes, of the same pattern as their ancestors did before them, and imagine that if they put on a coat or trousers of an English cut that it indicates a Christian; they think anything new or anything they don't understand must be meant in some way or other to affect their religion.'[59] Even as military service ensured their status and respectability of the *sepoys*, it was incumbent upon Indian troops in British service to publicly reject any attempts by their employer that could be perceived as undermining that very status.

The earliest and most serious rupture of this kind occurred at Vellore in the Madras Presidency in 1806, when a violent mutiny was triggered by something as seemingly unremarkable as the introduction of a new type of headgear for the *sepoys*. In order to make the appearance of the *sepoys* more uniform and in keeping with a Western military aesthetic, orders issued in 1805 stated that they could no longer wear caste-marks or jewellery while on duty, and they also had to trim their beards. These regulations interfered directly with most visible markers of masculinity and status, and were thus greatly resented by the *sepoys*. The following year a new type of headgear was introduced to replace the existing model, which the British considered to be impractical and altogether too similar to a turban. The new hat resembled the stovepipe shako worn by the musicians of the regimental bands, who were often Christians, as well as by the British troops. By wearing the hats of the Christians, the *sepoys* feared they would become Christians themselves, and would certainly be regarded as such by their relatives and caste members. Rumours circulated that no one would marry the *sepoys*, and some were apparently told by their own wives that they would no longer cook or sleep with them if they accepted the new headdress. The fear of being ostracised had an immense effect on the *sepoys*, who would do anything to avoid the odious appellation of 'topi-wallahs' or 'hat guys'—a common term of abuse for the British.[60]

The bond between the British and their Indian *sepoys* was in part based on the assumption that the rulers would never impose Christianity on their subjects, whose traditional beliefs they were obliged to uphold. Any new regulation or measure that could be perceived as impinging on religious issues was accordingly perceived as a breach of faith on the part of the British. Under such circumstances, the *sepoys* felt exempted from their oath of loyalty. The short-lived mutiny at Vellore was brutally suppressed, but highlighted the fact that the acceptance of British authority in India could not be taken for granted, not even amongst the *sepoys*. Shortly after the Vellore Mutiny, the British officer in command stated that 'there was an idea among the troops that it was the intention of Government to force them to relinquish everything that distinguishes one caste from another, and by degrees to convert them to Christianity; that they also suspected the Europeans intended to massacre the native troops'. This was, of course, to be a recurrent fear amongst the *sepoys*, and one which eventually came to dominate their rejection of cartridges in 1857.

By 1857, Alum Bheg could look back on a number of incidents where service in the Company's army put the ritual and social status of the *sepoys* at risk. During the First Afghan War (1839–42), the *sepoys* had had to forgo a number of their religious observances, such as washing before each meal, and they also had to accept food prepared by Muslims.[61] Their British officers personally supplied them with warm *poshteens* or sheepskin coats against the cold of the mountainous region, but wearing these was offensive to the high-caste Hindus. The Muslim *sepoys* also found it hard to reconcile the fact that they were serving an infidel government against other Muslims. The campaign was a catastrophic disaster, but once the *sepoys* who survived the gruelling retreat from Kabul returned, the real implications dawned on them as 'they had become outcaste to their religion.'[62] It is difficult to appreciate the profound implications being ostracised and shunned by family and kin had for *sepoys*, and for Alum Bheg, yet the following description, by an Indian officer, of the shame associated with corporal punishment is revealing:

'There is no soldier, Sir, that does not feel disgraced by being tied up to the halberds and flogged in face of all his comrades, and the crowd that may choose to come and look at him: the sipahees are all of the same respectable families as ourselves; and they all enter the service in the hope of rising in time to the same stations as ourselves, if they conduct themselves well—their families look forward with the same hope. A man who has been tied up and flogged knows the disgrace that it will bring upon his family; and will sometimes rather die than return to it; indeed as head of a family he could not be received at home.* (* Sleeman: The funeral obsequies, which are every where offered up to the manes[sic] of parents by the surviving head of the family during the first fifteen days of the month of *Kooar*, (September,) were never considered as acceptable from the hands of a soldier in our service who had been tied up and flogged, whatever might have been the nature of the offence for which he was punished; any head of a family so flogged lost, by that punishment, the most important of his civil rights: that indeed upon which all the others hinged; for it is by presiding at the funeral ceremonies, that the head of the family secures and maintains his recognition).'[63]

A *sepoy* who had suffered the public humiliation of being flogged, or had otherwise exposed himself to the accusation of ritual pollution, had not only jeopardised his own status but had also brought disrepute upon his entire family. Such concerns converged and were, to some extent, confused with similar issues emerging from the prison regimes of the colonial jail. When common messing was introduced in the colonial jails during the 1840s, it provided a further impetus to the fears of some that the Government was seeking to undermine the caste and religion of a part of the Indian population entirely in its power.[64] Another cause of contention was the removal of prisoners' brass vessel, the *lota*, which allowed high-caste inmates to maintain their purity— this was not possible with the earthenware vessels that replaced them. The prisoners' protests over these infringements of their dietary practices were widely supported by the Indian community outside, as the Indian police officer, Shaik Hedayut Ali observed:

'...that law must be very bad which by its infliction ruins our religion,— for instance, when any one is sentenced to imprisonment, immediately on his reaching the prison, his beard and moustache are cut; this to us is a great insult. In jail it is ordered that the prisoners should eat in messes, the Mahomedans by themselves and the Hindoos by themselves; this is no outrage to a Mahomedan, but it is a great one to the feelings and religion of a Hindoo. One Hindoo won't eat from the hand of another unless they happen to be brothers or cousins.'[65]

Sepoys openly voiced their fears that they might be the next to suffer the same fate at the hand of the Government. Like the prisoners, *sepoys* were subject to official rules and had their dietary habits disciplined by army regulations. In a show of solidarity with Brahmin and Rajput inmates who had rioted in the jail at Sahabad, several *sepoys* wrote to them that 'the day on which the English shall attempt to destroy our religion, every regiment will revolt.'[66]

The length of beards, or the nature of cooking utensils, might seem to be trivial matters, but they reflected broader concerns about the motives of British administration—and the wider implications of colonial rule. According to Hedayut, 'None of the Hindoos in Hindoostaan would eat with their comrades who went to Afghanistan, nor would they even allow them to touch their cooking utensils: they looked upon them all as outcasts, and treated them accordingly.'[67] The same applied to people who had been incarcerated. 'When a Hindoo is released from prison,' Hedayut explained, 'he is always tabooed by his family and looked upon as having lost caste: on this account both the prisoner and his relatives become disaffected towards the Government.'[68] It was accordingly not any one act of proven defilement that led to people being ostracised, but merely the fact that they had been in a position where their ability to maintain ritual observances had been compromised. The same applied to the greased cartridges. Once the ammunition served out by the British came to be identified as an object of pollution, any *sepoy* who accepted any cartridge exposed himself to the same opprobrium that had hitherto been associated with crossing the *kala pani*, eating food prepared by others, being in prison or wearing the skin of animals. It is for this reason that the exact composition of the grease on the Enfield cartridges, or which cartridges were even handled, mattered little to the *sepoys* in 1857.

Military service and an elaborate set of observances is what made the *sepoys* of the Bengal Army high-caste. The concern over pollution amongst the troops in 1857 was therefore a throwback to the social struggles and conflicts of the eighteenth century, during which Rajputs and Bhumihars had established themselves as high-status groups through the appropriation of Brahmin practices concerning ritual purity.[69] The exalted social status enjoyed by the high-caste Hindu majority in the regiments furthermore extended to the other *sepoys*, including the Muslims, Sikhs and other Hindus. Rather than stable or innate identities, caste, religion and social status were performative and the claim to high status had to be constantly affirmed through daily rituals and practices. Anything that might undermine the ritual purity of the *sepoys* thus had to be publicly disavowed by them, even if this entailed refusing to handle blank cartridges for the muskets they had been using for decades. Alum Bheg and the other *sepoys* were compromised by the mere fact of serving the British, and therefore they had to make a public display of their rejection.

At the most immediate level, service in the Bengal Army, which had formerly been a guarantor of high status, of high caste and martial respectability, had now become a social and ritual liability; it had become polluting rather than empowering. The cartridges should thus be regarded as tangible symbols of vague fears, and what the *sepoys* and *sowars* at Barrackpore, Berhampore, and later Meerut rejected was in essence the terms of their service with the British, rather than the small packets of lead-balls and gun-powder wrapped in paper. That is why the nature of the grease was far less significant than the British imagined it to be. By allowing the *sepoys* to prepare their own lubrication and by changing the drill for tearing the cartridges, the British did nothing to alleviate the real causes behind the *sepoys'* objections. There was, in other words, nothing that the British could have done to counter the rumours of pollution that spread with such speed across northern India in the spring of 1857. If the fears of the greased cartridges were largely symbolic, they nevertheless materialised to mobilise real resistance. The *sepoys* had no means by which to roll back time and renegotiate the terms of their service with the British, but they could refuse the cartridges.

In a petition written by the *sepoys* of the 43rd BNI at Barrackpore to their officers in March 1857, we can see how the specific objections to the greased cartridges merged with the wider rumours concerning the pollution of foodstuffs and the message identified in the circulation of *chapattis*:

'The representation of the whole station is this, that we will not give up our religion. We serve for honour and religion; if we lose our religion, the Hindoo and Mahomedan religions will be destroyed. If we live, what shall we do? You are the masters of the country. The Lord Sahib has given orders, which he has received from the Company, to all commanding officers to destroy the religion of the country. We know this, as all things are being brought up by Government. The officers of the Salt Department mix up bones with the salt. The officer in charge of the ghee mixes up fat with it; this is well known. These are two matters. The third is this: that the Sahib in charge of the sugar burns up bones and mixes them in syrup the sugar is made of; this is well known—all knows it. The fourth is this: that in the country the Burra Sahibs have ordered the Rajahs, Thakurs, Zemindars, Mahajans and Ryots, all to eat together, and English bread has been sent to them; this is well known. And this is another affair, that throughout the country the wives of respectable men, in fact, all classes of Hindoos, on becoming widows, are to be married again; this is known. Therefore we consider ourselves as killed. You all obey the orders of the Company, which we all know. But a king, or any other one who acts unjustly, does not remain.'[70]

All the different rumours that had troubled the *sepoys*, and the wider population, for months, here came together in the notion of a fully-fledged British conspiracy to undermine the religion of all Indians. Yet it was not simply the case that the *sepoys* and the population of northern India believed something absurd and demonstratively untrue to be true—the rumours of the greased cartridges, the pollution of food-stuffs and the stories associated with the circulation of *chapattis* were emblematic of what many feared from British rule. Rather than specific narratives of panic, in their own right, these rumours crystalised the fears and uncertainty that the governance of the East India Company instilled in its subject population after a century of political, economic and socio-religious intervention. At the purely symbolic level, the rumours of the greased cartridges and polluted foodstuffs all represented the same basic fear: that under British rule no-one would be able to maintain their religious and ritual purity, that everything Indians held dear would be undermined by colonial rule. The rumours presented an image of British rule which controlled all aspects of local life, and which therefore Indians could not protect themselves against. The very fact that such stories could be considered plausible and gain credence was an indication of the gap between rulers and ruled. This was, according to Ahmed Khan, a crucial factor in alienating the Indian population from the British government:

'Government could never know the inadvisability of the laws and regulations which it passed. It could never hear as it ought to have heard the voice of the people on such a subject. The people had no means of protesting against what they might feel to be a foolish measure, or of giving public expression to their own wishes. But the greatest mischief lay in this, that the people misunderstood the views and the intentions of Government. They misapprehended every act, and whatever law was passed was misconstrued by men who had no share in the framing of it, and hence no means of judging of its spirit. At length the Hindustanees fell into the habit of thinking that all the laws were passed with a view to degrade and ruin them, and to deprive them and their fellows of their religion. Such acts as were repugnant to native customs and character, whether in themselves good or bad, increased this suspicion. At last came the time when all men looked upon the English Government as slow poison, a rope of sand, a treacherous flame of fire. They learned to think that if today they escaped from the hands of Government, tomorrow they would fall into them; or that even if they escaped on the morrow, the third day would see their ruin.'[71]

* * *

The British confidence in their *sepoys* had reached the point of crisis by the end of March, and while the instruction in the use of the Enfield rifle was temporarily suspended, the military administration decided to modify the drill, so that the cartridges could be torn by hand rather than by using the teeth. At Meerut, the British commander decided to implement the new drill immediately, and ordered a firing parade for ninety skirmishers of the 3rd BLC on 24 April.[72] When all but five of the *sowars* refused to accept the blank, ungreased cartridges, for their old carbines, they were promptly dismissed and during a subsequent court-martial each given ten years of hard labour. One of the things that had contributed to the *sowars'* collective refusal to take the cartridges was the fact that the commander had promised to publicise their participation in the drill in the local papers.[73] This had been intended to demonstrate throughout the Bengal Army that there was no longer any cause for objection to the use of any cartridges, but the effect was quite the opposite. Considering the significance of peer pressure, and the fear of being ostracised, this was in fact the very last thing any Indian soldier would wish for. As the *sowars* themselves stated on the parade-ground of 24 April: 'If the other regiments will fire one cartridge, we will fire ten.'[74] It was accordingly the attempt to make the *sowars* at Meerut a test-case for the new drill that determined their absolute refusal to go through with the procedure. The punishment of the skirmishers resonated throughout the Bengal Army, as Ahmed Khan noted:

'The fatal month of May 1857 was now at hand, in which the army was punished in a manner which thinking men know to have been most wrong and most inopportune. The anger which the news of this punishment created in the minds of the Sepoys was intense. The prisoners, on seeing their hands and feet manacled, looked at their medals and wept. They remembered their services and thought how they had been recompensed, and their pride, which as I have before said was the feeling of the whole army, caused them to feel the degradation all the more keenly. Then the rest of the troops at Meerut were fully persuaded that they would either be compelled to bite the cartridges or undergo the same punishment. This rage and grief led to the fearful events of the 10th of May, which events are unparalleled in the annals of history. After committing themselves thus, the mutineers had no choice left but to continue in their career of rebellion.'[75]

Ultimately, the final trigger for the outbreak at Meerut on 10 May was much the same as it had been at other stations earlier that year: the rumour that British troops were preparing to disarm the *sepoys* caused a panic amongst the *sepoys* who turned on their officers. The *sowars* of the 3rd Cavalry took the initiative to free their comrades from the prison, and after the *sepoys* and local crowds had plundered and fired the station, killing dozens of European men, women and children, the mutineers left for Delhi.[76] The arrival of the Meerut mutineers, the next day, caused the *sepoys* stationed in the Mughal capital to rise up as well, and the British soon lost control of the city. In the early morning of 11 May 1857, *sowars* from Meerut rode up to the walls of the Red Fort, directly beneath the King's quarters, at a place called *Zerjharokhay*, meaning 'under the lattice', where the Mughal emperors traditionally showed themselves to their subjects and could be petitioned. In accordance with convention, the *sowars* called out: 'Dohai Badshah' or 'Help O King! We pray for assistance in our fight for the faith.'[77] When asked what had happened, the *sowars* responded:

'We have come from Meerut, where we have killed our officers, because they insisted on our using cartridges smeared with the fat of cows and pigs, and an attempt has been made to destroy our caste. Hindus and Mahommedans conjointly have created a mutiny (*bulwa*). There has been a fight, both Europeans and natives have fallen, and we have come here as complainants, seeking justice from the King. Advise us what we shall do, otherwise as we have been ordered, so we must do.'[78]

* * *

Throughout the tumultuous Spring and Summer of 1857, Sialkot had appeared to be strangely untouched by the unrest spreading throughout the cantonments of northern India. John Lawrence had personally visited in early May 'to see the new School of Musketry, as well as to judge with respect to the feeling among the Sipahis.'[79] Lawrence reported that the *sepoys* were 'highly pleased with the new musket, and quite ready to adopt it. They already perceive how great an advantage it will give them in mountain warfare.' The officers at the depot furthermore assured the chief commissioner that there had been no complaints from the troops and the troops and Lawrence himself 'could perceive no hesitation or reluctance on the part of any of the Sipahis.'[80] This might very well have been the British officers at Sialkot putting on a façade for a senior official, but Dr Graham similarly wrote to his nephew a few days later that 'our sepoys are quiet and well behaved notwithstanding the rumours you see in the papers to the contrary…'[81] With the outbreak at Meerut, and the fall of Delhi, all that was about to change.

If Alum Bheg and the majority of the Indian troops at Sialkot were undecided as to what course of action to take, a hard core of *sowars* in the A troop of the 9th were fully committed and prepared to force the turn of events.[82] It was subsequently discovered that while the British had been carrying on as usual after the dire news of 14 May, the *sowars* had drawn up a kill-list of the most unpopular British officers whom 'they were determined to destroy.'[83] Only later did officers like Wilberforce realise how close a call it had been, since,

> '…one very hot night (it was on May 20), when the officers of the 9th Bengal Cavalry entertained a good many guests at their hospitable mess-table—all windows and doors being open to catch any stray breath of air, and every one round the brilliantly-lighted table being distinctly visible to those outside—that in the darkness a number of cavalry were waiting for an agreed signal from the infantry lines to fire upon us, as signal which fortunately for us never came.'[84]

Nothing came of these plans, however, and for the moment Alum Bheg and his comrades in the 46th, 35th and 9th were biding their time, waiting for news of how things were progressing further south. The rebel stronghold of Delhi was hundreds of miles away, across several major rivers, and Sialkot furthermore had a strong contingent of British troops that had to be reckoned with.

3

COMMON FAME IS BUT A LYING STRUMPET

After news of the outbreak reached Sialkot, the British community was thrown into a state of extreme panic and Assistant Commissioner Jones remembered 'days of anxiety and nights of wakefulness, and pistol always at hand.'[1] As it was considered too dangerous for so many Europeans to be gathered within the church at the same time, Sunday service on 17 May was held within the lines of the cantonment instead, with armed guards standing watch.[2] Every British officer was on edge around the Indian troops, and Wilberforce recalled inspecting the outposts at night, accompanied by a patrol of *sowars* of the 9th:

> 'I was on duty, and of course had my patrol. On leaving the prison Guard I noticed that they were drawing very close to me, and in spite of orders continued to approach. Thoroughly alarmed, I turned my pony and led my patrol such a dance, through compounds, over low walls, &c., that I arrived at the Quarter Guard without my attendants, nor did I see them again; they may have meant nothing, but I had not been long enough in India to have a blind belief in the loyalty of the Mussulman, and I infinitely preferred their [absence] to their company.'[3]

For the Europeans at Sialkot, the worst part of the outbreak, which gradually engulfed much of northern India in May 1857, was the uncertainty. 'The mail being cut off, and the telegraph broken', Gordon noted, 'we are very much in the dark as to how the matter is going.'[4] Telegraph communication, the lifeline of Empire, could not be estab-

lished further south than Meerut, which meant that there was not contact between Punjab and either Calcutta or Bombay. The British nevertheless retained control over the lines of communication within Punjab,
where letters and local newspapers provided a steady stream of snippets
of news and hearsay. Verifiable intelligence was hard to come by and
Dr Graham laconically noted that 'I could fill a quarto sheet with
rumours, but it is no use, common fame is in these days but a lying
strumpet...'[5] Enough rumours had emerged from the south, however,
to allow the Europeans at Sialkot to imagine the worst. 'It makes one
shudder', Graham wrote, 'to think of the treachery and massacres that
have taken place at Meerut and Delhi.' As time passed, the circulation of
horror-stories only intensified. The fact that British women and children
had been killed at both Meerut and Delhi, in some cases in extremely
gruesome ways, allowed the colonial imagination to run rampant.
Writing from the safety of Calcutta, the noted missionary, Alexander
Duff, for instance, informed a friend back in Scotland:

> 'The public journals will furnish you with abundant details of the most
> harrowing description, though many of the most loathsome and revolting
> kind have been purposely suppressed, to spare the agonised feelings of
> distant mourning friends. Really, if the demons of hell had been let loose,
> with no restraint on their Satanic fury, they could scarcely have exhibited
> villainies and cruelties more worthy of the tenants of pandemonium.'[6]

The art of the innuendo thus found full expression in a distinctly
Victorian way of vague, yet unmistakable allusions, to the rape of white
women by Indian rebels.[7] This was the feverish atmosphere in which
Reverend Hunter and his wife, Dr Graham and his daughter, and everybody else at Sialkot now found themselves. 'What was there to hinder
us', one of the American missionaries lamented, 'from being every one
murdered by heathen, savage butchery, in another hour?'[8]

As soon as news of the fall of Delhi reached the British authorities
in Punjab, the entire colonial administration was mobilised to gather
enough forces to move southwards with the aim of retaking the Mughal
capital. In Punjab alone, however, there remained tens of thousands of
sepoys from the Bengal Army, none of whom were now considered to
be trustworthy. A number of these regiments were disarmed in the
immediate aftermath of the outbreak, but it was simply not possible for
the British to do so everywhere. The Punjab authorities thus came up

with the idea to form a 'Moveable Column' of British troops, augmented by new irregular forces recruited locally in the region. This task force was to take the field, the Commissioner of Peshawar, Herbert Edwardes, suggested:

> 'so as to get between the stations which have mutinied, and those that have not; and move on the first station that stirs next; and bring the matter, without further delay, to the bayonet. This disaffection will never be talked down now. It must be put down—and the sooner blood be let the less of it will suffice.'[9]

Crucially, the backbone of the Movable Column was to be formed of troops from Sialkot.[10] The plan was originally for the 52nd and Horse Artillery alone to join the Column, but Brigadier Brind, commanding the forces at Sialkot, protested that it was much too dangerous to leave three full regiments of Indian troops in one place without the check of any British forces. After some negotiation, it was decided that Alum Bheg and the 46th BNI should join the Column, but since Brind considered that regiment to be more trustworthy, the 35th BNI ended up being the one chosen.[11] On 25 May, the 52nd and Artillery, along with the 35th BNI and a wing of the 9th BLC, thus left Sialkot 'leaving us to the tender mercies of the remaining half of the cavalry and the 46th Native Infantry', as Jones described it.[12] For all intents and purposes, the British administration abandoned Sialkot to Indian troops suspected of being disloyal—a desperate gamble, but one that reflected just how precarious the British position in northern India was. Retaking Delhi and maintaining control of Punjab were essential to re-establish British authority in northern India and the concerns for the safety of a single station had to give way to wider strategic concerns. The official records noted that: 'Brigadier Brind protested; but as the column was much below the strength originally proposed and its efficiency was of paramount importance, his objections were overruled.'[13] There were many who thought the Brigadier was criminally negligent for not disarming the remaining *sepoys* at Sialkot, but once the last of the British force had left the station there was no way to enforce a disarmament. As the safety of the families of the officers and men at Sialkot could no longer be guaranteed, arrangements were made for the women and children to be brought down to Lahore.[14] These arrangements, however, only applied to the families of military personnel and no provisions were made for the rest of the Europeans, including the Hunters, Dr Graham and his daughter, or the American missionaries.

* * *

With Sialkot denuded of British troops, Brind set about making the most of an impossible situation by mobilising that most British of virtues: the stiff upper lip.[15] As Gordon described it:

'There was [...] a prevailing sentiment that we must not do anything that would betray our fears. The whole country was really in a very defenceless condition. The enemy, if posted as to all the circumstances, could doubtless have easily overpowered the government and the entire foreign population. To many, therefore, the safest course seemed to consist in putting on a bold front. They feared that if they should betray their fears they might embolden the enemy, and bring on an uprising which, through sheer force of numbers, would be irresistible.'[16]

The reality was that they had no choice but to put their faith in the loyalty of the 9th BNC and 46th BNI, the very troops whom Gordon described simply as the 'enemy'. The Brigadier instead went out of his way to assuage any grievances the *sepoys* may have harboured, while also avoiding doing anything that might provoke them. Alum Bheg and the *sepoys* of the 46th were thus allowed to keep their arms and perform their duties as before and, as the ultimate sign of confidence, the civil treasury funds were moved into their lines to guard, and the treasure chest of the executive Engineer was handed over to the 9th BLC.[17] Assistant Commissioner Jones, whose work in the civil administration continued as usual, described the precariousness of the new situation:

'sitting every day in Cutcherry with 40 Sepoys in the treasury, a few paces off. As treasurer, I had constantly to go among them to lock up and take out, and also to go to their lines to commit treasure to their main-guard, or to take it from them. Whenever we could we gave them rupees to guard, merely to please them by showing confidence in them. This was all we had left to do without any force at hand, and I can assure you that from the first nothing was omitted that could soothe them or tend to keep them right.'[18]

Monckton at the same time received instructions to raise a levy from among the local Sikh population to make up for the shortfall of regular troops at the station.[19] Police battalions were to take over the various guard duties previously assigned to the *sepoys*, and the new levies, known as *barkandazes* or armed guards, were to assume some of the police duties.[20] In compliance with Brind's instructions to give the *sepoys* no reason to believe their loyalty was doubted, Monckton had to be circumspect as he organised the new levies: 'The measures I adopted were first to form a levy, at first cautiously disguised as a town guard, and then as the men had been collected, to select such as would be fit for permanent military service and import to them some simple training.'[21] The strict non-interference policy instituted by Brind, eventually brought him into conflict with the missionaries. Preaching and educational instruction had already been suspended, but the Brigadier extended the ban to include private prayer-meetings within the confines of the cantonment. As one of the American missionaries described it:

'At the suggestion of some religious officers, we had established several prayer meetings in the bounds of the cantonments for the benefit of European soldiers. Whilst Hindu temples and heathen orgies were permitted to any extent, the Brigadier interposed his authority for suppressing our Christian prayer meetings, on the ground that they partook of the nature of *conventicles*. His authority was absolute at the time, and we were obliged to submit. Messrs. Hunter and M'Mahon, however, undertook to represent the matter by appeal to the Governor General in Calcutta.'[22]

Gordon later noted how furious the Brigadier was:

'one time he went so far as to threaten to hang Mr. Boyle, the Chaplain. It was in reference to his order forbidding us to meet together for prayer and conference, that Mrs Hunter said with much spirit and earnest feeling, *We will continue to hold our meetings, and I will attend them, if he should take off my head for it.*'[23]

Outside of Sialkot, however, Brind had no control over the way that British officials dealt with *sepoys* whose loyalty they questioned. Small detachments of the 46th had so far been providing the treasury guard in the nearby towns of Gujranwala and Shahpur, but the local authorities there no longer felt they could trust them. As one officer at Shapur put it: 'At the time the men of the 46th, knowing that their comrades had not committed themselves at Sealkote, still professed to be loyal; but even had they been otherwise disposed[,] the treasure was removed from under their charge so suddenly that they had no time to consult about not giving it up.'[24] The detachments were subsequently sent back to Sialkot to avoid them causing trouble or colluding with other nearby regiments.[25] This lack of trust in the men of the 46th BNI deeply angered Brind, since it undermined his desperate attempts to keep the rest of the regiment in Sialkot contended. One can only imagine what the *sepoys* of these detachments told their brothers in arms when they returned, but such measures were unlikely to inspire much loyalty.

* * *

Ultimately, none of these efforts made the people remaining at Sialkot feel any safer, or, indeed, give them much confidence in the ability of officers like Brind to be able to protect them should matters come to a head. Dr Graham wrote to his nephew how:

> 'Our sepoys here have shown no signs of open mutiny, but the Brig[adier]'s arrangements have been such that we owe their forbearance more to fear than love. There can be no doubt the mutinous feeling is universal, but we have not the means at our command to adopt strong measures, tho' every hour's delay is submitting to a prolonged disgrace showing and proclaiming to the whole world the slender hold we have on this mighty empire.'[26]

The vulnerability of their situation, and the tenuous grasp by which the British held India, was slowly beginning to sink in. Like Gordon and the other American missionaries, many had moved together in houses within the cantonment, so as to be near the safety of the British troops. Once the European troops had all left Sialkot, save for some sick soldiers of the 52nd in the artillery hospital, they began questioning the soundness of this strategy, as Gordon recounted:

> 'A few days later we began to re-consider our situation. The English soldiers were nearly all gone from Sialkot and the rest, with the exception of about twenty invalids, were under orders to leave; there was no organisation for self-defence; there was no concerted plan of escape; 1,400 armed Sepoys lay quartered within a rifle shot of us. The place, therefore, to which we had come for safety had now become the most unsafe one that could possibly have been selected.'[27]

The American missionaries accordingly moved out of the cantonment and down to their mission compound south of the city. It was not believed that the local population had much love for the *sepoys*, as Jones noted: 'Our great strength in the Punjab lay in the hatred that the Punjabee has to the 'down Easteners,' as they call the Sepoys, as an inferior and intriguing race, who have obtained offices all over the

Punjab which the Sikhs have a much better claim to fill.'[28] Jones himself moved out of Dr. Graham's house, in the heart of the cantonment, and joined McMahon in the Monckton house further away from the *sepoys'* lines.[29] And so, in an absurd twist of faith, the Europeans at Sialkot felt less safe in the proximity of their Indian troops, and placed more confidence in the local population. According to Gordon, there were serious doubts about the loyalty of the *sepoys*:

> 'we do not know how far they can be trusted. Still they have not been disarmed yet. The officers fear that this would create unnecessary alarm. The thought of their being armed is very unpleasant, to say the least, and what makes us feel still worse is, the fact that the guards around the treasury, around the officers' houses, and, I believe, all the guards in Cantonments, are native soldiers.'[30]

As May gave way to June, and the temperature continued to rise, the steady flow of rumours, and stories of new mutinies and more massacres, began to take their toll on the American missionaries. Gordon's companion at the Presbyterian mission, Stevenson, described the situation at Sialkot which seemed increasingly desperate:

> 'we have been treading, as it were, over the mouth of a dangerous volcano, not knowing at what moment it would burst forth and swallow us up. And now the order from the government is for all the European soldiers to leave this place, and march to Lahore, the capital of the Punjab. The order is also accompanied by the statement that all European residents, including ourselves, must leave or stay at the risk of their lives, as there will be no person left to protect them but a native regiment. In addition to all this, Mr. Gordon's youngest child is lying very sick, and brother G. himself is not at all well; in fact, I may say also, that all our ladies are more or less unwell, through excitement, and fear, and watching; and, as if to put the climax on the wretchedness, humanely speaking, of our condition, the hot season—the season in which we dare not venture out in the middle of the day, nor scarcely stir at any time—is upon us.'[31]

Andrew Gordon was no less despondent in his assessment of the situation as they saw their friends leave, one by one:

> 'The officers have also sent away their families, with a few exceptions. The most that remain here now, i.e., of white people, are these thirty soldiers, fifteen or twenty officers, and four families of missionaries, including the Rev. Thos. Hunter, who was lately sent here by the church

of Scotland. We have also been advised by some to leave, or at least to send away our families.'[32]

Gordon and his group were really too sick to travel, especially during the hot season, but as it gradually dawned on them that the situation was only going to get worse, they finally agreed it was time to send the women and children to Lahore. Unfortunately, they could not afford renting the carriage required for the two-day, seventy-mile journey. Both Dr Graham and the missionaries had lost their entire savings in the sack of the Delhi Bank, but while the affluent Doctor could shrug off the loss of several hundred thousand rupees, the loss of a fraction of that amount, Rs 1000, was nothing short of catastrophic to Gordon and the other Americans: 'we cannot avail ourselves of funds to enable us to remove. We have funds enough which will be available as soon as these disturbances are over. But just now nobody will exchange money, and nobody will lend.'[33] Meanwhile, Brind did not allow people to do much by way of preparations, lest this should send the wrong signal to the *sepoys*. The fort at Sialkot also offered little comfort for the increasingly anxious missionaries:

> 'There is a small and very inferior fort at Sialkot, in which there are two or three officers engaged in training up three or four hundred raw recruits, selected from among the simple countrymen of the Punjab; but there is only one dwelling house in it, and families are refused admittance because the fort is not suitable and safe for them.'[34]

Since the Americans literally could not afford to save themselves, they buckled down, borrowed some muskets and tried to fortify the isolated mission compound. The women also sought to prepare for any eventuality:

> 'Some of the ladies tried the experiment of disguising themselves by dressing like native women, and tying a little money in the corners of their *chadars* in native fashion; but they soon became discouraged, and abandoned the thought of escaping by such means; because, whilst they might succeed under the cover of night, yet when day would return they could neither escape detection nor endure the heat.'[35]

Much like Thomas and Jane Hunter, who were still holding out in their house in the cantonment, Gordon and his companions sought succour in the Bible. All the missionaries in fact sought to understand this crisis in predominantly Biblical terms and their letters home to their respective churches, in Edinburgh or Philadelphia, contained long quotes and invocations of the psalms that spoke to their current tribulations. Some, it seems, even welcomed this God-send opportunity to be become martyred, and Stevenson, in particular, fell into raptures in his letters back home:

> 'If God see proper to glorify himself by permitting us to suffer a violent death, let his will be done. Just and right are all his judgements.'

> '...we are not worthy to suffer for Christ on account of anything that we have done, or can do. But, blessed be God, our worthiness is not of ourselves. It is of our Elder Brother.'

> 'Such are my feelings in view of death. Let them be put on record...'

> 'I am yours, dear brother, in the hope of a glorious immortality.'[36]

While it was easy to speak of self-sacrifice in letters back home, daily life in the station, which was gradually being emptied of Europeans, wore on the nerves of those who remained. Dr Graham kept scouring whatever reports reached him for news about the Delhi Bank, and predicted the imminent fall of the Mughal capital almost every day after the siege had begun in early June—only to be repeatedly disappointed.[37] Amid the news of troop movements and the disarmament of *sepoys* across the region, the reports that rattled the missionaries the most were those that spoke of a grand conspiracy to drive the British out of India. According to Gordon:

> 'The country was becoming more and more unsettled, and the dangers of our situation were hourly increasing. The centenary day of the battle of Plassey—the 23rd of June, 1857—was at hand, and the impression was on the native mind that the British East Indian Empire, which had begun from the date of that battle, was to last exactly one hundred years, and no longer. Rumours were afloat of traffic in arms and ammunition being carried on in various parts of the country; conspiracies were being concocted; plans for a general insurrection, involving the massacre of the entire Christian population, were coming to light. And once more we took into serious consideration the question of making another attempt to reach a place of safety.'[38]

The irony was that those very rumours which so disturbed Gordon and the others at Sialkot, were themselves a reflection of the fears amongst the Indian population concerning the 'conspiracies' they ascribed to the British. The stories of contaminated cartridges, polluted foodstuffs, and a government plan to secretly undermine the religion of all Indians, thus found their counterpart in empowering rumours that abrogated such threats—often invoking divine retribution or Persian or Russian invasions that were said would defeat the British. What the British perceived to be the sinister plots of 'designing men', were really popular Indian attempts to imaginatively neutralise the sinister plots they believed the British were hatching; the story that the centenary of Plassey in June 1857 would signal the end of British rule was clearly wishful thinking, a sort of last hope of salvation for those who felt their entire world was under threat. Much of the antagonism that fuelled the uprising and its escalation was thus the result of mutually reinforcing fears that were exacerbated by reciprocal cultural misreading. Furthermore, when rumours among the local population were reproduced in British newspapers or disseminated through private letters, they were effectively given a second lease of life. A servant might very well overhear someone like Gordon talking about the centenary of Plassey and then repeat it in the bazaar, giving the story fresh momentum as it circulated among the anxious populace. Much of what was taking place throughout India at this point of time might perhaps be described as a 'conversation of rumours'—albeit a conversation 'in which neither of the interlocutors understood the others' language.'[39]

* * *

During the summer of 1857, the uprising continued to spread as new, localised conflicts erupted across northern India. Popular rebellion grew out of a longstanding climate of dissatisfaction, but assumed different regional characteristics, and was by no means universal across northern India. Some dispossessed rulers and landowners seized the opportunity to regain lost wealth and status, while others engaged in long-standing feuds over land and political power. What set the events of 1857 apart from the numerous smaller uprisings, that had regularly taken place during the previous half century or so, was the impetus provided by the *sepoys'* mutiny. The *sepoys* of the Bengal Army constituted a uniquely coherent group, cutting across religious and social divides, and as such they added a sense of unity to the outbreak that did not exist elsewhere in India. The British themselves recognised this and one officer later described how the Bengal Army had effectively provided the framework for the uprising:

> 'Brahman and Mussulman here met as it were upon neutral ground; they have had, in the army, one common brotherhood of profession, the same dress, the same rewards, the same objects to be arrived at the same means. They frequently joined each other in their separate festivals, and the union encouraged by the favour of the Government was finally resorted to as a measure to subvert it.'[40]

The outbreak was initiated by the *sepoys* and it was through their networks of communication, which predated 10 May 1857, that news of the rebellion was transmitted and the diffusion of resistance to the colonial state was sustained. The correspondence between the different *sepoy* regiments, which had been carried on ever since the first rumours at Dum Dum and Barrackpore in January, now assumed a more focused character. On 18 May, for instance, loyal *sepoys* of the 64th BNI at Shabqadar handed over a letter to their commanding officer, which had been sent to them by the 51st BNI stationed at Peshawar. The letter contained a warning that the greased cartridges would be distributed to them on 22 May and exhorted the 64th BNI to come to Peshawar the day before: 'O brother! the religion of Hindoos and Mahommedans is all one—Therefore all you soldiers should know this. Here all the sepoys are at the binding of the Jemadar, Soobadar Major, and Havildar major. All are discontented with this business, whether small or great. What more need be written? Do as you think best.'[41] Having been forewarned, the British moved quickly to disarm the affected regiments, but this kind of communication between *sepoys* was becoming more frequent throughout Punjab.

By June, the uprising had gained a momentum of its own and Alum Bheg, and the other troops at Sialkot, were now responding to actual events rather than just rumours from far-away cantonments. News conveyed by official reports, letters and the telegraph, however, was deliberately kept from them and they had to rely instead on whatever information did manage to slip through, including the rumours that reached the bazaars. Stationed in a foreign country, where the local population harboured little sympathy for the *Purbiya* troops, it is likely that Alum Bheg would have been as nervous and as desperate for trustworthy news as Dr Graham or Andrew Gordon. An anonymous

Punjabi letter-writer, who harboured strong sympathies for the resurrected rule of the Mughal Emperor, wrote of the difficulties in getting letters through to Delhi:

> 'The arrangements made for the stoppage of the postal communication of the infidels should be fully maintained, and no dàk should, as far as possible, be allowed to pass. I shall as far as practicable continue to communicate the news of the Punjab. But there is a strict watch kept and no well-wisher can communicate a detailed account.'[42]

This description gives the erroneous impression that the stoppage of the mail was due to a deliberate strategy on part of the rebels. The truth was that there was no rebel organisation in place dedicated to cutting off of British communications. In fact, postal correspondence and any other sort of communication via messengers were just as likely to be plundered by roving bands of Gujars or local villagers as being intercepted by mutinous *sepoys*. The British effort to stop local letters from reaching Punjab, on the other hand, was highly organised and very much part of a strategy to interrupt rebel communication, and prevent disaffection from spreading among the *sepoys*. In Gujrat, not far from Sialkot, a British officer reported that, after the outbreak in May, 'Strong guards were placed on the public roads and ferries, entrenchments being thrown up on the river bank opposite the latter. A strict system of passports and search was introduced; the highways were all patrolled; all travellers interrogated and vagrants apprehended.'[43] The British were particularly concerned by the unimpeded movement of religious mendicants and other itinerant figures, many of whom were suspected of being fugitive *sepoys* or rebels in disguise carrying messages.

Fakirs, *sadhus*, or *yogis* as they were also known, were a common sight in India as they moved between the large pilgrim sites with their braided hair and naked bodies covered in ash. They were usually regarded with the utmost suspicion by the colonial authorities, not least because they evaded official surveillance. During the 1830s, *sadhus* were considered to be part of the itinerant underworld that allegedly spanned the Indian subcontinent. Sleeman famously claimed to 'have had abundant reason to believe that religious mendicants of various denominations practice robbery in almost every part of India; and often murder persons before they rob them the better to conceal the robbery.'[44] Such allegations were never substantiated, and, yet, by 1857 mendicants were associated with religious fanaticism, anti-colonial conspiracies, and commonly believed to be spreading discontent under the guise of devout asceticism.[45] British fears verged on paranoia and 'orders were issued,' in some instances, 'for the apprehension of all fuqueers and vagrants found in the neighbourhood of cantonments.'[46]

There were also more deliberate attempts to intercept any treasonous correspondence between the *sepoys* in Punjab. At the head of the Movable Column, the famed General John Nicholson, for instance, 'made himself Postmaster-General, and all letters that passed along the road were intercepted; the native ones read, and sent on to allay suspicion.'[47] Not long after the outbreak, a Hindu *sepoy* of Alum Bheg's regiment had written a letter to a comrade in the detachment of the 46th BNI then stationed at Shahpur on the Jhelum river. The letter was intercepted by the commanding officer at Shahpur, who censored all correspondence to and from the *sepoys*, and who described its content:

> 'It said that every regiment had mutinied; that the Europeans were banded together in order of battle; that there was a great disturbance throughout India; and that the writer prayed that "Ram" would not stop this state of things. As for himself, the writer went on to remark it would be as well if he were to be allowed leave of absence, for that he did not intend to attend muster after the 1st of next month.'[48]

The *sepoys* were well aware that their correspondence might be read by their officers and the letter was accordingly carefully worded. The writer seemed to have only the most basic idea of what was going on in northern India yet clearly expressed his approval of the unrest, praying that it would be allowed to continue. There was no explicit call to arms, or any indication that he might be thinking of joining his brethren at Delhi, although the allusions to 'leave of absence' and 'attending muster' might very well have been a sort of code for desertion and an expiry date for his allegiance to the British. At times, however, the *sepoys'* letters contained more explicit plans. The entire 35th BNI, which had been part of the Sialkot brigade, for instance, were disarmed by Nicholson after he intercepted their mutinous correspondence. A British officer with the Movable Column approved of this pre-emptive move:

> 'No doubt can exist as to the wisdom of this measure; reports were current, and authentic information had been, I believe, received that the 35th

were in communication with the mutineers at Delhi, and only waited their opportunity, with the wing of the 9th Cavalry, to attack the column; the only reason the latter was not disarmed was the effect it might have had on the other wing at Sealkote.'[49]

The British conceived of mutiny among their *sepoys* in distinctly epidemiological terms, with seditious letters as the source of contagion: 'Mutiny is like small-pox, it spreads quickly, and must be crushed as soon as possible.'[50] Where the missionaries perceived the local population as being in league with the forces darkness, the military feared the effects of secret communication between the different bodies of disaffected soldiers.

Despite the British efforts to control the circulation of information, proclamations and letters issued from the centres of rebellion proved to be a remarkably effective mode of spreading rebel propaganda. With the fall of Delhi, and the ascension of Bahadur Shah to the throne, the dynamic of the uprising had changed dramatically: what had begun as a purely military mutiny now had political legitimacy. Numerous proclamations and royal decrees were circulated by the new government at Delhi, including one written in the name of Bahadur Shah addressed to local rulers throughout 'Hindustan', who had yet to offer their allegiance to the restored Mughal throne. Printed at Bareilly, the letter was probably written by Mirza Mughal, the eldest of the King's sons, who played a leading role in the rebel administration and defence of Delhi.[51] The circular called upon local rulers to assume the responsibility commensurate to their rank and position in society, in order to 'protect your faith' from the onslaught of the British, whom, the letter claimed, 'are people who overthrow all religions.' The various policies of the British were all described as part of one concerted effort to forcefully convert the entire population of India, and the retelling of the events that led to the outbreak is especially noteworthy:

'They resolved on compelling prisoners with the forcible exercise of their authority to eat their bread. Numbers died of starvation, but did not eat it; others ate it and sacrificed their faith. They now perceived that this expedient did not succeed well, and accordingly determined on having bones ground and mixed with flour and sugar, so that people might unsuspecting eat them in this way. They had, moreover, bones and flesh broken small and mixed with rice which they caused to be placed in the markets for sale; and tried besides every other possible plan to destroy our religions. [...] They...now ordered the brahmans and others of their army to bite cartridges, in making up of which fat had been used. The Mussulman soldiers perceived that by this expedient the religion of the brahmans and Hindus only was in danger, but nevertheless they also refused to bite them.[52] On this, the English now resolved on ruining the faith of both, and blew away from guns all those soldiers who persisted in their refusal.[53] Seeing this excessive tyranny, the soldiery now in self-preservation, began killing the English and slew them wherever they were found, and are now considering means for slaying the few still alive here and there.'[54]

In this circular we see many of the same themes contained in the rumours that circulated before May 1857, but now being deliberately mobilised for the purpose of propaganda.[55] The rumours and proclamations operated within a continuum of anti-British narratives. But whereas rumours had, by their very nature been transient phenomena, ephemeral and unprovable, the proclamations presented the very same stories as provable facts, authenticated by the alleged author. The power of such texts was thus partly derived from the sheer familiarity of the narratives they presented. While someone like Alum Bheg might have dismissed bazaar rumours concerning the greased cartridges as baseless, it was far more difficult for him to ignore the same claims being made in writing. This was especially so when the account was accompanied by a powerful call to arms by the Mughal Emperor, Bahadur Shah, himself:

'But there are some of my countrymen who have joined the English, and are now fighting on their side. I have reflected well on their case also, and have come to the conclusion that the English will not leave your religion to both you and them. You should understand this well. Under these circumstances I would ask what course have you decided on, to protect your lives and faith? Were your wives and mine the same we might destroy them entirely with a very little trouble, and if we do so we shall protect our religions and save the country. And as these ideas have been cherished and considered merely from a concern for the protection of the religion and lives of all you Hindus and Mussulmans of this country; this letter is printed for your information. All you Hindus are hereby solemnly adjured by your faith in the Ganges, Tulsi, and Saligram; and all you Mussulmans, by your belief in God and the Kuran, as these English are the common enemy of both, to unite in considering their slaughter extremely expedient, for by this alone will the lives and faith of both be saved. It is expedient then that you should coalesce and slay them. The slaughter of kine is regarded by the Hindus as a great insult to their religion. To prevent this, a solemn compact and agreement has been entered into by all the Mohamedan chiefs of Hindustan, binding themselves that if the Hindus will come forward to slay the English, the Mohamedans will from that very day put a stop to the slaughter of cows, and those of them who will not do so, will be considered to have abjured the Kuran, and such of them as will eat beef will be regarded as though they had eaten pork; but if the Hindus will not gird their loins to kill the English, but will try to save them, they will be as guilty in the sight of God, as though they had committed the sins of killing cows and eating the flesh.'[56]

The emphasis on religion in proclamations such as this, and in much of the rhetoric deployed by the rebels of 1857, served as a powerful tool of propaganda. It also reveals how the events were understood by those who rose up against the British. Rather than a politically illegitimate rebellion, religious rhetoric cast the uprising as a just struggle in defence of their way of life, both physical and spiritual. Just as the danger posed by the British was conceptualised through the consumption of polluting meat or other adulterated foodstuffs, the repercussions for those who did not heed the call to arms were conceived as similarly polluting. Joining the rebels gathered at Delhi under the Mughal banner thus became a divine duty, not merely a political choice. Bahadur Shah represented true authority, and those who served him became the honourable defenders of *deen* and *dharma*, of faith and social duty and obligations. The rebels, in short, fought to preserve the moral order and fabric of north Indian society.[57]

While the original rumours concerning the greased cartridges had merely implied a shared bond between Hindu and Muslim *sepoys*, based on their being equally threatened by the British, the proclamation explicitly emphasised the unity of the two faiths produced by the common danger posed by Christianity. The reference to the slaughter of cows by Muslims pointed to one of the recurring causes for conflict between the two communities. Hindu-Muslim unity was accordingly not something that could simply be taken for granted as the norm within north Indian society, but had to be actively encouraged. The proclamations thus sought to forge a close relationship between Hindus and Muslims, and to mobilise both against a common enemy. The references to 'Hindustan' in this, and other similar, proclamations, furthermore suggested a cultural and geographically-bounded sense of solidarity—an imagined community that extended beyond the walls of Delhi, beyond the ranks of the *sepoys*, which encompassed what may be described as the Mughal heartland. This was more than local patriotism yet less than the fully-fledged nationalism of a later age. Like rumours, the proclamations projected hopes and aspirations in equal measure, describing as fact a future still to be achieved.[58]

In mid-June, the *sepoys* gathered at Delhi sent a letter to their brothers in the regiments of the Bengal Army stationed in Punjab, castigating them for not yet having cast off their allegiance to the British.[59] As such the letter may be regarded as an unofficial counterpart to the proclamations issued in the name of Bahadur Shah, one which was addressed directly to Indian soldiers such as Alum Bheg. In full, it read as follows:

'From your Brother Soldiers, Hindoo and Mahomedan, who have assembled at Delhi,

To our brothers, Hindoo and Mussulman, who are employed at Lahore and other places in the Punjab.

Peace be to you! Ram! Ram![60]

It is a matter of much regret that although we have for the sake of our religion revolted from the English, and considering you our associates have collected treasure from every place and made arrangements for fighting, and moreover have killed all the European Soldiers, the enemies of our faith, and through the assistance of God been victorious, why then are you, who are our relatives and connections and brothers in arms, sitting idle there? Such conduct is unbecoming. In whatever way you can, destroy the enemies of your religion and come to Delhi. It is proper to fight in defence of our faith; thousands of Hindoos and Mussulmans have joined us for the purpose. Don't remain there on any account, and if the European Soldiers should oppose you on your way kill them by all means.

Don' think of your pay and services; through the blessing of God there are appointments of Rs 12 per month[61] here and food and drink in abundance. Those who are slain in this contest if Mahomedan will become a martyr, and if Hindoos, will become "Bykont Bashees."

Do not entertain any fears, but come at once. All the sepahees have in consultation issued a proclamation throughout Hindoostan. All the country, Hindoo and Mussulman, &c., is with us. A copy of the proclamation is forwarded to you with this. Hear its contents and become acquainted with the particulars. You should have 10, 20, 50 or more copies of it written in

a legible hand and suspended in every place where there may be a cantonment, so that all our brothers, both Hindoo and Mahomedan, in the
Punjab may be put on the alert and may perform whatever they are
capable of. Do not fail in this.

The arms of a soldier are his hands and feet. Never at a verbal order resign
your arms and thereby, rendering yourself helpless, suffer the imputation
of cowardice. While you have life do not give up your weapons, and should
European soldiers oppose you on your way do not let them escape: you
should be ashamed of your conduct. We are all assembled at Delhi while
you are scattered at various places. What is the cause of delay? Act up to
the instructions contained in this proclamation.'[62]

Similarly to the official proclamations, the uprising was thus described
in distinctly religious terms and both Hindus and Muslims were encouraged to join. Much like the original letters sent out by the *sepoys* of the
34th BNI at Barrackpore in the spring of that year, the main purpose of
this proclamation was to rally the troops and shame those *sepoys* who did
not heed the call.[63] Casting doubts about the bravery of the troops in
Punjab was akin to long-distance peer pressure. But the letter also
reflected the purely professional concerns of the soldier: double pay was
promised those who joined the rebel army, in addition to better food and
drink. The mutiny had in other words not dissolved the military organisation or ethos of the *sepoys*, who perceived themselves simply as having
changed allegiance to a new ruler, who could offer better terms. Yet this
was not merely about the level of pay and that those who fell in combat
were promised martyrdom and an honourable death. Speaking to physical as well as spiritual needs, the rebel soldier was promised a reward in
both this world and the next. The letter was clearly intended to be reproduced and further disseminated as a sort of chain-letter—giving some
indication as to how such material was designed to be spread throughout
'Hindustan', or northern India.

Alum Bheg and the troops at Sialkot were thus torn between loyalty
to their regiment and officers—the life they knew—or the choice to
risk everything by joining a rebellion far away, the reality of which must
have seemed very distant from the frontiers of the Himalayas. A poster
found in Sialkot later that summer, for instance, claimed to be a royal
firman, or decree, by one Maharajah Shere Singh, 'Ruler of Hind and
the Punjab.' According to the poster, the British had been driven almost

entirely out of India and the king of Burma was supposedly in Calcutta with 140,000 troops.[64] Who was to say that that was any less true than the proclamations supposedly coming from Delhi, or the stories the British officers told about executions and the disbandment of disloyal regiments? Apart from the departure of some of the European families, and the suspicious looks of the remaining Sahibs, daily life in Sialkot had changed little. What was Alum Bheg to believe? The *sepoys* had no access to concrete information and were thus unable to distinguish fact from fiction. Alum Bheg and the other *sepoys* and *sowars* of the 46th and 9th BLC at Sialkot were evidently conflicted about their loyalties, and on 14 June submitted a written petition to their officers, 'offering their services against the mutineers' at Delhi.[65] This was far from a unique occurrence and several similar petitions exist from other regiments. One submitted by the Indian officers and *sepoys* of the 39th BNI, also in Punjab, read as follows:

> 'Whilst we deeply regret that the Govt has lost all confidence in the Poorbea Sepoys, owing to so many Regiments having proved unfaithful to their salt, we heartily rejoice to hear that those scoundrels who have repaid the favors and bounties of the Govt with the basest ingratitude and treachery, will soon reap the first reward of their villainous and traitorous conduct, and we sincerely and earnestly pray to be sent against the exciters of mutiny and sedition to Delhi or elsewhere, wherever they may be, that we may prove to the Govt and to the world, our zealous and devoted loyalty.'[66]

This was not a calculated attempt at duping the British by *sepoys* already committed to joining the uprising but reflected the indecision of so many Indian troops during these crucial months. That there was considerable tension amongst the Sialkot troops, who were probably far from unanimous in their declaration of loyalty, also became apparent a few days later, as Dr Graham noted on 19 June:

> 'Here we continue quiet. A sepoy of the 46th [native infantry] used threatening langue to the subadar major yesterday. He was tried immediately by a native [regimental court] martial. It proved a case of mere black-guardian, and want of temper. The court however did its duty [and] quite ready to hang the fellow if occasion required, and gave him five years with hard labour on the roads, and got rid of the rascal.'[67]

As long as the British openly demonstrated their faith in the Indian troops, and did not give them any cause for alarm, the *sepoys* and *sowars* remained contented. Furthermore, there seemed to have existed a remarkably close relationship between at least some of the British officers and the Indian troops at Sialkot—personal ties that ultimately allowed the precarious stalemate to continue for the time being. Up until this point, Brind's desperate strategy had paid off and even as Alum Bheg and the others kept receiving letters and proclamations urging them to rise, life continued at Sialkot, perched as it seemed on the edge of a volcano.

ESCAPE AT ONCE FROM THIS HORRIBLE PLACE

Sometime during the summer, a warning note was found attached to a garden gate between Sialkot Cantonment and the town:

> 'This order is addressed to the English blackguards.
>
> Beware that when we advance towards Lahore you will find it difficult to escape. The Punjabee Troops will join us. Rest assured the Punjab shall never be yours. We know that your bones will be reduced to powder in this country.
>
> If you wish well to yourselves, fly immediately to your country. You may then perhaps escape, but you are powerless. God has misled you. You can do no good.'[1]

Though obviously fanciful in its depiction of the political situation, the note nevertheless reinforced the pervasive sense of vulnerability amongst the Europeans at Sialkot. Spurred on by the rumours and threat of Indian conspiracies, Gordon and the Americans finally managed to borrow some money from Captain C. M. Fitzgerald, which was not the first time this officer had helped them out. With these funds, they could rent two carriages to send the women and children to Lahore—one carriage drawn by bullocks, and one by coolies. Since a man was required to accompany the women, and Gordon's little son was still desperately ill, it was decided that he should go while Hill, Stevenson and the two Indian converts, Swift and Scott, remained behind to look after the mission compound.[2]

Due to the heat, Gordon and the women and children would have to travel at night and they aimed to make the journey in two days, stopping half-way at the *dak* bungalow at Gujranwala. Before leaving Sialkot, Gordon wrote to the Hunters, asking them to join their small party on the journey to Lahore—Thomas and Jane, however, declined the invitation.[3] Late in the evening on 11 June 1857, the Americans set out on their own for what they expected to be safer quarters. Travelling in the dark, at a snail's pace and through an unknown countryside, Gordon was too concerned about his precious charges to be afraid himself:

'…these mothers, with darling babes in their arms!—how could they thus cast off fear? As I moved down the road towards Gujranwala with my precious charge, in the solemn stillness of that fearful night, it was most painful to witness the forebodings of approaching danger from which some of our little company continually suffered. A Persian-wheel creaking in the distance, the hoot of some lonely owl, a bat flitting by in the air, would cause them to quake. Imagination transformed almost every object that met the ear or eye into a murderous Sepoy; and it was difficult often to persuade them that these imaginary enemies were not actually pressing upon us.'[4]

Twice during their journey, the fearful party was overtaken by Indian troops, whom they expected would attack, but nothing happened. After two days of travel they finally reached the safety of Lahore. Gordon had spent fourteen hours in the saddle during the final leg of the trip, holding on tightly to his revolver the entire way. The spacious fort at Lahore offered a welcome change from their previous situation at Sialkot: hundreds of Europeans had also sought refuge there and the presence of British troops provided a much-needed sense of security. Having effectively abandoned the mission he had originally founded, Gordon was now at pains to explain himself to the elders of the church back in Philadelphia:

'Had it not been for the sake of the women and children, none of us would have left the Mission premises to come so far—seventy miles—but having heard of the horrible manner in which women and children have been abused, tortured, and murdered, by the rebels at Delhi and some other places; knowing also that the mutiny is every few days breaking out in some new place, and that our families would be quite helpless in case it should break out at Sialkot, we unanimously concluded that we ought to take them to the nearest place of safety.'[5]

The Americans who had remained behind at Sialkot, however, did not last long and after more alarming rumours reached Sialkot, they hastily joined their friends at Lahore. Before leaving, one of the missionaries, Stevenson went by the Hunters to persuade them to join the party, but they declined as Gordon later recounted:

'They offered no good reason for not yielding to his entreaties. They had a small bundle of clothing and other necessary articles in readiness. Even the nursery lamp for baby and a supply of such articles of food as it would require, were placed every night by their bed-side. They were just "biding their time," as poor Mr. Hunter said, and holding themselves "*in readiness to start at five minutes' warning.*"

Mr. Stevenson still urged them to come along with him, and insisted that if it should come to a matter of only five minutes' warning, he feared it might then be too late. Failing finally, to accomplish the object of his visit, he reluctantly bid them farewell...'[6]

Although they were now all safely gathered at Lahore, the American missionaries felt guilty for having fled. As Gordon put it: 'I always felt as if it were wrong for us all to leave our post while some civil and military officers remained at theirs. It appeared like affording the enemy an occasion to reproach.'[7] To stay or to flee was really a spiritual question for the missionaries who regarded the Indian rebels as the forces of evil incarnate. Thomas Hunter, however, was adamant in his decision to stay in Sialkot with Jane and their baby, as he reported to his church back in Scotland:

'My earnest desire has been to preach the Gospel among natives, directly and widely. Just as my way seems clear, all the doors are unexpectedly closed. I forebear laying before you our positive danger—about fifty Europeans to defend us against more than 1200 sepoys. We have not followed the example of almost everyone, and taken refuge in the Fort of Lahore. We hope still to continue at our post. May the Lord be our Keeper!'[8]

Remaining at their post, as Thomas and Jane Hunter did, was not only an act of solidarity with the military personal who had no option but to stay, yet it was also an affirmation of faith: they had not been sent into the world to spread the word of God only to flee and abandon their work in the face of danger. While everyone else was leaving, they saw it as their divine duty to stay.

Dr Graham and his daughter had also remained behind, though for very different reasons. 'This station is deserted, nothing but empty houses,' the Doctor noted as he and Sarah found themselves increasingly alone as Sialkot slowly turned into a ghost-town.[9] The daily correspondence with Graham's nephew at Landour offered some respite from the sense of isolation and Sarah described in one letter why she had not yet left:

'We keep quiet here still, altho' one does not feel quite so comfortable now the Europeans have all left us, with the exception of thirty sick men who could not be moved and a guard of forty for them. I have not gone to Lahore after all. I was twice on the point of going Papa thinking it better for me to do so, but the parties with whom I was to have gone *viz*. Mrs Fitzgerald and Mrs Graham[10] both changed their minds, thinking we might as well remain until there was some cause for alarms, but nearly all of the ladies have taken flight, but the accounts of the barrack's life at Lahore is so dreadful that I feel quite glad I am not there, altho' I had an invite from Capt. Lawrence, but every lady I believe is obliged to sleep in the barracks, and after all one is as safe here as there where they seem to have been in an frightful state of alarm, altho' they have had up to the present moment such a number of our guns, and only allowed to go to their houses from 6am to 6pm and then alarmed to do so. W[ilia]m on arrival went to [Mian Mir] but could only see *one* European who was ready armed for an attack with revolvers etc., so I intend to enjoy the comforts of life quietly as long as I can, but the best of natives are not now to be trusted.'[11]

With the dangers of the unfolding rebellion reaching Sialkot only through letters—and thus never personally experienced—Sarah found the idea of life at Lahore, shoulder to shoulder with people that might have been of a lesser social standing than her, abhorrent and ultimately chose comfort over safety. Life at Sialkot was nevertheless beginning to wear on her nerves: 'This station looks so deserted—not a buggy or a single individual scarcely to be seen in the evenings.'[12] The exception was Friday nights when, keeping up the pretence of normality to the point of absurdity, the band of the 46th still played cheerful tunes for what remained of the European community.[13] What Alum Bheg and the other Indian NCOs of the regiment, who attended these semi-social gatherings, thought of such occasions can only be imagined.

The more vulnerable their position in Sialkot became, the greater powers Dr Graham seemed to attribute to the near-mythical figure of

John Nicholson, whom he described as 'just the man for the crisis now existing.'[14] Where others had found solace in the Bible, Dr Graham instead indulged in histrionic fantasies of revenge which he outlined in his letters to his nephew:

> 'I fancy you will ere long hear of some sharp and decisive punishments amongst the mutinous prisoners at Lahore, Ferozpore and Peshawur. Mercy to them is out of the question; firmness and decision, and the fate of our empire all require the last penalty, and die they must. Maudlin humanity and over indulgent sentimental feelings have placed us in our present position. Had we been rigid, stern and unhesitating in our rule our present difficulties would never have shown themselves, but it is folly now to speculate, for change our ways we must. The only good order I have yet seen is that of hanging the authorities, and burning the villages at all places where the electric wire had been cut or injured. Had the 19th and 34th regiments received their reward—sharp and short as the cannons roar, we would have had no massacres to chronicle. Humanity and forbearance in this country are put down to fear! Might is right, and when not exercised is put down to pusillanimity. Our timid conciliating orders and policy are a lasting disgrace to our rule and will be so recorded in history.'[15]

Brind's cautious and conciliatory attitude towards the *sepoys* at Sialkot, which Graham was railing against, were indeed becoming a rarity as the uprising slowly spread across northern India. With every mail bringing new stories of mutinies and massacres, few Englishmen any longer pretended that British governance could maintain its veneer of benevolence. Maintaining control of Punjab was of utmost importance to re-establish British rule to the southeast, and as regiment after regiment broke out in mutiny, the colonial state unleashed its entire arsenal of exemplary force. On 9 June, the British for the first time took recourse to a particularly brutal form of execution by blowing two *sepoys* of the 35th from the mouth of a cannon near Lahore. An artillery officer witnessed the gory spectacle:

> 'On the 9th of June, at Anarkullee, two sepoys of the 35th were tried by a drum-head court-martial for mutinous language, and sentenced to be blown away from guns. The execution was a terrible one. Having been directed to carry it out in my battery, I was close to the wretches, and could watch every feature; they showed the most perfect apathy: one man merely saying that he had some money in the hands of the non-commissioned officer of his company; the other never uttered a word. (Since this

execution I have seen many men hung and executed in various ways. They all evinced the same indifference as to life or death; one man bowed his head to me as he was being tied to the gun and said, "Salaam, Captain Sahib, Sallam, gora log," "Good-bye Captain, good-bye Europeans.") This was the first tragedy of the kind carried out, and must have struck awe and terror into the minds of all who witnessed it.'[16]

This scene would be repeated many times over as the British fought to regain control over northern India—only a few days later some twenty-four *sepoys* of the 55th BNI were executed at Peshawar in the same manner. Moral outrage was quickly replacing the soft rhetoric of Evangelicalism and Utilitarian reform, and colonial officers such as John Nicholson, whom one writer has described as an 'imperial psychopath', rose to prominence during this time, embodying a new and militant ideal of vengeful Christianity.[17] There was much self-fashioning on the part of Nicholson, who was said to have expunged the word 'mercy' from his vocabulary, and who at one point proposed a bill 'for the flaying alive, impalement, or burning of the murderers of the women and children...'[18] When asked to report on the different types of punishment he had inflicted on captured rebels, Nicholson's reply was allegedly curt and concise: 'THE PUNISHMENT FOR MUTINY IS DEATH!'[19] Such anecdotes played well to the likes of Dr Graham.

While it seemed that the rest of the world was going up in flames and people everywhere else were either killed or killing, the strain was beginning to show at Sialkot. 'Our Padre Boyle', Dr Graham noted of the priest, who had been on edge ever since May, 'is the greatest of the horror stricken here.'[20] Boyle was in such a state that Sarah found it difficult to hide her contempt:

'The poor padre here sets us all a very bad example. *He* ought to be ready to die but he is in *such* an excited and alarmed state. He came to call on us the other morning with his leather belt with two pistols on. He went to Lahore under the pretence of escorting Mrs Baker and Bourchier over, but in truth trying to try and get ordered with the moveable column as its chaplain. He telegraphed[21] Sir John Lawrence to know what he was to do, when the reply was *to do as he liked*. In the mean time he had an order from the Brigadier *here* to return immediately, asking him if he was not the chaplain of *Sealkote*. He has now applied for the chaplaincy of Fort William...'[22]

Boyle was clearly desperate to get away from Sialkot and go anywhere large numbers of British troops might be found, even if it meant joining the siege at Delhi. Dr Graham and his daughter nevertheless carried on the bluff of Empire, as the doctor himself described it: 'We continue quiet here and not only occupy our own homes, but take our drivings [sic] morning and evening as if the whole country was serene.'[23] The whole country was clearly not 'serene', and yet the father and daughter went through the motions as if an adherence to the routine of everyday life might in and of itself bring about the sense of normality that was so evidently missing. On the last days of June, the rains broke, offering some relief from the relentless heat.[24]

By early July, Thomas and Jane Hunter were beginning to waver in their conviction and the tone of his letters had become desolate rather than hopeful: 'Two months ago the country seemed profoundly tranquil, and bright schemes for the future were formed. How these are doomed to disappointment is now apparent...We are very anxious; the season is far advanced and the heat becomes excessive.'[25] After their friends had left for Lahore, Jane, the ever-devout evangelical, wrote to Gordon and the other Americans and confessed her fears and growing doubt, couched, as always, in religious language: 'These texts have been constantly in my mind: Lord, increase our faith.'[26] She ended her letter with another Biblical reference: 'Soon the day will break and the shadows flee away.'[27] A few nights later, Jane had a disturbing dream 'in which she saw the dead bodies of her husband and baby lying before her,' which she took to be a warning from God.[28] This was apparently the final straw, and the couple began to prepare to leave for Lahore immediately. Having been warned against undertaking the journey on their own, they, arranged to leave the very next day, 8 July, along with Rev. Boyle, who had managed to get attached to the Movable Column at Amritsar. Unfortunately, the letter confirming Boyle's new assignment had not arrived in time, forcing him to postpone his departure. Though they were desperate to leave, the Hunters agreed to wait until they could travel with Boyle. This unexpected delay at the eleventh hour was a hard blow to the couple: 'When Mrs. Hunter heard that it was impossible to leave Sialkot, she picked up her baby of eleven months, and holding it to her bosom exclaimed "O do let us escape at once from this horrible place!"'[29] By the time Boyle received his orders with the morning mail on the 8th, it was too late in the day to leave, and so the anxious missionaries were yet again persuaded to postpone their departure until the following day.

The situation at Sialkot, however, was about to be overtaken by a dramatic turn of events. On the 8th, Dr Graham unexpectedly received a letter marked 'secret' from an acquaintance at Gujrat, thirty-six miles west of Sialkot.[30] The 14th NI at Jhelum had apparently mutinied the day before, and at Gujrat they had been hearing the distant thunder of artillery for a while. Other than those brief details, the correspondent had no further information, but Dr Graham expected his adored Nicholson to save the day, as he wrote his nephew:

> 'It is not improbable that this affair will lead to the disarming of all other native regiments in the Punjab. Nicholson and his movable column will make a desperate effort to cut these rascals up. Mercy is not a word to be found in his vocabulary.'[31]

In his obsession with vengeance and retribution, Dr Graham seemed certain of the ultimate outcome of the struggle and noted, almost in passing, that 'the 46th here...appear all right.'[32] It is nevertheless possible to detect a creeping sense of doubt at the very end of the same letter—while most others had fled, he and Sarah had perhaps waited too long at Sialkot: 'At present I feel it impossible to decide on what I shall do. The chances for and against going are equal, showing the mutability of all human schemes!'[33]

The outbreak at Jhelum had, in fact, been the outcome of a botched attempt to disarm the *sepoys* there, and although the mutiny was quickly contained, the fallout proved disastrous. For some time already, the detachment of the 14th stationed at Jhelum had been suspected of being on the verge of mutiny, but as there were no British troops nearby, nothing could be done. By early June, the situation was nevertheless deemed to be critical and three guns and 285 British soldiers of the 24th, along with a number of newly recruited Punjabi troops, were dispatched to disarm the 500 *sepoys*. The plan was for the British troops to arrive during the early morning when the *sepoys* were on parade, but the appearance of the column sent the *sepoys* into a panic and they immediately armed themselves and retreated to their lines. The *sepoys* were able to hold back the British troops with a sustained fire and although the artillery was brought to bear on the men ensconced in their quarter guard, the encounter lasted for several hours before the mutineers were driven out of the cantonment. The fleeing *sepoys* were pursued through the countryside and offered a determined resistance from a village to which they had retreated. The encounter lasted into the night and at one point the *sepoys* even managed to capture one of the guns. In the end, however, the survivors dispersed. The British troops suffered severe casualties during this confusing engagement, but that was nothing in comparison to the fate of the *sepoys* of the 14th: 167 were killed during the fighting, 25 drowned while trying to escape across the nearby river, and of those later captured, 108 were promptly executed.[34] Out of the 500 *sepoys* who resisted disarmament at Jhelum, only 39 managed to get away.[35] While the outbreak at Jhelum was thus quickly contained, the concern was that any fugitives might reach Sialkot, which was on the direct route to Delhi. In the absence of any British troops, the fragile trust that Brigadier Brind had maintained with the 9th and 46th might easily be upturned by the fallout of the mutiny at Jhelum.

When Boyle received his orders to join the Moveable Column in the morning of the 8th, he had also received an invitation to join Mr Jones, the Assistant Commissioner, for dinner at Monckton's house in the Civil Lines, where Captain McMahon was also staying.[36] Boyle thus went home to house in the cantonment and made the final preparations for his departure along with the Hunter family next day. The Reverend then went to the civil lines and spent all afternoon and evening in the company of the officials. Just as he was about to leave at 8pm, Jones said to him: 'You are not to return to-night; you must sleep here.'[37] Boyle protested but his hosts insisted and despite the fact that Brigadier Brind had 'bound them to secrecy,' they eventually told him of the outbreak at Jhelum, to convince him to stay at the house.[38] Boyle, who had long been on bad terms with Brind, later described his response in a letter to his wife:

> 'The Brigadier from the first has made wonderful mistakes. He never disarmed the force, and for two months we have been as it were waiting the pleasure of these brutal devils to put us to death. When the Brigadier heard of the mutiny at Jhelum, and of the escape of the survivors of the 14th, he became alarmed, but not before, having miraculously maintained confidence in the Sepoys. When the danger was hinted at I could no longer contain myself. "The Brigadier's policy from the first," said I, "was wrong. He has put too much faith in the villains. He ought to have made a stand against all the Queen's being taken from us by the authorities. Before they went the Sepoys should have at least been disarmed. I was aware, I said, he

93

did not approve, but that was not enough, he ought to have made a stand, and I now assert, and if he and I live shall say it, that he alone will be anywhere responsible for all the blood that, in my opinion, will be shed to-morrow."[39] After thinking and cooling down as became, I hope, my clerical character, I said to Jones, "Good God, are the women and children to be butchered; are the valuable lives of God's creatures to be lost, lost without one word of caution? Must no hint be given? Cannot they be brought away in the night to the fort?" "No, the suspicions of the Sepoys are not to be raised, and he wishes all to be kept quiet."[40]

Boyle wrote this almost a week later, when the benefit of hindsight allowed him to pretend a greater level foresight than he really possessed. The truth was that although the Brigadier had forbidden any officials to speak of the news, last-minute precautions were being taken. On the eve of their departure, Thomas and Jane Hunter, and their baby, were in a particularly precarious situation, according to Gordon:

'Their house was in the south-east corner of the military Cantonment. South-west of them, between their house and the city fort, lay the Chief Bazar [*Sudder bazaar*], with a large native population. Should they even succeed in reaching the City in safety, they could enter the Fort only after passing through several narrow streets, which were thronged with natives. Along the north border and down the west end of the cantonment were the Sepoy lines; and when once these armed Sepoys should begin their bloody work, escape would seem almost impossible.'[41]

Captain McMahon accordingly invited the Hunters to move out to Reverend Hill's house, that had stood empty since the Americans had left for Lahore, which was a quarter of a mile west of Monckton's residence and just next to the police lines. Since the police consisted of local Punjabi recruits, they were thought to be more reliable than the *Hindustani sepoys*. Moreover, with Monckton, Jones and McMahon virtually next door, they would be able to warn the missionaries in case of trouble.[42] By the evening of the 8th, an outbreak seemed imminent. Staff-sergeant Greenwood, who had the administrative oversight of the Sudder bazaar, had for several days heard rumours in the bazaar 'to the effect that there would be a rising in the near future.'[43] He duly reported this to the Brigade Headquarters, but this information was disregarded as unreliable and the sergeant was ridiculed for his efforts. Rumours ran rampant among the Anglo-Indian communities through-out northern India, and many at Sialkot had become inured to their increasingly alarmist content; Jones, for instance, mentioned the 'dozens of rumours, most of them more or less true, of the bad state of the troops here.'[44] Yet just as rumours could spark a panic if they reinforced pre-existing anxieties, they could as easily be dismissed if they did not align with what people wanted to hear. Brigadier Brind, who had for so long maintained his faith in the *sepoys*, was certainly not going to let 'bazaar gup' shatter the pretence of normality. The nuns at the Convent, however, were explicitly warned by Indian friends during the evening of the 8th that 'they would do well to leave the place as promptly as possible with their pupils, as the insurrection was to commence the next morning at break of day, and the insurgents had resolved to kill every European.'[45] As a result, the nuns began packing up their belongings in several carriages, prepared to leave at any moment. Meanwhile, in the military lines, everything seemed as calm and quiet as usual. The seventeen-year-old Lieutenant Arthur H. Prinsep of the 9th BLC, who was on guard duty, found nothing unusual to report:

> 'On Wednesday night [8 July] it was my turn for duty at the guard, and accordingly I went down after mess, went through the lines, and, having found all quiet, took off my jacket and lighted a cheroot. I had a long talk with the native officer and troopers on guard, who were all very cheerful; after which I turned in and went to sleep.'[46]

5

TENANTS OF PANDEMONIUM

The apparent calm in the cantonment on the eve of the 9th was decep-
tive. Just as the news of the outbreak at Meerut in May had reached
Alum Bheg and the *sepoys* at almost the same time as it did their officers, so too had the news of the outbreak at Jhelum made its way to the
'native' lines on the evening of the 8th. The authorities had done everything in their power to keep any information, and any fugitives, from
reaching Sialkot: along the Jhelum and Chenab rivers, all bridges had
been broken and all boats had been seized. Yet these efforts merely
delayed the news travelling the 70 miles from Jhelum to Sialkot.[1]

Alum Bheg and the other Indian troops were already uneasy. After
their former friends, the 35th BNI, had been disarmed by Nicholson,
they had sent letters to Sialkot 'requesting the 46th and 9th Cavalry to
come down and free them.'[2] If the Sialkot troops were to make it to
Jandiala, just outside of Amritsar, the 35th there promised they would
'murder their officers with their bayonets,' which they still retained.[3]
These were the desperate pleas of disarmed *sepoys* with no options
left, but they struck a strong cord with Alum Bheg and the others at
Sialkot, since they were much more immediate than the distant sham-
ing by the rebels at Delhi. When news of the outbreak reached the
troops at Sialkot late on the 8th, they did not rejoice or plan to join
their friends; they knew that the 46th and 9th would be next on the list
of regiments to be disarmed. That very evening, two *sowars* of the wing

97

of the 9th BLC which had been attached to the Movable Column, arrived at Sialkot on furlough.[4] These men regaled their old comrades with stories of the disarmament and executions they had witnessed, and crucially 'reported that the Column was moving up, had reached Umritsur, and was probably coming to disarm the Sealkote troops.'[5] Once they had disarmed the *sepoys*, it was said, the British troops would 'blow away several men from guns.'[6] Alum Bheg and the other *sepoys* had very clear examples before them of what would happen if they allowed themselves to be disarmed—whether it was the fabled massacre at Barrackpore in 1824, or any number of more recent cases. At both Berhampore, Ambala and Meerut earlier in 1857, the mere rumour that British troops were approaching to disarm the *sepoys* was enough to cause a panic, and in the latter case actually triggered the final outbreak. According to one of the nuns at Sialkot, 'the native soldiers heard they were to be disarmed the following day. They became furious, and secretly planned a revolt.'[7] Very few Indian troops were at this point fully committed to mutiny, but the situation was sufficiently tense for the rumours to tip the balance. According to Ahmed Khan, the *sepoys* cursed their fate after they had rebelled in 1857: '"What could we do," said they, "except rebel? We were never sure what punishment was in store for us, as Government had no confidence in us. On an opportunity offering, we should have been compelled to do anything."'[8]

Before sunrise the next morning, 9 July 1857, the A troop of the 9th BLC woke up and saddled their horses. These were the very men who had prepared a kill-list and who had been poised to rebel back in May. As had been the case at Meerut and elsewhere, it was the cavalry *sowars* who seized the initiative and became the ones to force events. The *sowars* were highly mobile, and since they were almost exclusively Muslim, they formed a much more tight-knit unit than even the high-caste majority *sepoy* regiments. Within a small company, it was also possible for just a few individuals to take action and effectively force the rest to join in. According to one Indian officer of the Bengal Army, 'there is one knave and nine fools; the knave compromises the others, and then tells them it is too late to draw back; they either actively join, or run away for fear of the Europeans' vengeance.'[9] Thus at daylight, the men of troop A 'mounted their horses and dispersed about the station shooting at whoever they met in European garb, the 2 other troops, namely B and C troop were forced by threats to do likewise.'[10] *Sowars* were simultaneously despatched to the lines of the 46th.

Captain Caulfield had been on guard duty during the night with a picket of the 46th and was just returning for the morning parade. As his wife later described it:

> 'The next morning, when it was the time for taking the pickets off, C— observed a body of troopers coming towards our lines, and thinking it suspicious and our men getting unsteady he collected them and marched to the parade, but as they came near it they fairly left C—and rushed down to their lines.'[11]

In the lines of the 46th BNI, Alum Bheg and the other *sepoys*, along with most of the British officers, were assembling for the morning parade, when suddenly the *sowars* came riding down. They 'flashed off their pistols, shouted rebellion, yelled about religion, cursed the "Feringhee kaffirs,"[12] and intentionally committing themselves they committed the best intentioned others.'[13] There were also rumours that a letter had arrived from the Mughal Emperor, and one account even mentioned that *sepoys* had been 'seduced by spies from Delhi and other quarters.'[14] Whether another proclamation from Bahadur Shah had indeed reached Sialkot is unknown. What is certain is that the *sowars* riding down to the lines of the 46th, called out that 'the *chhuppa* (printed letter or circular) had come.'[15] One Indian officer of the 46th thus explained 'that four Sowars of the 9th Cavalry had early that morning been in our lines telling the men to get ready, for "the letter" had come.'[16] The very claim that a letter had arrived could be mobilising in and of itself; in the Mughal capital, the local head of police, Mainodin described how 'In every instance the Kings *perwanah* had the effect of causing the soldiers to mutiny and make their way to Delhi. At the sight of the King's *perwanah* the men who had fought for the English forgot the past, in the desire to be re-established under a native Sovereign.'[17] At Jhansi, for instance, the outbreak was also triggered by the arrival of a letter from Delhi. In this case, a servant: 'brought a chit from Delhi station that the whole army of the Bengal Presidency had mutinied and as the Regiment stationed at Jhansee had not done so, men composing it were outcasts or had lost their faith. On the receipt of this letter, the four ring leaders … prevailed upon their countrymen to revolt and to carry out their resolution.'[18] Alum Bheg and the men of the 46th were also cowed by the sudden arrival of the excited horsemen, and one Indian officer later explained that 'What could we, unarmed and on foot, do against armed men on horseback?'[19]

Meanwhile, a party of forty to fifty *sowars* led by the quartermaster Havildar headed down to the jail, mid-way between the cantonment and the city. As it turned out, the *sowars* were well-acquainted with the *darogha* of the jail, and the thirty prison guards, most of whom were '*Hindustani*', did not put up any resistance as the troopers went about liberating the prisoners.[20] The mounted police, who were locally recruited, remained inactive and at no point intervened in the events that were unfolding. The breaking open of prisons was a recurrent pattern in the outbreaks that had taken place ever since Meerut, and the local police and jail guards had almost invariably joined with the mutineers. British rule in India, it should be recalled, was entirely dependent on the collaboration of local allies and in the absence of British troops, the power of the colonial state rested exclusively with the *sepoys* and *sowars*. British authority, which was precarious at the best of times, and tolerated rather than accepted by the local population, collapsed in a matter of hours when the 9th and 46th rose up at Sialkot. Much of the turmoil and violence during the events of 1857 was a direct outcome of this sudden implosion of the entire structure of British authority, and local police and prison guards were not going to oppose the rebellious *sepoys*, who ultimately held the real power.

The prison was of course one of the most potent symbols of the colonial state, and therefore an obvious target for the mutineers. Freeing the prisoners released them from the condition under which they had become socially ostracised due to British policies—just as the *sepoys* had, by the very act of rising, prevented the British from forcing the greased cartridges upon them, as they feared they would. There was furthermore a strategic purpose to breaking open the jail: by releasing the prisoners, 366 in total, the *sowars* not only added to the general confusion at Sialkot, but also unleashed an angry and impoverished crowd, intent on plunder and with a grudge to settle with the colonial authorities.[21] After their release, the prisoners joined forces with the prison guards, and at Meerut, for instance, one officer of the jail guard was actually seen leading a group of freed convicts.[22] With the British as a common enemy, the very circumstances of the outbreak allowed for unexpected alliances to be forged among different group of Indians. We should not, however, make too much of the solidarity between the *sepoys* and the prisoners, since released convicts were afterwards often forcefully conscripted as labourers for the rebels. For many prisoners, their freedom was short-lived.

During the outbreak at Sialkot, it was not just the Indian troops of the Bengal Army who played a central role; Hurmat Khan, the former flogger of the District Court, emerged as an unlikely leader during the turmoil. 'This man,' according to Gordon, '"breathing out threatenings and slaughter"[23] against the local authorities, and being in sympathy with his fellow Purbias, was a chief mover in the horrible business of the 9th of July.'[24] Khan was a Pathan from Bareilly and 'a man of great size and strength and a renowned swordsman.' He had been employed as the official flogger of the Court, but Monckton had recently demoted him to the Kotwali, or town police, after he had a quarrel with a clerk about a woman.[25] Evidently expecting the outbreak, the first thing he did early that morning was to dispatch men to kill the Commissioner. He then went to the cavalry lines where troop A was still trying to convince the other *sowars* to join them, and was 'instrumental in forcing them to break out.'[26] With his work completed in the cantonment, Hurmat Khan took advantage of the complete chaos that reigned and, according to Gordon:

> 'went down to the city to murder a court clerk, with whom he had had a quarrel about a woman, which had resulted in his own degradation from his late position as flogger. Not finding the clerk at home, he cut down a servant at the door, and then came up to the jail, where he, in company with others, was liberating the criminals.'[27]

As the official flogger, Khan was used to inflicting violence with moral impunity, and this made him a central figure at a time of crisis. His social position was similar to that of a European executioner, in that he was both feared and shunned, yet he possessed a unique skill-set, and a willingness to deploy it, which was indispensable during the outbreak. At Meerut, for instance, it had been a local butcher, with some skill in using a knife on carcasses, who during the outbreak very deliberately killed and mutilated the pregnant Mrs Chambers.[28] The same was the case during the infamous massacre of European women and children at Bibighar in Cawnpore, just a few days after the outbreak at Sialkot, where at least some of the men who did the killings with swords were butchers.[29] Violence, and especially the killing of Europeans, was required to transform the panic and tumult into an open mutiny that went beyond the point of no return. This was an important mental barrier to breach, and only someone like Hurmat Khan could be relied upon to bloody his hands without hesitation.

And so it was that the reverberations of the original outbreak at Meerut eventually reached Sialkot after two full months. While mutinies were spreading and the uprising was raging all over northern India, Alum Bheg and the Indian troops had essentially remained true to their salt. Now an entirely contingent series of events—the mutiny at Jhelum, their seemingly imminent disarmament, and the rumoured arrival of a letter from Delhi—finally pushed them over the edge. Yet even at the moment of mutiny, just as Alum Bheg and his brothers of the 46th BNI cast off their allegiance to British rule, and burned all bridges behind them, their actions were far from unequivocal.

* * *

It was as yet dark during the early morning hours of 9 July 1857 when the first stirrings of the outbreak began. Brigadier Brind was up and about, drinking coffee at his house with Joint Magistrate Chambers and Captain Balmain of the 9th BLC, discussing how best to intercept any of the Jhelum mutineers that might make their way to Sialkot. These fugitives were expected any moment, and Brind was actually thinking of deploying the 9th and 46th against them. Suddenly, the window was shattered by a bullet, putting an end to any illusion that the storm might pass Sialkot over.[30] While Chambers remained with Brind, Balmain rode off to see what was going on in the lines of the Indian cavalry. Noise and gunshots could be heard from the direction of the lines, which were just next to the Brigadier's house. Lieutenant Montgomerie of the 9th, who was fast asleep in his quarters at the time, later recalled:

'I was awoke by a woman running in screaming. This was the wife of our Sergeant-Major, who was followed shortly after by her husband, with a wound in his forehead. He said that he had had five or six shots fired at him by our men. By the time I had dressed and got my pistols and sword on the

Havildar-Major came and said that early that morning the Mussulmans of the 1st troop began saddling their horses, and as there was no parade ordered he asked them what they were doing, when they told him to mind his own business. I rode to the Brigadier's, and in a short time he came out with Chambers, the joint magistrate.'[31]

Balmain had gone down to the lines along with the young Lieutenant Princep who had only just finished his duties for the night and was preparing for a morning ride, when he became aware of the tumult. Princep had already been warned off by one trooper of his regiment, yet he and Balmain went back again:

'We went down, intending to go to the stables, but, as we passed the men's houses some rushed out, and said, "Come in here, Sahib; come in here." We went in, and found some six men with a native officer, who said that all the rest had gone, and if we did not go into their house we should be killed immediately. B—returned to inform the Brigadier, while I stayed some minutes longer.'[32]

At the Brigadier's, Montgomerie and the other officers were still trying to convince the station commander that it was time for them to leave and seek refuge in the fort, when Balmain returned and recounted how he had been warned off by the Hindu *sowars*. Brind finally gave in, and they all left for the fort. The delay, however, proved fatal to the Brigadier and 'soon after leaving his bungalow a trooper fired his carbine at him from behind, the ball entering his back close to the spine. [Brind] turned on the man, but his pistols had been previously unloaded by his Khansamah (cook), and clicked harmlessly. He then seized the barrel of his pistol, and riding the trooper down, broke his jaw with the butt-end of the weapon.'[33] Montgomerie later described their ignominious flight:

'Brigadier Brind, Balmain, Chambers, and I rode out of the compound, and then we perceived a large body of our men posted so as to cut us off from the fort in the city, who immediately they saw us commenced chasing and firing at us. We first of all made straight for the cantonments, so as to bring them after us, and then on a sudden we turned off to the right and rode for a bridge which was between the cantonment and the city. By this manoeuvre I found myself leading, and being mounted on a good horse I could have gone off without coming into collision with the rascals again. As I was nearing the bridge Balmain, who was close behind me, called out, "Stop and make a stand, or the Brigadier is lost!" We both turned on the

103

bridge, and I then saw the Brigadier trying to get across the nullah with a number of our men after him. The foremost of them, who was a little in advance of the others, as soon as he saw me stop, turned from following the Brigadier and came at us. I had just time to draw and cock my pistol when down he came on me at full gallop, with carbine levelled. I could have almost touched him when he fired, and the bullet whizzed past me. At the same moment I fired, but, owing to the pace he was coming, I missed. I was perfectly cool, and made up my mind not to fire until he had done so and was close on me. If I had used my sword instead of my pistol I must have killed him. Balmain had two shots at him but also missed. All this did not take half a minute, but it gave time for the Brigadier to cross the nullah, and we then rode on to the fort without interruption.'[34]

It was only after the officers arrived at the fort, which was held by the new Sikh levies, who were not involved in the outbreak, that they realised why Brind had been lagging behind: he had been mortally wounded 'and it was only with difficulty he bore up.'[35] Montgomerie, meanwhile, did not stay at the fort, and, putting his faith in the speed of his horse continued riding to Gujranwala, 33 miles away, which he reached by 9 am 'more dead than alive' some five hours later.[36] Back in Sialkot, Lieutenant Princep was still in the lines of the 9th but found his situation becoming increasingly untenable:

'I heard shots fired right and left; and the few men remaining not seeming much inclined to protect me, I thought it time to go too. I was then mounted on a troop-horse with my parade saddle. I galloped back to my bungalow, to try to get some powder to load my revolver from B——'s servants, having none of my own. Found that it was all locked up. I found a few grains in an old flask of mine, and loaded one of the chambers. I then went to join the Brigadier, but found that he had gone down to the fort in the city. I followed and met one of his servants, who was crying and wringing his hands, saying, "They are killing the Brigadier." I asked which way he had gone and, putting spurs to my horse, dashed after him.'[37]

Prinsep, however, found his way blocked by the same troopers who had pursued Montgomerie and Brind a little earlier:

'About half-way between fort and cantonments I saw six troopers drawn up on the side of the road. I drew my revolver, though of no use, and there being no other escape proposed to run the gauntlet with my horse at full speed. I came opposite the first, who fired his pistol; the rest did likewise as I came opposite them, but without effect. The last gave chase, drawing his second pistol. I covered him with my revolver, which kept him off for some time, but suddenly closing in two yards he took steady aim at my head and fired. I felt as if I had been hit a severe blow with a stick on the right arm, having covered myself as well as possible with it. He gave a shout and closed; I thought it was all up with me; but, finding I could draw my sword, began to feel rather jolly again. When he came alongside I rammed it into him, but, having no strength, could only get it in about two inches into his side. He knocked it out with his pistol. I struck him again, but with like effect. He then shot ahead. I put spurs to my nag, and as I came up banged at him. He bent forward to avoid, and I only got about one inch into him, but he almost lost his seat, and pulled up. I had almost done so, too, but pushed along and he fell behind. I now thought I should reach the fort, but was disappointed. Seeing some more men ahead of me I turned to the right, and took a pull at my horse.'[38]

With his path to the safety of the fort cut off, Princep set out for Wazirabad. Despite his wounds, he managed to reach it safely later that morning and eventually joined Montgomerie at Gujranwala later that evening.

From the lines of the 9th BLC, on the western side of the cantonment, the unrest spread to the 46th BNI, whose quarters were right in the middle on the northern side. In the official report, Colonel Farquharson described the moment he and the other officers lost control:

'It appears that early on that morning a few troopers came to the light company of the 46th N.I. and the whole of the left wing soon rose and armed themselves, as did also the right wing after some hesitation. Most of the officers were by this time on the parade, but their endeavours to check the men were unavailing.'[39]

The *sepoys* had already been in a state of excitement, but the arrival of the *sowars* seemed to decide the matter: 'The men asked permission to get to their arms to keep our troopers off', one officer recorded, but 'As soon as they obtained it they rushed to their lines, instead of to the places where the arms are usually kept, and then came out and began firing at their officers.'[40] One officer of the 46th had run down to the lines of the *sepoys*, dodging the groups of mounted *sowars* who were sweeping through the cantonment:

'In a short time I was joined by some more officers and the Colonel. We tried to reassure the men, and gave them order to take their arms and fire on the cavalry' instead of firing on the cavalry, they fired on us. A Sepoy of my regiment seized the bridle of a brother officer's (Smith's) horse, and led him under shelter, telling him to gallop for his life; he started off immediately, followed by Horsford, another of ours, and I came last. In passing a side street I was fired at, but most providentially missed; the ball passed close to my nose.'[41]

This officer also relied on his horse to carry him to safety at Wazirabad. What was remarkable was that even though Alum Bheg and the *sepoys* of the 46th were disobeying their officers, and for all intents and purposes breaking out in mutiny, they did not actually attack their officers. These officers were completely outnumbered and could easily have been overpowered, as happened in many other instances during the uprising. Instead, it seemed as if Alum Bheg and the *sepoys* were throwing off allegiance to the East India Company, but without the usual accompanying violence against their officers to mark this dramatic shift in loyalty. Even as Alum Bheg and his men were abandoning their loyalty to the British, they did not completely sever the relationship between officers and subalterns.

This bond was to be demonstrated in even more remarkable ways. After most of the officers of the 46th had either escaped on their own, or been led to safety by *sepoys*, the regimental commander, Colonel Farquharson, along with Captain G. Caulfield, remained at the quarter guard of the grenadier company. Caulfield's wife described her husband's peculiar situation as he remained in the lines of a regiment, which had ostensibly cast off its loyalty to the British:

'The grenadier company would not let C—go, but forced him into the Kote havildar's hut,[42] declaring he would be killed by some of the excited Sepoys, and promising to escort him to the fort in the evening if he would trust them. He remained, for he had no choice, as the work of devastation was going on everywhere; and presently the colonel and sergeant-major were brought in. The men were of his own company, and were kind, even carrying their kindness to the length of offering him 1,000r. a month, and the colonel 2,000r., if they would accompany and command them!'[43]

The *sepoys*, in other words, offered employment to their officers 'if they would remain with them and lead them to Delhi against the English.'[44] Farquharson and Caulfield were furthermore promised 'six months leave in the hills every hot weather, and only to be stationed in the best Cantonments once the English had been defeated.'[45] This peculiar offer is highly revealing in terms of how Alum Bheg and the other *sepoys* of the 46th perceived the struggle they were caught up in. This was evidently not a conflict determined simply by race or religion, and the *sepoys* perceived their officers as essentially mercenary in nature. The political vision of the *sepoys*, if it can be described as such, was moreover one that did not preclude them being commanded by British officers after the uprising, and where British officers could still retreat to comfortable hill-stations in the summer. Tellingly, the conditions that Alum Bheg and the others imagined after 1857, did not seem that different from what they had been under British rule. Despite their situation, Farquharson and Campbell politely turned down the generous offer and the *sepoys* seemingly accepted their decision. The wife of the quartermaster sergeant had also been brought to the quarter guard, and she was sitting and weeping by herself:

> 'The havildar in charge of the guard came forward and asked her what was the matter; to which she replied that though they had saved her life, she was penniless as everything had been left behind in her bungalow. The havildar at once got some men together, and with fixed bayonets marched her back through the Cantonment to her house, where she was given time to collect her cash and other valuables. They then returned to the quarter-guard.'[46]

Although the power dynamics of the colonial state were rapidly collapsing, some bonds evidently remained intact. Caulfield, for instance, sent his wife to the fort accompanied only by a trusted *sepoy*, Maharaj Missur, while he himself went to the lines of the 46th. Later in the day, the *dobee*, or washerman, of the Caulfield household, also served as a go-between, carrying messages between the worrying wife in the fort, and her husband in the *sepoy* lines.[47] Some personal relationships, in other words, were unaltered by the mutiny and general breakdown of colonial order. These expressions of affection between the British officers and their men were later to raise questions as to why British officers had not warned the civilians at the stations about the impending outbreak. The mother of Thomas Watson, an artillery officer at Sialkot, wrote to her son on this matter: 'While you were soundly sleeping on your bed…Captain Caulfield was protected by the men; while your property was destroyed, his was untouched. With an almost Indian wife it was far more likely that he had intimation than you had but we know *no-body* had warning given him.'[48] Caulfield's wife was probably half-Indian, and during the crisis of 1857, that was enough to make the *sepoy's* protection of him seem somewhat suspicious.

The ethnic background of Caulfield's wife, however, had little to do with the way the Indian troops treated their officers, and in the cavalry lines, where the outbreak had originated, a similar scene played out. At 5am, Colonel Campbell, the commander of the 9th BLC, and his wife had been woken up by loyal *sowars* who came to warn them of the outbreak. The two quickly got dressed and made their way to the Brigadier's house. During their approach, they saw Brind and the other officers in headlong flight, being chased by a group of *sowars* who were firing their pistols. Campbell's wife described what happened next:

> 'We immediately rushed into the mess-house and out at the back door, which is opposite the cavalry lines, when troopers met us, and said they would not kill my husband, and begged us to go with them and they would try and save us. I thought every moment would be our last. Oh! the expression of their faces was awful to behold. Two of them hid us in a mud hut of a native officer, when in a minute the door was surrounded by the soldiers demanding us. L.[49] kept out of sight, and held his revolver ready to fire at them when the men who protected us said "It is the Colonel and his wife; don't kill them." They said, "we will not kill the Colonel if he comes out;" so we were obliged to go out among them, and they declared if we would follow them to the quarter-guard that they would protect us from the infantry and police. How can I describe our feelings—running along among horses' feet, and the men firing at all Europeans! We got into the quarter-guard, and I saw five or six police at the door, and when they saw me sitting on a charpoy, they waved about their swords and wanted to get at me, but the troopers kept them off, and said "The Colonel and his wife are to be saved, as he has always been kind to us."'[50]

In the lines of both the 9th and of the 46th, British officers and their wives were protected by the very Indian soldiers who had cast off their allegiance to the rule of the East Indian Company. But it would be a mistake to assume that the mutiny at Sialkot was characterised only by the bonds of friendship and loyalty—as indeed the attacks on Brigadier Brind and other officers had shown. As Mrs Campbell and her husband were sitting in the quarter guard, with nothing to do but wonder about their fate, and with men running to and fro and shots going off in all directions, a distraught Sarah Graham was brought in by a pair of troopers.

Early that morning, at the palatial Graham residence, the neighbours, Dr Guise and Mr Smith, had rushed over to warn the doctor of the outbreak. Dr Graham was already up and getting dressed but Sarah was still in bed. Since she had only just recovered from her fever, her father did not want to alarm Sarah and merely told her it was time for their morning ride. As she was slowly getting ready, her father calmly prepared for their departure. 'The Doctor was perhaps too much averse to either taking or giving alarm', Gordon noted, 'and there was no hurry in their movements.'[51] Waiting on the veranda, Dr Guise and Mr Smith were now getting increasingly nervous about the delay and hearing shots being fired in the *sepoy* lines close by, they decided to make a run for it on their own. Guise started off on foot but was soon picked up by Smith, who had fetched his buggy, and together they hastened through the Sudder Bazaar and along the road down the eastern side of the city. They could see *sowars* riding through the cantonment behind them and drove furiously until they reached the bridge at the intersection of the roads to Gurdaspur and Pasrur, on the southeastern corner of the city. Smith had thought of continuing towards Lahore, but Guise disagreed—an exchange later described by Gordon:

"'No,' said the Doctor, "there is danger of the villagers rising, and danger from sunstroke, if we should drive out into the country; let us turn back to the fort."

"Perhaps we may not be able to get through the city," said Smith; "a mile through the public streets is very hazardous; but I'll try it, Doctor, if you say so."

The Doctor began to doubt, and hesitatingly inquired: "But can you guarantee that the people of the city have not risen?"

"*Guarantee?*" said Smith. "No, I can't guarantee *anything* just *now*." Then, turning the horse, they dashed through the narrow streets of the city, and finding themselves still alive on reaching the fort entrance, they dropped the reins, leaped from the buggy, and passed inside the massive gates.'[52]

As Guise and Smith made it to safety, and with the mutiny in full swing a few hundred feet away, Dr Graham was still trying to gently nudge his daughter out the door without raising her suspicions. Having called for servants to prepare their buggy, Dr Graham and Sarah finally left the house and drove westwards, to the end of the cantonment and then turned south along the main Pucka Road. A little past Brigadier Brind's house, which now stood empty, Sarah noticed *sowars* galloping off to the right near the jail and started getting nervous:

> "'I fear,' said she, 'the Sepoys have mutinied.'
>
> "O, no," replied her father, endeavouring to quiet her fears.
>
> "But do you see those *sowars* coming across the race-course?"
>
> "Yes, my child, but do not feel alarmed; they have been at the riding-school, and are returning."
>
> "But, papa, dear, that is not the place for the riding-school; and I see two of them coming in this direction. Oh, I am so much afraid! See! They are coming at a gallop, and coming straight towards *us*.'"[53]

Dr Graham, however, continued to drive on at a leisurely pace in the direction of the fort. The approaching *sowars* at first appeared to be veering off toward the cantonment, and for a moment it seemed as if they would pass by the buggy. On reaching the road, however, they suddenly turned round, and riding up close, one of them shot Dr Graham in the back of the head with a pistol.[54] According to Gordon's account, 'The wound was mortal, and he sank heavily against his terror-stricken daughter, in a dying condition. Miss Graham seized the reins and endeavoured to support her dying father as well as she was able, whilst his life-blood flowed fast, and the frantic horse ran back into the cantonments, not coming to a halt until after reaching the compound of the Gen. Hearsey's house.'[55]

General Hearsey's house was a massive Georgian house, even grander and more imposing than the Graham residence, which stood in a large park-like garden with several outbuildings and servant's quarters, in the western end of the cantonment, and a stone's throw from the Brigadier's bungalow. At the time, the house was occupied by Dr J.H. Butler and Captain J. B. Saunders, medical officer and quartermaster, both of whom belonged to the 9th BLC. Along with their wives, children, nannies and servants, more than a dozen people were gathered at the house. Like so many others, Butler had been woken up early that morning by a servant who came rushing into his bedroom, calling out: 'sahib, sahib! Jildee utho sowar log bundook chalata, aur pultun bigra hai ['*Sir, Sir! Quickly those troopers are firing carbines, and the troop has become disaffected*'].'[56] Butler immediately roused his family and Captain

Saunders armed himself with a revolver and went out on the veranda, from where much of the Pucka road was visible. Here he 'saw several sowars riding about, some leisurely, others furiously, and heard pistol shots in several places.'[57] The families had already planned what to do in the event of an outbreak and prepared their carriages, packing only a few spare items to take with them. Before leaving, however, Saunders rode down to the mess of the 9th BLC. Upon passing three *sowars* on the road outside, he asked them what was going on, but they simply responded 'bag jao'—'*run away*'.[58] The *sowars* continued and stopped outside the compound of the Hearsey house and after a minute's discussion, turned around and headed for the lines of the 46th, as did several other parties of cavalrymen. Butler was still standing on the veranda, trying to gauge the situation:

> 'About half an hour elapsed from the time I came out to the moment when things had progressed so far—a pistol shot was heard to our extreme left, when some of our servants (most of whom were congregated in one part of the house) said, there is the Doctor Sahib's buggy coming. I looked in that direction and saw Miss Graham coming in the buggy apparently alone, screaming and crying most piteously. I helped her alight, the pistol shot I had heard was fired by a trooper (she afterwards told me) who rode after them, passed her side of the buggy, and went round to her poor father's and shot him. She told me the sowars had possession of the bridge along the road to the fort. I assisted in taking her father's body out of the buggy, and had it placed in one of the verandahs of the servant's houses, and then we determined upon not venturing out in that direction and knew not, in fact, what to do.'[59]

By now, they had now all but given up the plan of trying to leave the house, and Sarah's story showed just how dangerous it would be to venture out on the road. In the event of an outbreak, Butler had anticipated that the mounted police would be deployed to guide people in the cantonment to the safety of the fort, and he kept waiting for this escort—which, as it turned out, never came. In a later letter, Butler put this down to the fact that the mounted police and the *sowars* of the 9th cavalry had been allowed to fraternise.[60] So far, none of the *sowars* had taken any notice of Butler and the others, but that was about to change as Saunders suddenly returned, with several *sowars* in hot pursuit. When he entered the compound, Saunders was riding so fast that the horse did not stop outside, but barged through the front door and entered the house with the officer still on its back.[61] The pursuing *sowars* did not approach the house just then, although one of them did ride up and, pointing his carbine at the servants, told them to leave if they valued their lives. He also directed the coachman to take the carriages to the lines, definitively ruling out the chance of the families escaping. Butler and the other Europeans, including Sarah Graham, were now convinced by the servants to go back into the house and shut the doors, since *sowars* were bringing *sepoys* of the 46th down to the house.

Just as the Indian troops were favourably disposed to some of their officers, they also harboured an intense dislike of others, and Saunders was one of them. We do not know exactly why the *sowars* bore such ill-will towards their quartermaster, but Butler did state that 'the mutineers had vowed to take Saunders' life for the part he played in the Moonshee case.'[62] Apart from this cryptic allusion, we have no further details about the 'Moonshee case'. The regimental *munshi*, or clerk, whom this presumably referred to, was responsible for paying the soldiers their salaries, paying out advances and keeping the books for the regiment.[63] As quartermaster, Saunders would have played an important role in the day-to-day administration of regimental affairs and he may have been responsible for the dismissal of a well-loved *munshi*, or possibly have protected a *munshi* perceived by the troops to be corrupt. Whatever the case might have been, it seems clear that Saunders was one of the officers on the *sowar's* kill-list. Now that he was hiding in the Hearsey house along with Sarah Graham, Butler and all the women and children, his presence put everyone at risk. What is particularly noteworthy, is how organised the hunt for Saunders was. Butler described how ten minutes after the *sowar* had entered the compound and threatened the servants, a party of *sepoys* of the 46th arrived, 'brought up by the sound of the bugle, to do their bloody work.'[64] The actions of the *sepoys* who put their lives on the line to protect those officers they respected, was mirrored by the persistence and commitment to hunt down those against whom they held a grudge.

Butler and Saunders, who had been joined by Mr Garrard, a veterinary surgeon, prepared to defend their lives at all costs. Armed with revolvers, they slowly retreated into a bathroom, where the women and children had taken cover. According to Butler:

'the men of the 46th now were breaking open the doors and firing as they came along the corridors and into the rooms. On one making his appearance in the bathing room, I pointed my revolver at him, this was not a *sepoy*, but apparently one of the servants pointing out where we were, for on seeing my pistol and hearing it snap, he cried out, "Sahib log wahan haen, hun naheen jahye, marna ko moostaid haen" ["The Masters are over there, they cannot escape, they are preparing to fight till the end."]'[65]

Meanwhile the women and children fled into a small godown, or lumber room, attached to the main building by a side door. However, upon seeing the cramped space, Sarah Graham decided to try her luck elsewhere. Never one to compromise her comfort, she could not stand the prospect of being cooped up in such a small space with so many people, and instead left to hide in the big garden.[66] Here Sarah was immediately discovered by two *sowars*, who dragged her away. In stark contrast to the many horror stories of rape and violence allegedly perpetrated against white women by Indian rebels during 1857, Sarah nevertheless managed to negotiate with her captors: 'Able to speak the Hindustani language [*Hindi*] fluently, she made a pathetic appeal to them, which touched their hard hearts, and promised besides to reward them liberally if they would spare her life.'[67] Not only did Sarah convince the *sowars* to spare her life, but she also got them to fetch her a carriage and eventually escort her down to the Quarter Guard of the 9th, where she joined Mrs Campbell and the others.[68] Against all odds, Sarah had proved to be quite capable of looking after herself.

Back at the Hearsey compound, Butler and the others were still hiding in the lumber room, while the *sepoys* were turning the house upside down, firing into every room and breaking doors and furniture. At one point, Butler recounts, 'a sepoy of the 46th with a most fiend-like expression I ever saw', fired at the door to their hiding-place, but quickly retreated when Garrard fired at him with a revolver. They now expected more troops to gather, but the *sepoy* did not return. It was a nerve-wracking experience for the small group:

'The yell that ever and anon arose, and the crashing noise caused by the plunderers breaking open the wardrobes, almirahs and chests, kept us in a constant state of alarm as we could hear the troopers riding about; the chowkidar said our only security was in keeping quiet, which was no easy task with eight young children, as the least noise might reveal to the villains our hiding place.'[69]

The desperate parents had to gag the children to prevent them from crying out.[70] At one point they heard the soldiers trying to force the *chaukidar*, or watchman, Abdul Razak, to reveal their hiding place—but the old servant, the only remaining member of the household, claimed that they had all left. Razak later brought them some chapattis and a pitcher of water, to alleviate their thirst and hunger. As the hours passed and the sun rose higher in the sky, the small dark room grew increasingly hot and stuffy as Butler described it:

'In this godown there were most providentially two small windows, the glass of one was broken, and we were able to have some ventilation, but the heat and stench of the place was most trying. The godown adjoining was broken into, and when the magazine exploded, we thought, such was the shock we felt, they had mined the wall, and were going to blow it in; when the second magazine was blown up, there was so much noise and riding about that we imagined the mutineers had brought the cannon to bear upon the place to induce us to come to be massacred. The suspense and anxiety was awful'[71]

Razak would come from time to time to tell Butler and the others what was going on, but with soldiers still milling about and searching for Saunders, he did so at considerable risk to his own life. Gordon described how,

'Again and again the faithful watchman, Abdul Razak, was pressed to tell where the English refugees were. The four sowars who thirsted for Major Saunders' blood took Razak away for the 9th Cavalry lines, and offered him one thousand rupees if he would tell where they were concealed; but he insisted that he knew not. They then threatened to kill him if he would not inform them. At that juncture a man whom he had at some former time befriended, stepped forward and deliberately affirmed that he had just seen Major Saunders lying dead in Palkhu creek, north of the cantonments.'[72]

Razak was ultimately released and able to make his way back to the house. Throughout the day, several people came near to where the Europeans were hiding, but no concerted effort was made to flush them out. At one point Butler heard someone just outside the door: 'and then a savage looking man give it a tremendous blow, but not succeeding he looked through the grating. I took a steady aim with my revolver and fired, he fell back and groaned, but never spoke more, he was dead…'[73] The *sowars* may have suspected where Saunders and the others were hiding but Razak managed to divert them and apparently no one wanted to risk their lives approaching the lumber room. And so Butler and the others remained hidden in the sweltering heat of that small dark room.

6

THEIR BLOOD HAVE THEY SHED LIKE WATER

Outside the cantonment, the British residents did not escape the turmoil. At Monckton's house, Jones, who had the second watch of the night, fell asleep just as things went off in the Cavalry lines. A servant heard a disturbance in the direction of the jail and woke up McMahon, who had to stir his unreliable friend: 'At half-past 5 M'Mahon came into my room, saying, "There's a row at the gaol;" I offered to go down with him, but he said "Do not trouble."Two minutes later he came in, saying, "Well, J——, it is come at last."'[1] Stepping outside, they were treated to the spectacle of several *sowars* galloping through Monckton's garden with their swords drawn, and Lieutenant Princep fleeing for his life in the direction of the Wazirabad road. The sound of musket fire could now be heard from the cantonment, so they alerted Monckton and Boyle and assembled their guard of newly levied Sikhs.[2] While McMahon and Jones went to the lines of the Mounted Police, Monckton and Boyle ran over to Hill's house to alert the Hunters, but discovered that they had already left. After looking through the house, Boyle found himself 'left among the trees in the grounds, peeping out to see how near the wretches came; after staying and occasionally moving and again hiding, I made up my mind to take my heels across the plains.'[3] The good Reverend eventually made it to the safety of the fort, while Monckton, who was quite ill, managed to escape to a nearby village.[4]

Meanwhile, McMahon and Jones had hastened down to the Police lines, a few hundred yards away from the house, along with twelve brand new Sikh recruits. Once they arrived, McMahon ordered the one hundred-man-strong force of the mounted police to saddle up and follow them. To their surprise, they found that not a single man was prepared to follow orders—'they responded only by angry and sullen looks.'[5] There were at the time several *sowars* of the 9th riding about within the police lines and the two officers realised that these Indian troopers were the ones in charge. One of the *sowars* even called out to the recruits of McMahon's tiny force: 'Come you also and join us.'[6] Realising that their survival rested entirely on the recruits remaining faithful, McMahon addressed his men earnestly: 'Fifteen years' service on good pay,' he said, 'with a liberal pension the rest of your lives. Are you ready to forfeit all this, and be hanged besides?'[7] After some wavering, the recruits finally declared their loyalty, and McMahon and Jones carefully led them out of the police lines, giving up on the men there as a lost cause. When they learned that the Hunters had already left, they too set out for the fort and Jones later described their tense march past the jail where the *sowars* were in the process of releasing the prisoners:

'I and M'Mahon walked off at the head of our raw recruits, going slowly for the rest to come up, and then having to stop and make them load, and see that they did it well, as it was the first time many of them had put a cartridge into a musket. We then went slowly across the plain, till two or three cavalry rode up very close, calling to our men to come with them, and at first, taken in by the *ruse*, they moved a few paces towards them. We told them they were mutineers, who wanted to take away their bread from them, and, patting one or two of them, told them that this was a time when we and they were going to be brothers. They then marched on as pluckily as possible, laughing and joking with us, though we felt in anything but a laughing humour. Twice, as we moved along, bodies of cavalry came very near. We made our men face round to them, and, telling them that Punjabees were not to be alarmed at the sight of such cowards, they showed so bold a front that the wrenches went off, though they might with ease have cut us all up. Our horses were led after us, but we thought it best not to mount, lest it might discourage our men. After getting past the gaol we found no difficulty in reaching the fort, where we found numbers of officers had preceded us.'[8]

It was only after they reached the fort, that McMahon and Jones found out that Thomas and Jane Hunter never made it. The anxious missionaries had probably stayed awake the previous night, in anticipation of their departure, and were thus likely to have been among the first to be alerted when the *sowars* rode down to the prison before the break of dawn. Following this, they had immediately packed up the carriage and left Hill's house with the baby, quietly passing the Monckton house where Jones was sleeping on his watch; the others were as yet unaware that the outbreak they had all been anticipating had commenced.[9] Rather than heading straight out of Sialkot, and westwards towards Wazirabad, Thomas Hunter stuck with their original plan to make for Lahore, which meant they had to drive south and down through the city. Accordingly, they took the road that led down past the jail, court-house and treasury, and unbeknownst to them, the same path the *sowars* had taken just shortly before.

As they crossed the bridge over the Palku Creek, the Hunters came within sight of the *sowars* and jail *chauprassis* who were in the process of releasing the prisoners from the jail. When the carriage was spotted, a *sowar* resolutely rode up and fired his pistol at Thomas at point-blank range, the ball 'passing through Mr. Hunter's face and entering Mrs Hunter's body about the neck.'[10] No one now seemed willing to finish the job, but after some discussion Hurmat Khan, the demoted *chauprassi* with a grudge, stepped forward and 'completed the murder with a sword, killing the child also.'[11] According to Indian eye-witnesses questioned by Monckton, the Hunters 'and their child were then dragged out of the carriage and hacked to pieces by the Kutcherry and Jail Chupprassees.'[12] At least one account claims that the bodies were subsequently stripped naked by Hurmat Khan as an act of public humiliation—but this is not corroborated by any other sources and was indeed a standard trope in contemporary accounts of rebel atrocities.[13] What is certain is that the bodies were left 'weltering in their blood upon the ground.' After news of the murder of the Hunters reached McMahon at the fort, he went out with some of the Sikh recruits and recovered the bodies. Even in death, Jane still clutched the body of her baby and, according to Gordon:

'Mr Hunter was found lying with his head pillowed upon his arm, a position he seemed to have taken after he had received his mortal wound.

Captain McMahon distinctly states that their bodies were not mutilated. Some Panjabi peasants who had seen them lying unguarded, drew near, and watched over them until they were removed to the fort.'[14]

In their desperation to leave, Thomas and Jane Hunter, along with their baby, might very well have become the very first European victims of the outbreak at Sialkot.

Back in the lines of the 9th BLC, Mrs Campbell, Sarah Graham and the others were still being protected by the *sowars*. They knew that the Scottish missionaries had not gotten away since a wounded horse had been brought in by a servant who said it belonged to Mr Hunter, 'and that he, his wife and child, had been killed in their carriage, and were lying dead on the roadside.'[15] Though afraid for what might befall her husband, Mrs Campbell managed to keep up a brave front and tried to comfort Sarah. Gordon later described, with some poetic license, how Sarah Graham had mourned her father:

'As she sat sadly reflecting upon what had happened, her eyes rested accidently on a pair of diamond bracelets which adorned her fair hands, and caught a glimpse of blood-stains. The tragic events of the awful morning were instantly before her; and these thoughts flashed across her troubled mind: "How gently my father urged me to rise, disregarding what his courageous spirit deemed unnecessary alarm! How tenderly he sought to dispel my rising fears at the sight of those murderous troopers! Alas, how leisurely I arranged my toilet when moments were worth millions! Oh that we had made *haste!*"—*and she dashed the bloody ornaments from her sight in horror!* Poor bereaved child!'[16]

There was little time for such sentiments, however, and they kept getting news of various people who had been killed. There were also more Europeans being brought in, including one officer of the 9th who, along with his wife, was wearing the clothes of an Indian woman to avoid detection.[17] The French nuns and their young female pupils had to escape from the convent on foot when their carriages were commandeered by *sowars* who also plundered all their valuables. None of them, however, were hurt and they were allowed to seek refuge at the Quarter Guard; although by their own accounts this was due only to divine intervention and a series of miracles worthy of a medieval chronicle.[18] When the *sowars* at the Quarter Guard were distracted by the arrival of cash removed from the treasury, a Christian drummer of the regimental band helped the nuns and their wardens escape to the fort.[19] At one point during her miraculous delivery, the Mother Superior also had to cover herself with a sheet, and, pretending to be a soldier's wife, *salaamed* two *sowars* who were passing by.[20] Considering how pervasive the image of the colonial officer disguised in local dress became in colonial literature after 1857, famously exemplified by Rudyard Kipling's 'Kim' or 'Inspector Strickland', or indeed any of John Master's characters, the reality of such attempts at cultural cross-dressing is noteworthy. Where the fictional sahib in disguise personified the colonial state's power and unhindered access to local society—spying on the secret plotting of 'Thugs' or rebellious rajas—the British reliance on disguise at Sialkot in 1857 reflected their vulnerability and complete helplessness during this moment of crisis. 'Going native' was not an expression of cultural mastery, but the desperate acts of people fleeing for their lives.

The wrath and violence unleashed against the British at Sialkot was neither random nor unique, but followed a well-established repertoire common to urban riots. The *sowars* and *sepoys* deliberately destroyed official buildings and institutions that symbolised colonial authority: they blew up the magazines, with its stores of ammunition; they burnt the court-house, and all the records and files; and they also plundered the treasury.[21] While the local Punjabi population remained largely uninvolved, most of the *Hindustani* servants and camp-followers of the station immediately joined the *sepoys*. As one official report described it: 'Khitmutgars, syces, grass-cutters, bazaar people, all appear to have joined them.'[22] These were the subalterns and menials who serviced the military establishment, and most of the camp-followers, including prostitutes, blacksmiths, and merchants, lived in the Sudder Bazaar under direct British supervision. Like Alum Bheg and the other *Purbiya* troops, they were alien to Punjab; they lived under much the same conditions as did the Indian troops, and their fate was intimately tied up with that of the *sepoys* and *sowars*.

What might appear as mindless plunder and destruction at Sialkot during the outbreak, was the result of the carnivalesque excitement of the world being turned upside down: released prisoners, now standing shoulder-to-shoulder with prison guards, could do as they pleased, and servants suddenly found themselves in possession of their masters' house and belongings. Under such circumstances no real distinction can be made between the attack on the authorities and plunder for personal enrichment. For the *sepoys* and servants systematically destroying the Hearsey mansion, in which Butler and the others were hiding, there would have been little difference between smashing the china, or pocketing the silverware. It was furthermore not just the European bungalows that were plundered and torched. In the Sudder Bazaar the shops owned by Parsis appear to have been deliberately targeted by the *sepoys*, while those owned by Muslims were untouched.[23] The details of this remain somewhat unclear, but there does seem to have been a sectarian aspect in the targeting of merchants. One particular merchant fared badly despite his support for the rebels:

'One merchant who had private information of the intended mutiny at Delhi, and who gave information to the King of Delhi respecting our forces, stood on the bridge leading to the Fort and threw dirt at the ladies as they came up. The [*sepoys*] fined him 2,000 rupees, promising not to loot his shop, which was at that time well filled; having got the money they treated his shop worse than the others.'[24]

Later in the day, villagers from the surrounding countryside began to pour in. These were essentially poor peasants taking advantage of the outbreak to loot and their actions should thus be considered as separate from those of the *sepoys*. The involvement of villagers from the countryside nevertheless reflected the expanding dynamic of the outbreak, and what had started as a purely military mutiny, quickly came to involve other parts of the population. Yet how much Alum Bheg and the villagers of the countryside surrounding Sialkot really had in common was far from clear.[25]

Amidst the noise, smoke and general confusion of the outbreak, the Quarter Guard became an unlikely haven to the British men and women who found themselves caught up in the mutiny. The presence there of Lorne Campbell in particular appears to have been a deciding factor in how the *sowars* acted. By the afternoon of the 9th, the *sowars* finally seemed to be preparing to leave, as Mrs Campbell recounted:

'The troopers told L. they would accompany him to the fort, and protect us from the infantry. They said he and the Colonel of the 46th were the only two they would preserve. Just as they were ready to march, we got into our carriages (we took Miss Graham into ours and Mrs Graham[26] went in her own) and set off for the fort with four troopers to keep people from destroying us. What a sight to behold! many of the houses on fire, and men standing on the road ready to take our lives! When we got near the fort we saw Sikh soldiers on the ramparts, who were protecting the Europeans that had escaped. We made signs for them not to fire; but an accidental shot went off, which frightened the troopers, so they fled as fast as they could to the station. We did not mind, as we were then safe so near our own people; and when we got to the gate our officers met us. On our entering the fort a fearful scene of distress met our eyes—our Brigadier (Brind) lying mortally wounded, and the Brigade-Major lying dead.'[27]

The brigade-major, Capt. W.L. Bishop, and his wife and children, had earlier that morning fled the cantonment in a carriage and took the main road through the Sudder Bazaar as Guise and Smith had also done. As they approached the fort along the road that brought them close to the court-house and treasury, they were suddenly pursued by several *sowars*. The British assembled in the fort observed the desperate race from the ramparts, as Gordon recounted:

'On came the carriage and pair as fast as they could be urged. On sped the murderous troopers, "swift as the eagle that hasteth to the prey." The fugitives seemed almost to have won the race. Shots were fired from the fort to check the pursuers, but without effect. Near the spot now occupied by the Sialkot Railway station, was an excavation in the road, washed out by the rains, over which one of our light "American traps"[28] would have skimmed like a swallow; but English carriages are heavy, and though very elegant, are only adapted to toll majestically along smooth roads. The carriage plunged in, and was upset.'[29]

In order to save his family, Bishop jumped out of the carriage and sought to draw the *sowars* away as he tried to escape on foot. The pursuers fired and wounded him, and Bishop staggered into a ditch full of water—'a trooper then rode up and deliberately shot him through the head.'[30] Meanwhile Mrs Bishop and the children managed to save themselves and fled into the safety of the fort.

As the pre-arranged rallying point, the fort was now crowded with survivors of the outbreak.[31] Aided by the Sikh levies, the British officers had thrown up earthworks to reinforce the gate; muskets and ammunition had been served out and the bastions manned: 'no time to eat,' as McMahon put it, 'and a burning sun over us.'[32] From the relative safety of the fort, Reverend Boyle and the others could do little more than watch as their homes and the station were destroyed. When Alum Bheg and all the *sepoys* and camp-followers eventually left during the afternoon, they marched right past the ramparts in a surprisingly orderly column, leaving Sialkot in a south-easterly direction along the road towards Gurdaspur. Boyle described the spectacle:

> 'I stood on the north bastion of the fort for hours, watching all they did, and when the artillery magazine blew up it was grand and fearful. They then collected all our carriages, horses, buggies, and loaded them with the spoils of all our bungalows. Then they mustered the Government camels, and loaded them, and at 4 o'clock, the hour we were to have started, they took the road I was to have taken for Goojeranwalla, passing along by the fort, and so affording us a full view. They took away our dear Edward's pony, and my only companion, the dog Charlie.'

Although the Europeans at Sialkot had only barely survived the out-break, what seemed to grieve them most was the loss of their material possessions: clothes, jewellery, a favourite horse, a piano or regimental plate. Apart from the distraught Sarah Graham, several of the other survivors were deeply traumatised by their experience, including the wife of the civil surgeon, whose grief was 'most painful and heart-rending, and while in the fort she nearly sunk from sorrow.'[33] Bishop's wife was also said to have lost her mind.[34]

* * *

After the departure of Alum Bheg and the *sepoys* and *sowars*, the survivors slowly emerged from their places of hiding and began trickling in to the fort. Mrs Caulfield was reunited with her husband, who came along with Farquharson directly from the lines of the 46th BNI. Missing since the morning, Monckton now appeared as he was brought in from a nearby village, 'covered up on a *charpai*, and carried as if dead on the heads of four coolies.'[35] Butler and his party spent more than twelve hours in the lumber room before they ventured out at six o'clock in the evening and made their way to the fort. Shortly before, when they thought they were about to be discovered, Butler and his wife had actually handed over their infant boy to the Sikh wet-nurse to save his life. The woman came to the fort the following day with the baby, and the parents were reunited with their child.[36] Campbell's wife described the situation at the fort:

'All the ladies and children are here, with the exception of Mrs Hunter and her child, who were killed. The mutineers blew up both the magazines before marching, and we saw the explosion. The prisoners were let loose from the jail, who, with the natives, villagers, &c., broke into our houses, smashed all our furniture, and stole every article we possessed; so here we are without a stitch of clothes, shut up in a place with only one room, containing nearly one hundred, and the heat excessive. We have a hard native bedstead to sleep on, without sheets or anything of the kind, which we take outside at night, as every one chooses to sleep in the open air.'[37]

Outside the fort, the locals were left to fend for themselves. Mohamet Ismael, the Muslim convert who had been a companion of Thomas and Jane Hunter right from the beginning, when they first arrived at Sialkot, had remained at their house in the cantonment, and it was here that he first learned of their deaths:

'It was on the morning of Thursday, the 9th [...], that Mr. Hunter's bearer came to me with the melancholy news that they were all murdered by the rebellious and cruel sepoys. This heartrending news excited grief and terror in my mind, and I began to cry aloud, when Mr. Hunter's servant, who was a well-disposed man, advised me not to do so, adding that my life was also in danger, I being a Christian, and having often preached to the natives. So he, though compassion, took me to a neighbouring village, where we both stayed until I heard there was peace and quiet in Sialkot'[38]

As was usually the case during 1857, the suffering of the local population was barely noticed by the Europeans, and for all the melodramatic details we possess on the experiences of white men, women and children, the archives are largely silent as regards the fate of everybody else. One letter from an officer of the 52nd briefly mentions that, at the time the Hunter family was killed, the prisoners who had been freed also killed 'several half-castes'.[39] People of mixed background, usually known as Eurasians, were often targeted during the uprising, as were Indian Christians, whose very religion marked them as collaborators with the British. According to the French nuns, the Christian drummer who helped them was later 'maltreated' by the *sepoys*, and his hut and possessions burnt.[40] Probably referring to the actions of Hurmat Khan, McMahon also stated that the rebels 'also killed several natives, against whom they had a spite.'[41] There is, however, no way of knowing exactly how many Indians and Eurasians were killed during the outbreak at Sialkot.

* * *

The Indian Uprising of 1857 was widely regarded by the British as the outcome of a vast conspiracy. The rumours of the greased cartridges had been no more than a convenient ploy, they believed, used by religious leaders and power-hungry maharajas to manipulate the gullible *sepoys*. The insidious nature of the conspiracy was further exacerbated by the peculiarities of the 'oriental' character, as Reverend Duff of the Church of Scotland described it:

> 'Throughout the ages the Asiatic has been noted for his duplicity, cunning, hypocrisy, treachery; and coupled with this,—and, indeed, as necessary for excelling in his accomplishment of Jesuitism,—his capacity of secrecy and concealment. But in vain will the annals even of Asia be ransacked for examples of artful, refined, consummate duplicity, surpassing those which have been exhibited throughout the recent mutinies. In almost every instance, the *sepoys* succeeded in concealing their long-concocted and deep-laid murderous designs from the most vigilant officers to the very last.'[42]

At Sialkot, most of the European residents who had lived through the outbreak could not bring themselves to believe that it had been anything but the result of a plot.[43] One of the sisters at the Jesus and Mary Convent claimed that once the *sepoys* heard they were being disarmed, they 'secretly planned a revolt. They carried their plans into execution at an early hour on the following morning.'[44] The young Lieutenant Princep of the 9th BLC similarly stated that 'the whole business was evidently preconcerted, although we were quite unprepared for it.'[45] The idea of ringleaders guiding events at Sialkot found its full expression in the narrative of Deputy Commissioner of Amritsar Frederic Cooper, written in 1858. Cooper, who himself played a key role in the suppression of the uprising in Punjab, described in great detail the circumstances of the conspiracy—and the devious mindset of the plotters, as he imagined it:

> 'Up to the date of events at Jhelum everything had been still and quiet as deep waters at Sealkote. The band played as usual; society partook of its evening recreation. In fact the sepoy did not find it worth his while, as at

Jullundar, to test by insolence and incendiarism the temper of the authorities; for he was already master of the situation. Society knew, however, the corruption that lay beneath that shining and polite exterior. The sepoys, too, felt himself suspected, and knew his power. Besides this a hopefully hypocritical aspect had to be worn. By a temporising policy, every day without fresh evidence of "overt" disaffection was of a week's political value. And though every resident in the ill-fated station had his or her forebodings, none liked to dilate upon them, when every gesture and look was commented upon. Thus on the night of the rising, the Superintending Surgeon begged a friend with whom he was dining, who had remarked on the contemptuous demeanour of the sepoys, not to let "his fears get the better of his senses." The next morning the slaughtered body of Dr. Graham fell into the arms of his daughter, shot dead by a trooper as he was driving her to the fort!'[46]

According to Cooper, everything that happened on 9 July had been planned the previous evening, after the arrival of the *sowars* from Amritsar, and the outbreak itself was thus merely the climax of a well-prepared conspiracy:

'a second conclave was held with delegates from the 46th N.I. that very night. The whole plan of the morning's bloody proceedings must have been laid out. The sepoys invited their officers to hold an inspection parade, the invitation was complied with, and the right at once commenced firing on them.'[47]

Of course, none of this was true, and Cooper could offer no evidence to back up such claims, but many of the newspaper reports that subsequently circulated about the outbreak at Sialkot were no less misleading and no less sensationalist.[48] *The Times*, for instance, reproduced a letter from an Englishwoman writing from the safety of the hill-station at Simla:

'At Sealkote three of the native Cavalry rode up to the Brigadier Brind's house, and giving information of an intended meeting and an impending attack from without, asked for a parade, that they (the loyal) might be prepared to receive and defeat the mutineers. A parade was ordered, and these loyal gentlemen fired on their officers! The poor brigadier was shot dead through the body. His widow is two doors from us. Captain Bishop and a third fell. The others escaped with their lives into the fort, finding the station guarded by pickets. The missionary and his wife were murdered. The wretches first cut off the head of their little child of two years old; they then ripped up the mother, and threw her body and child's out into the road.'[49]

Another news report claimed that, at Sialkot, 'some of the European women were violated and other atrocities committed. We shall never hear publicly of half the villainies perpetrated by these Poorbeas throughout the country.'[50] Not only were these reports factually inaccurate, but by inventing episodes of Indian treachery and barbarism they also provided the implicit justification for any retributive violence visited on the rebels.

* * *

The truth was that the outbreak at Sialkot was a highly contingent and confusing event, and one that in many ways differed from the mutinies that had taken place earlier that year at Meerut, Delhi and elsewhere. At Sialkot, there were no angry mobs chasing European civilians, no random lynching of isolated *sahibs*, no sexual attacks on *memsahibs* and no mutilation of their corpses. There had been numerous opportunities for *sepoys* and other locals to rape white women should they so have wished, but it never happened. Jane Hunter and her baby were indeed the only woman and child to be killed.[51] According to one contemporary newspaper report, 'the insurgents had resolved to kill every European.'[52] The opposite was actually the case, and according to Gordon, who later talked to many of the survivors:

> 'The 46th Native Infantry Regiment mutinied with the 9th Cavalry, and marched away with them, but took no part in murdering their officers or other English people. On the contrary, they had entered into a positive agreement with the 9th Cavalry not to murder any of the English; and when the latter violated the engagement they threatened to turn about and fight *them*.'[53]

The notion that there was an agreement not to kill any Europeans seems incompatible with the existence of a kill-list—yet both were true, which reveals just how complex the dynamics of the mutiny at Sialkot really were. Within each regiment, there were evidently different cliques, not necessarily in agreement with one another: it was the elite grenadiers of the 46th BNI who protected Farquharson and Caulfield at their quarter guard. Two of the NCO's of the grenadier company were also the only ones out of the entire 46th to remain loyal and to stay behind at Sialkot when the rest left.[54] In the 9th BLC, the division appears to have been along religious lines: the *sowars* of A troop were explicitly described as 'Mussulmans', while Balmain referred to the warning he was given by the Hindu *sowars*.[55]

Since the relationship between at least some of the Indian troops and their British officers was so strong within both the 9th BLC and 46th BNI, those *sowars* committed to the rising, had to make a very deliberate effort to sever the bond of loyalty. Unless all the troops joined in, the mutiny would fail, and those who had taken the initiative would have risked their lives for nothing. They had to do something irreversible to implicate everyone, and this is why a seemingly small group of the *sowars* were so active and the ones almost exclusively responsible for the attacks on their officers and other Europeans. When the quartermaster Havildar and *sowars* of A troop, who were the main instigators, chased Brigadier Brind and the other officers, or shot and killed Dr Graham, it was thus calculated and deliberate. Hurmat Khan's killing of the Hunters, and especially of Jane and the baby, however, was far more transgressive. Carried out up close with a sword, rather than from the distance of pistol-shot, these murders went beyond any of the violence inflicted by the mutineers. Although it was an individual act, it was furthermore one that had a profound collective impact, effectively sealing the fate of all the Indian troops at Sialkot. Colonel Campbell tried to convince the loyal *sowars* of the 9th not to join their comrades, but 'as some of them had committed murder they said it was impossible for them to remain.'[56] A mutiny required complete solidarity amongst the troops and once officers had been attacked, and women and children murdered, there was no going back. They knew that none of them could expect any mercy from the authorities: their only hope of survival was to stay together and defeat the British.

In his report on the outbreak at Sialkot, McMahon provided another more specific explanation for the murder of Jane Hunter:

> 'Mr Hunter and his family had gone on some time before, and had all been murdered on the road. It seemed to have been no part of the Sealkote mutineers' plan to massacre ladies and children, but perhaps Mrs Hunter had offended the fanatical Mohammedans by establishing a small female school—a crime, in their eyes, deserving death.'[57]

This is not implausible, but there is also the possibility that when Hurmat Khan could not get hold of Monckton, against whom he held a grudge, he took out his revenge on the Hunters instead when they happened to drive past. During the uprising, personal animosity merged with general discontent, and personal vendettas and political conflicts became virtually inseparable. Apart from buildings, such as churches, prisons and court-houses, every European man, woman and child, were seen to embody the colonial state; during 1857, Europeans were thus often attacked indiscriminately, as if they individually represented an existential threat to the moral order of Indian society. This accounts for the retributive nature of some of the more brutal acts of violence and mutilation that took place at Meerut and Delhi. In other instances, Indian servants simply felt empowered to strike back at their former masters. The sudden implosion of colonial rule ultimately allowed men like Hurmat Khan to take advantage of the chaos and seek revenge for personal reasons.

Yet just as personal animosity might feed into the broader violence of the outbreak, so too did personal friendships and ties of loyalty save lives and shape the course of events at Sialkot. Contemporary accounts made much of the fact that some servants had sided with the mutineers at Sialkot, but the truth was that many of the Europeans owed their lives to *sepoys* and Indian servants. For every servant who sabotaged his master's pistols, or pointed out their hiding place, there were those who risked everything to help the frightened and vulnerable Europeans cowering in the intense July heat. During the upheaval of the outbreak, however, the bond between *sepoys* and *sahibs* was not enough to prevent even the most loyal troops from throwing in their lot with their brothers in arms. Of the *sowars* who had spent the entire day protecting Colonel Campbell, his wife and several other Europeans in the Quarter Guard, only one, *Havildar* Subhan Khan, remained with the officer and went into the fort while the rest of his comrades left Sialkot. Of the more than 900 *sepoys* in the 46th BNI, just three stayed behind at Sialkot, remaining at the side of Colonel Farquharson. Ultimately, the Indian troops at Sialkot functioned as a tight-knit unit, and their sense of solidarity and cohesion remained firm even as they cast off their loyalty to the East Indian Company. When Farquharson and Caulfield left the Quarter Guard, and headed for the fort in the afternoon, the *sepoys* of the 46th BNI were genuinely upset:

4.

5.

1.

MR. AND MRS. JOHN MANTLE of The Lord
Clyde, Walmer, with the Indian mutiny skull
discovered in a lumber room.

2.

Skull of Havildar "Alum Bheg," 46th Regt. Bengal N. Infantry
who was blown away from a gun amongst several others of his Regt. He was
a principal leader in the mutiny of 1857 & of a most ruffianly disposition. He
took possession (at the head of a small party) of the road leading to the
fort to which place all the Europeans were hurrying for safety. His
party surprised and killed Dr Graham shooting him in his buggy by
the side of his daughter. His next victim was the Rev. Mr Hunter
a Missionary, who was flying with his wife and daughters
in the same direction. He murdered Mr Hunter, and his
wife and daughters after being brutally treated were
butchered by the road side.
    Alum Bheg was about 32 years of age, 5 feet 7½ inches
high and by no means an ill looking native
    The skull was brought home by Captain Costello who was
on duty when Alum Bheg was executed.

3.

6.

7.

8.   9.

10.   11.

12.

13.

14.

15.

16

17.

18.

19.

20.

21.

22.

23.

24.

25.

26.

27.

28.

29.

30.

31.

32.

33.

34.

35.

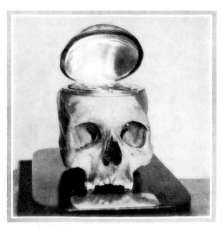

36.

37.

38.

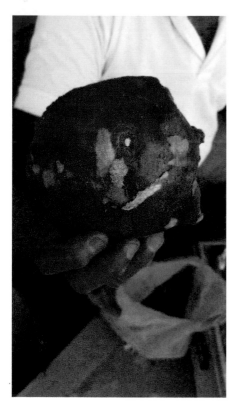

39.

40.

'On parting with them several of the men shed tears, touched their feet, the most respectful mode of native salutation, and deplored the separation between them. On being urged not to join in the mutiny, they said they could not avoid doing so. They must fight for the general cause.'[58]

Within a matter of hours, Alum Bheg had gone from being a soldier in the Bengal Army, to being a mutineer, and one who was moreover tainted by the blood others had spilled. Whatever his personal feelings were, he was swept along by the current of events bigger than himself.

One of the most persistent myths of the outbreak at Sialkot, was the story that the mutineers had strategically placed pickets all around the cantonment to intercept any Europeans trying to flee. The Hunters had supposedly been stopped by one of these pickets when trying to leave Sialkot via the Wazirabad Road, which is why they turned around and went south past the jail and to their death.[59] But apart from the *sowars* riding around along the two roads leading from the cantonment to the fort, there had been no such 'road-blocks' deliberately set up—and dozens of fleeing Europeans made it to safety along those very roads. Crucially, this also means that the description of the outbreak in the note found with Alum Bheg's skull is in essence incorrect. The note claimed that Alum Bheg had been a 'principal leader in the mutiny,' and that he:

'took possession (at the head of a small party) of the road leading to the fort, to which place all the Europeans were hurrying for safety. His party surprised and killed Dr Graham shooting him in his buggy by the side of his daughter. His next victim was the Rev Mr Hunter, a missionary, who was flying with his wife and daughters in the same direction. He murdered Mr Hunter, and his wife and daughter after being brutally treated were butchered by the road side.'

The existing evidence makes no mention of a party of *sepoys* waylaying British fugitives, and the Hunters and Graham were also killed on different roads leading to the fort. There is also nothing to indicate that Jane Hunter and her two-year-old son (not daughters), were 'brutally treated,' as a euphemism for sexual assault, before they were killed. We do not know exactly where Alum Bheg was during the outbreak on 9 July, nor what role he played in the chaotic events. He might have been one of the loyal NCO's who protected Farquharson and Caulfield at the Quarter Guard in the lines of the 46th, or he may have been with the party that tore the Butler mansion apart in their search for Saunders. What is clear, however, is that Alum Bheg was not responsible for the murders of Thomas and Jane Hunter and their baby, nor of Dr Graham; these were all very explicitly recorded as having been killed either by *sowars* of the 9th BLC or by Hurmat Khan, the *chauprassi*. Several of the key eyewitnesses to the outbreak were furthermore clear on this general point: the men of the 46th BNI did not kill anyone at Sialkot. Alum Bheg, in other words, was innocent.

7

GORGING VULTURES AND HOWLING JACKALS

By nightfall on 9 July 1857, Alum Bheg and the other mutineers from Sialkot were heading towards Delhi where British rule had been over-turned and the Mughal Emperor reinstalled. Further south, at Banda, the *sepoys* asserted their role when the local Nawab proclaimed his rule with the words: 'Khulq khodi ki, mulk Badshah ka, Hukm Subahdar sepoy Bahadur ka'—'the world is God's, the country is the Emperor's, and it is the rule of the soldiers.'[1] This reflected the belief among the mutinying *sepoys* that they constituted the real power behind the throne—a somewhat lofty role the British had never accorded them. To their former employers, the *sepoys* were merely an instrument of power, but the *sepoys* saw themselves as kingmakers. By reinstating Bahadur Shah, the Meerut and Delhi mutineers had created the possi-bility of an alternative source of legitimate authority. Elsewhere the *sepoys* gathered around local figures of power such as Nana Sahib at Cawnpore or Lakshmi Bai at Jhansi. When *sepoys* and civilians offered their allegiance to these new rebel governments, it was not, according to Ahmed Khan, considered a betrayal:

'It must be borne in mind that for centuries past the condition of India has been unsettled, that from time immemorial its people have been accus-tomed to flock in thousands to the standard of any powerful noble (Ameer) who attained any success in the field, and that they never held their doing so to be criminal, accepting responsible posts in the administration of his country for the time being. It is well known in India that the taking of service is no offence. Whoever pays is served. It is thought wrong not to tender allegiance to a king who may have been proclaimed king in the place of another deposed. The various kings and princes of Hindustan have never, on conquering an enemy's country, attached any blame to the servants, whether civil or military, of that enemy, and the people were aware of this.

When the leaders of the rebellion called for recruits, thousands of poor men, wanting service, flocked in and took it. They thought there was nothing wrong in doing so, as their livelihood was procured by such service. Many thought that the British rule in Hindustan was at an end, and that therefore it was their duty to tender their allegiance to the reigning powers, i.e., to the rebels.'[2]

In one sense, the mutiny at Sialkot was not so much an anti-colonial uprising as much as it was the suspension of a contract of service. The next step was to receive the blessings of a new patron—one who would could offer political leadership and safeguard their status and honour. Without that, they were merely a mutinous rabble of mercenaries. Alum Bheg and the men of the 9th and 46th did not simply plunder the treasury at Sialkot, throw off their uniforms, and then scatter to the four winds with as much loot as they could carry home. Their shared *Purbiya* identity tied them together, especially since they were thousands of miles from their villages back in Awadh. More than that, however, it was their shared military identity that provided a sense of cohesion even at the moment of mutiny. The Sialkot troops remained together as functional military units and they chose not to divide up the cash taken from the treasury. Instead, they intended to take it to Bahadur Shah, and somewhat ironically, offer it to him so that he could provide them with a formal salary for their service.[3]

Since the Movable Column was known to be at Amritsar, the rebels planned to circle around Lahore and Amritsar, and then travel via Gurdaspur and Jallandahr down to Delhi. The plan was to join forces with the various regiments along the way—the 2nd Irregular Cavalry at Gurdaspur, 4th BNI at Nurpur, and the 16th Irregular Cavalry at Hoshiapur—and thus arrive at the Mughal capital with a substantial force.[4] The distance between Sialkot and Delhi, however, was more than 300 miles, and they would have to cross both the Ravi and the Beas Rivers, which were at their highest during the rain season. The *sepoys* had plenty of horses, camels, carriages and other modes of conveyance, but they also had hundreds of camp-followers and other *Hindustanis* from Sialkot in tow—including women and children. They were additionally weighed down by their loot, which included everything from the regimental mess plate of the 52nd, to the old signal gun from the cantonment, a heavy old 12-pounder.

Alum Bheg and the Sialkot mutineers knew that there was no British force in pursuit, and since their route took them far from any of the bigger stations, they did not hurry. On the day of the outbreak they only marched ten miles before making camp, and after three days they had made it no further than the Ravi River, fifty-six miles from Sialkot. Their progress was halted at the river since the British had destroyed the boats and placed guards at the ferries and fords between Madhopur in the north and Lahore to the south.[5] Two *sepoys* of the 46th were sent ahead to Gurdaspur to alert the 2nd Irregulars of their arrival, and a *sowar* from that regiment later rode out to show the rebels where the river was fordable at a place known as Trimmu Ghat.[6] There was an island in the middle of the river at Trimmu Ghat, but as luck would have it the water levels were so low that it joined up with the mainland on the north-western side. On the side closest to Gurdaspur, the water was sufficiently shallow to be crossed on foot. The entire body of *sowars*, *sepoys*, and camp-followers, along with the carriages and animals weighed down by plunder, now hurried across the river; only the cannon was too heavy to drag across the channel where the water was chest-high, and so it remained stuck on the small island. While the *sowars* could easily cross mounted on their horses, the *sepoys* had to wade across the ford, carefully holding their rifles, cartridge-pouches, and reserve gunpowder above their heads, to prevent them from being soaked and ruined by the water. Just before noon on 12 July, shortly after everyone had finished the crossing, scouts from the 9th BLC, who had been sent ahead in advance, came galloping back to report that a sizeable force was approaching from the direction of Gurdaspur. It was unclear who these troops were, since Amritsar was more than forty miles away, but soon Alum Bheg and the others spotted mounted sentries advancing in the distance. The rebels now scrambled to meet this unseen foe, its approach revealed by a cloud of dust like the smoke from a burning field.

By the time the Sialkot mutineers had reached the Ravi, Alum Bheg and most of the men would have replaced the white trousers with the loose *dhoti* commonly worn by men in northern India. Many, however would have also kept their red uniform and probably also the white Kilmarnock or forage cap with the regimental insignia. We know that the *sowars* of the 9th BLC were still wearing their flamboyant, instantly recognisable, French-grey uniforms, which had earned them the nick-name the 'Ornamentals'.[7] The rebels represented a sizable force: the 46th consisted of almost a thousand men, while the wing of the 9th was at least 200 strong. In other words, this was no ragtag group of rebels or armed peasants—this was a highly-trained military unit, which had furthermore maintained its operational cohesion. While they no longer had any senior commanders, which invariably consisted of British offi-cers, the entire Indian staff, including NCOs like Alum Bheg, was there to lead the troops.[8]

The entire Sialkot brigade deployed in formation, across the road leading from the ford to Gurdaspur, just as they had been drilled to do for years. Alum Bheg and the *sepoys* of the 46th formed a line, two men deep, both of which kneeled until they had to fire when the rear line would stand.[9] As was the norm at the time, the cavalry formed on the flanks.[10] Immediately on their left was a tiny village, Allowal, while their right flank rested on an old dilapidated *serai* and another village, named Nutteree.[11] They had the Ravi to their rear, and the landscape before them was flat, but green with fields that were irrigated by small canals and water from the river and were lined by trees. The simmering heat, heavy with humidity, was steadily climbing towards its peak of around 45 degrees Celsius. The position of the rebels was not a bad one, however, and many of them were under the cover of trees, while their enemy would be out in the open.[12] Across the fields, they could now clearly see Sikh cavalry materialising out of the dust in front of them, and an indiscernible mass behind, infantry and what might be some artillery. Judging from the khaki uniforms what was clear to Alum Bheg and the rebels was that the force that now blocked their route to Delhi seemed to consist mainly of Punjabi soldiers.

Waiting in the stillness of the midday heat, the rebels allowed the opposing force to cross the creek that separated them, the cavalry and infantry wading across the knee-deep water, while the artillery crossed using a small bridge. The sight of more than half a dozen artillery pieces unnerved Alum Bheg and the others, since all they had was the old 12-pounder signal gun that was now stuck on the island well to their rear. As the enemy slowly deployed, the Punjabi horsemen in front moved back, revealing no less than nine horse-drawn cannon being unlimbered, as well as what now turned out to be an entire regiment of British soldiers. This was an unpleasant surprise to Alum Bheg and the other *sepoys* and *sowars*, none of whom had ever faced European troops in battle before. Contemporary British accounts assumed that Indian troops simply could not stand up to white soldiers, but this says more about the racist assumptions of the time than anything else. British soldiers, however, were well-disciplined and did indeed have a fearsome reputation.

* * *

The force facing Alum Bheg and the other mutineers on the banks of the Ravi was none other than Nicholson's Movable Column, including the very troops who had left Sialkot in late May. Back then, the 52nd Oxfordshire Light Infantry had been dressed in white uniforms, but they had since changed to the new khaki colours, which is what the Punjabi Sikhs usually wore. This was one of the first times that khaki was ever used by British regiments, and in this instance, it had served well to hide the identity of the troops until the last moment.[13]

As soon as the British authorities were alerted to the outbreak at Sialkot, the wing of the 9th BLC, along with another *sepoy* regiment, were disarmed.[14] Nicholson, who was then at Amritsar with the Movable Column, learned of the outbreak in the morning of the 10th and immediately put into action a long-prepared plan: British infantry were loaded onto no less than 200 pony *ekhas*, or small carriages, while the cavalry horses of the disarmed wing of the 9th were handed over to some of the newly recruited Sikh soldiers.[15] Using this configuration, the Column could move much faster than usual, especially considering the temperatures, which Ensign Wilberforce of the 52nd estimated was 'a tremendous' 54° Celsius.'[16] The British force consisted of 658 men of the 52nd, horse and light artillery, 184 men of the 3rd and 6th Punjab Infantry and two troops of newly recruited Punjabi levies.[17] Nicholson's plan was to cover the more than forty miles between Amritsar and

Gurdaspur by forced marches in order to intercept the Sialkot mutineers. This would have been considered a risky move at the best of times, but during the hottest month of the summer is was little short of reckless. Against all odds, the Movable Column managed to reach Gurdaspur before the rebels did, but not without paying a high cost:

> 'The heat during the previous day had been so excessive that it was difficult to grasp the brass sword-handle; many horses died of sunstroke during that day, many men were invalided, and some died of heat apoplexy on that march of forty-two miles in twenty-one hours, most of it in the full blaze of a July sun.'[18]

Nicholson seemed quite prepared to risk the lives of his men for what he saw as the greater good, and he drove them onward without mercy. As one officer of the 52nd put it in a somewhat understated manner, 'our Brigadier did not consider the season.'[19] The plan worked, yet by the time the Movable Column deployed against the Sialkot rebels along the banks of the Ravi, the effective strength of the more than 650 men in the 52nd had been reduced to just 220.[20] Nicholson ordered those men to deploy on both flanks in skirmishing order, with his nine guns in the middle. In the rear, the rest of the 52nd, many of whom were still recuperating from the march, the Punjab infantry and the cavalry levies were kept in reserve. The British force then slowly advanced across the open field.

It was too late for Alum Bheg and the rebels to avoid a battle. Moreover, their path to Delhi was now blocked by the approaching force. Maintaining their cool, the rebels allowed the enemy to advance to within 250 yards of their position. The rear ranks of the 46th now stood up and the regiment 'poured in a rattling volley, which lasted two or three minutes'.[21] Alum Bheg and the *sepoys* were still armed with the old smoothbore musket, yet they still managed to inflict a deadly blow against the British lines. As one British officer described it, 'they opened a fusillade, and in about five minutes we had about 40 casualties in the force.'[22] The rebels still had their buglers and regimental colours, and one eyewitness described the salvo as being 'delivered as simultaneously as if on parade at Sealkote.'[23] The 52nd were on the receiving end of this volley and had not seen action since Waterloo in 1815. According to one of their officers:

'The men behaved very steadily, considering it was the first time they had been under fire. The first volley astonished them. They made a sort of swerve at first, when the bullets whistled about their heads, as if looking for cover; and some of us felt very much as if we should like to take up a position under a gun-waggon too.'[24]

Immediately after the volley, the rebel cavalry charged on both flanks; the infantry, Alum Bheg and the 46th BNI, followed right behind them. It was now the turn of the British to unleash a devastating volley of fire using grapeshot from the cannon and the new Enfields which the 52nd had recently been equipped with. The grapeshot, which consisted of clusters of smaller balls bound in canvas rather than solid round shot, tore through the ranks of the *sowars* and their horses like a giant shotgun. Nevertheless, the rebel cavalry charged on, speedily covering the ground between the two forces, and riding right in amongst the artillery where they 'cut right and left at the gunners and drivers.'[25]

One contemporary account of the battle, by John Cave-Browne, dramatised the clash between the two forces as the culmination of the outbreak three days before:

'With what feelings must the Column have thus confronted its old acquaintances of Sealkote! The Sealkote brigade, for such virtually it was, facing the Sealkote mutineers! The blood of the brave old Brigadier, of the kind-hearted *generalé doctor*, the respected Mr Hunter, and others, each and all of whom had friends in the Column, called aloud for vengeance. Thus they met—the murderers and the avengers of blood.'[26]

The truth, however, was more complicated. One of the Indian officers of the 9th BLC who charged the guns was Havildar Mirwan Singh, who, on the morning of the outbreak at Sialkot, had been the one to wake up and warn Colonel Campbell. Now, this same man 'led one of the attacks on the guns and fought with great desperation. Failing to shoot a horse artilleryman with his pistol, he hurled the weapon with so strong an arm and so true an aim as to knock out several of his opponent's teeth and bring him to the ground.'[27] Men who had put their own lives on the line to protect their officers on Thursday, now fought the British in desperate battle on the following Sunday. Some of the soldiers who clashed at Trimmu Ghat were even personally acquainted, and in the midst of the fighting, Gunner James Brabson heard his name called out by one of the *sowars*. As Cooper recounts, 'One desperado of the 9th

Cavalry galloped up to an artillery sergeant, saying, "Salaam, Brabazon Sahib," and slashed him over the head, inflicting a wound of which he afterwards died.'[28] The battle of Trimmu Ghat reflected the confusing nature of the outbreak at Sialkot, and the unexpected intrusion of personal relationships exacerbated the usual chaos of the battlefield.

The British artillery and infantry bore the brunt of the ferocious charge of the *sowars*. According to Wilberforce, the soldiers of the 52nd had barely had time to get into formation to receive the charge:

'On the right the cavalry were received in squares of companies; they rode round and round, firing their pistols point blank at us; at length they had had enough and retired. In doing so, one cavalry trooper seized an artilleryman by his shoulder-belt and was riding away with him, when they crossed the path of fire of one of the nine-pounders; at that instant the charge of grape was fired, it struck the three of them at a distance of some fifteen yards, blowing the horse, the rider and the captive literally to pieces.'[29]

Nicholson and his devoted bodyguard of Pashtun horsemen were positioned right behind the artillery, and as the rebel attack seemed to flounder, they decided to join in the combat. Wilberforce described the scene that played out right in front of him and his men:

'we saw two of the body-guard come out on our right and apparently challenge two of the Bengal Cavalry to single combat; anyway, the challenge was accepted, and the four rode at each other, the Pathans on their ponies, their tulwars waving in circles round their heads, their loose garment flowing; the Bengalees sat erect on their big horses, their swords held ready to deliver the "point," a stroke no irregular cavalry man comprehends, as he does not in his sword exercise learn to parry and thrust. For a moment all eyes were on the four combatants: the thrust was delivered, but instead of piercing the bodies of the Pathans it passed over them, for they threw themselves back on their ponies, their heads on the crupper, their feet by the ponies' ears, and in that position swept off the heads of the Bengal Cavalry men; instantly the ponies wheeled round, the men straightened themselves in their saddles, and they passed away from our vision. Then Nicholson came into view; he too was going to kill his man. The scene was a brief one, the mutineer thrust at the great swordsman, who parried the thrust, and with apparently the same motion clove his assailant's head in two; he also passed away from our sight.'[30]

At the time of the battle, the British attributed the sheer frenzy of the assault to the rebels' alleged consumption of *bhang*, a common intoxicant based on the cannabis sativa plant. One officer at Trimmu

Ghat claimed that 'they were all "bang-ed," or they would never have done so much,'[31] while another dramatically described how the *sowars* were 'gnashing their teeth, and worked up to the utmost with intoxicating drugs.'[32] Along with other cannabis-derived drugs, such as *ganja* or *charas*, *bhang* was the *sepoy's* favoured poison of choice. It was often used to muster a sort of 'Dutch courage,' much as British soldiers did with rum; it also reduced hunger and numbed pain.[33] The British found it very convenient to explain the bravery of Indian troops, who were supposed to be racially inferior to Europeans, by their use of drugs. As had been the case with Mangal Pandey's one-man mutiny at Barrackpore earlier that year, the use of drugs delegitimised the *sepoys'* resistance to colonial rule. It is indeed unlikely that Alum Bheg and the rest of the Sialkot mutineers were all on drugs during what became known as the Battle of Trimmu Ghat. The truth was that they were fighting for their lives, and really had nothing to lose. They could not turn back and risk running into the forces they knew had disarmed their friends at Jhelum, and so the only way was forward. Very few of the approximately 200 *sowars* of the left wing of the 9th BLC, who had mutinied at Sialkot, survived their desperate charge on the Movable Column. According to Bourchier, who commanded the artillery, 'not a trooper of the 9th Cavalry who charged the guns left the batteries alive.'[34]

Wilberforce and his men soon had other things to worry about, as the Indian infantry, including Alum Bheg with the 46th, advanced and closed in on the British lines: 'In the smoke and noise it was impossible to see what was going on on our left, but soon an urgent message reached us, our square opened out, and with fixed bayonets we charged down on the left.'[35] Despite the heavy fire, the *sepoys* had managed to reach the British formation, driving part of it back. Wilberforce and his men then charged headlong into the turmoil of the close-quarter fighting:

'I saw one Sepoy pierced through with a bayonet, and borne to the ground, the bayonet going into the ground and twisting so that it could not be withdrawn. One of our men, an Irishman, who was also a spectator of this incident, immediately took off his bayonet, and, putting it in the ground, went on with his butt, which he flourished to some purpose, one swing of it felling no less than three of his opponents. The Sepoys were forced backward, and breaking, fled to the river in confusion, leaving, however, many dead and wounded in their flight.'[36]

The deadly and effective fire kept up by the British had taken its toll on the Sialkot mutineers, and, as a British artillery officer put it: 'In about twenty minutes the fire of the enemy was subdued; in ten minutes more they were in full retreat towards the river, leaving between three or four hundred killed and wounded on the field.'[37] The companies of the 46th who had led the charge, were entirely wiped out as one British officer described: 'so desperate were the fellows that they were all killed within 15 yards of our line. The left subdivision behaved equally well, and were all killed in covering the retreat of their main body.'[38]

The British noted several instances of bravery amongst the *sepoys*, and an officer of the 52nd described how 'some of them behaved very pluckily. We saw one fellow about one hundred yards from the guns, all around him having been killed, loading and firing all by himself, till he was knocked over.'[39] Alum Bheg and the Sialkot mutineers had been fatally outgunned from the outset and no amount of valour could change that. Once their ranks had been decimated and their charge repulsed, the discipline and cohesion with which they had begun the day gave way to sheer panic, turning their retreat into a rout. The Punjab levies with the Movable Column had fled the battlefield almost as soon as the firing began, so Nicholson had no cavalry with which to follow up the victory. This allowed many of the surviving *sepoys* to re-cross the river and get back to the island. The rebels still had the old signal gun which at a distance of some 1100 yards kept the British at bay as they advanced right up the river bank. Any plans that Nicholson may have had to attempt a crossing of the river that evening in order to inflict a decisive defeat were soon abandoned.[40] Following the forced march and the exhaustion of the fight, the Movable Column could barely follow up their victory, but they eagerly took possession of the loot left by the fleeing rebels:

'Had the General but possessed a squadron or two of Cavalry, not a man could have escaped. The Sikhs, less done up by the sun than the Europeans, advanced, gallantly led by Lieutenant Boswell. The horses were nearly as much done up as the men, and could hardly get up a canter to the river bank; where we took possession of all the baggage and stores crossed over by the enemy, consisting chiefly of arms, ammunition, and clothing, the property of Government; and carriages, furniture, and property belonging to the officers at Sealkote.'[41]

Many of the officers of the 52nd searched in vain for their own possessions, which they had left behind at Sialkot when they left the station in May. One of them noted how 'it was curious to see the motley collection of articles the rascals had brought with them in the way of plunder. After murdering the Brigadier and several of the Europeans, and burning down the station, they had taken everything from a knife and fork up to carriages and buggies.'[42] The rebels had indeed plundered everything they could lay their hands on; inside one of the carriages, a British officer found 'a bottle of eau-de-cologne and a Bible, and an unfinished overland letter'.[43]

For Alum Bheg and the other rebels the defeat was truly disastrous. Wet and bedraggled, the survivors of the first day of the battle had made it onto dry land on the island in the middle of the river. They were safe for the time being, but they had lost half of their force, in addition to most of their loot and equipment. Many had also thrown away their uniform and muskets as they fled.[44] Their wounded comrades were left where they fell, and those who made it down to the banks 'were swept away in trying to recross the river, which at the ford was more than breast-high, and was rising every minute.'[45] Those who did not drown fell into the hands of the British forces and were unceremoniously executed. 'Short thrift awaited all captures,' a British account noted: 'The motto of General Nicholson for mutineers was "*a la lanterne*." ["String them up"].'[46] According to one newspaper, 'The prisoners were not, in the General's opinion, even worthy of a rope, but were simply turned loose amongst the Sikhs, who very soon cut them to pieces.'[47] Compared to the veritable slaughter of the *sepoys*, the British losses on 12 July were negligible: the 52nd had just five rank-and-file killed, with two officers and an additional sixteen wounded; the artillery and Punjabi infantry had about the same number of casualties.[48] Besides the losses sustained during the actual fighting, however, should be added those caused by heatstroke; the 52nd lost twenty men due to the heat, six of whom died.[49] The two opposing forces had been almost evenly matched in terms of numbers, but the disparity in casualties reflected the lopsidedness in their armament.

Unfortunately for Alum Bheg and his comrades, their situation was only getting worse: rain and melting snow from the Himalayas caused the Ravi to rise considerably during the interval of just a single day. With a *schadenfreude* typical of the British of the time, Cave-Browne described the precarious situation of the rebels stranded on the island:

'Here, however, they found themselves in a dilemma they had little anticipated. The bank or strip of land by means of which they had crossed, and where they had been driven back, divides the river into two channels— the southern one a deep and strong current, the other at times little more than a marsh, and almost always fordable; but when the water rises (and it was now rising rapidly from the melted snow), this channel becomes flooded to such a depth as to be quite impassable. Thus it happened that the water which the rebels were able to wade through with some little difficulty on the 11th, was utterly unfordable two days after. The bank of land had now become an island. Here, with the dreaded Nicholson in front, the fear of a pursuing force from Jhelum in their rear, and the whole country around eager to catch and fleece them, they were in noenviable position. If, by chance, some clever student of one of the Government colleges, where mental culture is the *summum bonum*, and Christianity has no place, happened to be among them, he might have recalled to mind, and have translated into choice Oordoo [Urdu], to his blood-stained companions, as aptly illustrating their own position, the reflection of that prince of traitors and murderers, Macbeth,

– "there is nor flying hence, nor tarrying here."'[50]

With nowhere to run, the rebels decided to make the most of their position and built a defensive breastwork behind which they could use the cannon. Having dug themselves in, all they could do was wait and watch anxiously across the river and the 'wide desolate plain deserted by everything except the gorging vultures and the howling jackals.'[51]

After the battle, Nicholson marched his force back to camp outside Gurdaspur, where they enjoyed a much-needed rest; although the British casualties had been comparatively small, they lost as many men to the heat as they did in actual combat.[52] During the next two days, as the men of the Movable Column rested and regained their strength, Nicholson's Pashtuns and Punjabi mounted levies scoured the countryside for fugitives. Wilberforce recalled how the prisoners brought in were 'paraded in a line in the evening, and then Nicholson would walk down the line. Every now and then he pointed to a man, who was immediately taken out. Those pointed at were Sepoys, and ordered for instant execution; the remainder, mere country people, were let go.'[53] Such summary justice was commonplace during the uprising, and yet not everyone approved of Nicholson's ruthlessness. Lieutenant Ommaney of the artillery wrote in his diary:

> 'A man of the 2nd Irregulars who showed the Sialkot Mutineers the ford, had his 2 hands cut off, a bayonet run through his body and then hung; batches of prisoners with their hands tied are taken out into the jungle and the Sikhs let at them. Such cruelties must tell against us in the long run, and because these men have done the same to us...is no reason that we should emulate them. Kill them by all means by hanging and shooting the really guilty [but the innocent should be spared].'[54]

In the evening of the 15th, Wilberforce and the of the 52nd marched down to the river once more, passing the scene of the heavy fighting two days earlier: 'Clouds of vultures rose from or hopped about on the ground; they had been satiating themselves with the dead Sepoys and with dead horses; the stench as we marched across the scene of the encounter was horrible.'[55] They encamped near the river bank, and early next morning, while it was still dark, they silently crossed over to the island a mile further south, where they were out of sight and out of range, of the rebels and their entrenched gun. To distract the rebels, the British artillery shelled the earthwork and few huts that made up the only habitable spot in the dense forest of the island. Wilberforce's company took the lead of the small assault force, which also consisted of some Punjabis, and slowly advanced in skirmishing order through tall grass that provided complete cover. Once they got closer to the *sepoys'* position, however, they came into the open, and soon came under fire after being spotted. Nevertheless, the strategy had worked and the rebels were caught off guard. As one British artillery put it: 'At last the true state of things glimmered on their understandings, "their stronghold was invaded".'[56]

The rebels, whose attention had been diverted towards the mainland, were frantically trying to turn the old gun around to face the attackers. With shots whizzing over his head, Wilberforce found himself advancing towards the earthworks, while Nicholson rode next to him and regaled him with a story about how he had once killed a tiger with his sword on horseback. The final moments of the attack were dramatic, as Wilberforce recalled:

'When about 200 yards distant from the gun they fired grape at us; we closed on our centre, leaving a gap for the fire of the gun, charged, and in a few moments took the gun. A revolver given me by my father saved my life, for being a fast runner, and from my position in front having a start, I was over the bank on the left just before my Captain jumped in on the right, and was brought up by a huge horse-pistol held to my forehead. I fired instantly, not aiming, and the bullet went through my assailant's heart, the discharge of his pistol blowing off my solar topee. All the Sepoys but one in charge of that gun died at their post; the one who ran away was pursued by Nicholson, who overtook him, and rising in his stirrups dealt him such a mighty blow that he actually severed the man in two!'[57]

The man cut down by Nicholson was the old *khansamah*, or cook, of Brigadier Brind, who allegedly unloaded his master's revolver at Sialkot, and who had been working the cannon expertly throughout the engagement.[58] The crew kept firing right up until the last moment, when they were overrun by the British force and 'were in such a hurry, that the man who was ramming down the charge was blown to pieces.'[59] The presence of the twelve-o'clock signal gun at Trimmu Ghat was something of a historical coincidence: it had originally been used by the Sikhs at the Battle of Gujrat in 1849 near the end of the Second Anglo-Sikh War—a battle at which the 46th BNI, and possibly even Alum Bheg, fought for the British.[60] Now, in 1857, the very same gun was used by the remnants of the 46th BNI against the British, who were now supported by Sikh troops. The elevation screw on the old gun was described as 'an old Sikh affair', which the *sepoys* had been unable to operate efficiently, meaning that all their shots went high during the final attack.[61]

Once the earthworks and gun had been taken, the rest of the island was soon cleared of its temporary occupants. As one officer of the 52nd described it:

'It was now helter-skelter; they ran to the head of the island, were followed up by our fellows, and took to the water; many of them must have been drowned; numbers were like mud-larks on sandbanks and small islands; and how poor Pandy is to get out of it I do not know. There is deep water on the other side, and the villagers are up; there are only two or three places on this side where they can cross; these are all watched...'[62]

The *sepoys* were, of course, '*Hindustanis*' and as strangers in the land they could not rely on the support of the local population, even if they managed to escape the British bayonets. After the island was cleared, the junior officers of the 52nd went over the ground where the rebels had been encamped while they were stranded and a curious incident occurred:

> 'a lot of us youngsters saw a small house, one of the few dwelling-places situated on the island, and to it we repaired to see what was inside. There was nothing visible, the one room of the little house was empty; the room had a plank ceiling, and while we were standing about talking some one heard or thought he heard a noise above the planks. Placing therefore his revolver in a crack of the planks he fired, and on search discovered he had killed a Sepoy, who had selected that place for his refuge, and would doubtless have escaped had not nature compelled him to reveal himself.'[63]

The final stage of the battle of Trimmu Ghat on 16 July had been a decidedly one-sided affair, as Wilberforce recounted: 'The clearing of the island was speedily accomplished; most of the Sepoys sought for safety in the swollen waters of the Ravee and found death, only a very few being captured and of course shot.'[64] The Sialkot brigade was thus complexly annihilated; the British suffered just six wounded.[65] After the final defeat of the Sialkot mutineers, Nicholson, who, according to Wilberforce, 'hated Sepoys with a hatred that no words could describe', demonstrated an uncharacteristic respect for the enemy he had defeated and had the bodies of the rebels buried according to Muslim tradition.[66] No mention is made of the fact that most of the *sepoys* were Hindus, whose funeral rites involved burning, but the gesture was genuine: Nicholson also set up a makeshift monument at the side of the *sepoy's* last stand around the earthwork on the island, testifying to their valour.[67] At times, it seems, the British could display a surprising degree of respect towards their enemy—albeit an enemy they had slaughtered indiscriminately.

The British perceived Nicholson's victory over the rebels at Trimmu Ghat as a just punishment and as little different from the spectacular mass-executions that were then taking place all over Punjab. One contemporary observer noted that:

> 'It was butchery, no doubt, and the 46th Native Infantry, who had protected their officers, hardly deserved annihilation, but the holocaust was necessary. That the 52nd Foot should have executed sentence on their former comrades at Sialkot was a curious Nemesis.'[68]

Even in the absence of any semblance of due process, justice was still invoked as an almost divine attribute of British actions, and this allowed free reign for indiscriminate violence. The 'condign punishment' of the Sialkot rebels at Trimmu Ghat was thus repeatedly described not as a military victory but as the execution of justice pure and simple:

'We now hear that these men have been totally destroyed—that they are swept from the face of the earth—that the mutiny brought the sentence of death on the regiments, and that capital punishment has been strictly and fully executed. Justice so prompt and so vigorous will give its lesson to every ear in which the word Revolt has been whispered.'[69]

Not all of the Sialkot mutineers, however, were killed or captured by Nicholson's forces. By the time of the final attack, several hundred of the rebels had already abandoned their hopeless position on the island. Alum Bheg was most likely amongst those who were reported to have braved the currents and fled into Gholab Singh's territories in Kashmir on 14 July 1857.[70] Following the outbreak, the dreams of Alum Bheg and the rest of the Sialkot mutineers of joining the uprising down south, and entering the service of Bahadur Shah had lasted exactly five days. The Indian soldiers of the 9th BLC and 46th BNI never escaped British service long enough to experience what it meant to be masters of their own destiny, let alone help build and defend a new rebel government in defiance of the East India Company. Their mutiny was cut short, as were the lives of so many of their comrades, by Nicholson and the Movable Column at Trimmu Ghat. Yet, even as Alum Bheg and the other survivors staggered ashore on the western side of the Ravi, and literally ran for the hills, their fates were sealed. From then on, they were fugitives on the run, beasts to be hunted down.

8

JUSTICE SO PROMPT AND VIGOROUS

On 10 July, at Lahore, Andrew Gordon and his fellow American missionaries were gathered around the death bed of his young son, Silas,
who had never recovered from his illness. Gordon later recalled the
moment their sad vigil was suddenly interrupted:

> 'The next moment Mr. Barnes entered the room in haste with an open
> letter in his hand, saying, with deep emotion: *"Brethren, the Sepoys in Sialkot
> have mutinied! General Brind, the commanding officer of the station; Doctor
> J. Graham, the superintending surgeon; Dr. J.C. Graham, the civil surgeon; Captain
> Bishop, and poor Mr. and Mrs. Hunter and their babe, have all been murdered!"* My
> heart fills, and my eyes moisten, at the remembrance of that moment as I
> write these lines, more than a quarter of a century after the events.'[1]

True to character, Gordon had the appropriate Bible quote on hand:
'Help us, O God of our salvation, for the glory of thy name; and
deliver us, and purge away our sins for thy name's sake. Wherefore
should the heathen say, Where is their God? [Psalms 79:10]'[2] Back at
Sialkot, Dr Guise had tried in vain to care for Brind, but the wound
was fatal and the Brigadier died early next morning.[3] This brought the
number of casualties of the outbreak to seven: Brigadier Brind, Captain
Bishop, Dr James Graham, Dr John Graham, Thomas Hunter, Jane
Hunter and her baby.[4] Because the British had not yet re-established
control over the cantonment, their bodies could not be laid to rest in
the European cemetery. Instead they were buried three days after the

outbreak, in a small garden under the western wall of the fort. Reverend Boyle conducted the service.[5]

When Gordon, Hill and Scott returned to Sialkot two weeks later, they found to their surprise that the small Presbyterian mission had been protected by local villagers during the outbreak and had suffered no damage. After they had examined the possessions they had left behind, confirming everything was there, they walked up to the cantonment and European lines to see for themselves the extent of the damage. With most of the Europeans still cooped up in the fort, the station appeared completely devoid of human life.[6] When an officer of the 46th claimed that 'no city was ever more completely sacked than the station of Sealkote,' it was a gross exaggeration, especially given the later destruction of Indian cities such as Delhi or Lucknow at the hands of the British.[7] As Gordon and the others made their way through the empty streets, however, Sialkot was hardly recognisable from the lively and orderly station they had left just a month before.

Most of the European houses were made from brick and had not been set on fire. Once Gordon and the others ventured inside the former homes of their friends, the devastation nevertheless became apparent: 'everything like furniture, dishes, books, and glass, were torn to bits or dashed in pieces in the most barbarous manner.'[8] The well-kept bungalow, with their pristine gardens, were now little more than empty shells. 'Into many houses we merely looked through the windows,' Gordon recalled, 'observing merely that the windows were broken, an evidence that if we would look in we would see nothing but ruins.'[9] Gordon went to inspect the house occupied by the Hunters and found it had been ransacked and destroyed like all the rest. 'Sad, indeed, was the thought', he reflected, 'while looking on these ruins, that those lovely people had been so cruelly murdered.'[10] Sialkot had become a colonial ghost town, and with its streets strewn with abandoned loot it was a place of 'sorrowful desolation'.[11]

The final house they visited, was Mr Hill's, where Thomas, Jane and the baby had spent their last night. The house stood isolated a mile west of the cantonment and 'of all the houses we have seen,' Gordon wrote, 'this seems to have suffered the most.'[12] Everything, including doors and windows had been removed or broken, and only the walls and the roof were left intact. As Hill walked through the wreck of his home, his eyes caught a piece of paper amongst the debris on the floor, which turned out to be one of his own sermons written long ago. The theme of the sermon was from Corinthians and, considering the circumstances, rather poignant: 'For the fashion of this world passeth away. [1 Corinthians 7:31]'[13] Picking up a few odd items that had survived, including Hill's Greek grammar and a manuscript of Thomas Hunter's, they finally left. 'Everything was in such a sad state,' Gordon noted, 'that we felt as if we would much rather have seen nothing at all.'[14]

* * *

The peasants of the surrounding area had been led to believe that British rule was over and had flocked into Sialkot to make the most of the unexpected withdrawal of law and authority after the rebels left. On 10 July, McMahon entered the cantonment along with the levies from the fort, shooting more than twenty villagers, and driving away the rest who were still engaged in plundering the abandoned houses.[15] A gallows was erected in the fort, and MacMahon proclaimed that unless all plunder was immediately returned within twenty-four hours, the headman in every village where loot was found would be hanged. This had the desired effect, as Gordon later described:

> 'The next day Captain McMahon, as he surveyed the country from the high walls of the Sialkot fort, witnessed a most interesting spectacle. Long processions of men and beasts of burden laden with the plunder were seen wending their way towards the city from north, south, east, and west, like so many extended caravans. Some were loaded down with tents, chairs, tables, trunks, doors and window-blinds; some carried books, clothing and bedding; others were the bearers of teapots.'[16]

With the arrival of Captain Richard Lawrence, sent up from Lahore, the task of punishment began two days later.[17] Lawrence' investigation initially focused of the old officer of the mounted police, the *Rissaldar*, and the two officers of the jail guards, the *Subadar* and the *Darogha*, all of whom were suspected of having colluded with the mutineers.[18] Most of the jail guards and wardens were in fact '*Hindustanis*' and, unknown to the British, had maintained close links with the *sowars* of the 9th BLC. During his investigation, Lawrence discovered that, during the months prior to the outbreak, two *sowars* of the 9th had been in the habit of visiting the jail guards and smoking with them. 'No doubt', he concluded, 'matters were arranged during these interviews and the Soobadar was won over to assist.'[19] The old *Rissaldar* of the mounted police, who otherwise 'bore an excellent character', had not personally taken any part in the outbreak, but he kept his troopers inactive throughout and prevented them from aiding the British—as had been noted at the time. A few of the mounted police were also Hindustanis and were known to Monckton's *chuprassis*, including Hurmat Khan. 'I can only imagine,' Lawrence noted, 'that he [the *Rissaldar*] was corrupted by four or five designing Hindoostanee scoundrels in the Ressala [mounted police].'[20] The links between different personnel employed by the British, combined with a shared *Purbiya* identity, as well as the confusion of the outbreak itself, had all contributed to the apparent disloyalty of the police and guards at Sialkot. The conclusion of the enquiry was that 'it was clearly proved that the Soobadar of the Guard and the jail Darogha had a good understanding with the mutineers of the 9th Cavalry, and that they opened the jail gates and let loose the prisoners without even a show of resistance.'[21] All three were promptly hanged, the old *Rissaldar* 'within a quarter of an hour of the conclusion of his trial.'

The executions were tense undertakings and tested the strength and resolve of British control, which was so precarious in the immediate aftermath of the outbreak. Because the *Rissaldar* was a Sikh, there were concerns that the execution might cause resentment among the local population, as one British soldier described in a letter:

'It was a very ticklish affair, as we were hanging Sikhs when we only had Sikh levies about us. The ropes broke, and the guard was ordered to shoot the half lifeless bodies; then followed three or four volleys of musketry. Those not looking on thought that it was "all up," and that the guards had turned upon us. I never felt so alarmed all through the affair.'[22]

This was only the beginning, though, and over the following days and weeks various types of punishment were meted out. The policemen and guards who had not run away were all given prison sentences or simply discharged. After the rout of the rebels at Trimmu Ghat, servants and camp-followers were daily being brought back, as the same officer noted:

'Lots of servants who went away with the mutineers have been punished. In one day we had to flog 125 men—40 lashes each. We have some hang every day, from one to six in number [...] We have a hard day's work before us again to-day, for another batch have come in. They are nearly all "down-easterners," as we in the Punjaub call them—i.e. men of the north-west provinces.'[23]

Those Indians who had remained loyal, and who had saved the lives of Europeans, were given promotions and other financial compensation. Rewards were offered for those locals against whom particularly grave crimes could be attributed, including Hurmat Khan, for whose apprehension the sum of Rs 1000 was offered.[24] By 18 July, exactly a week after he arrived, Lawrence reported the following numbers of 'cases dealt with':

Shot: 24

Hanged: 10

Imprisoned: 8

Dismissed from service: 22

Flogged: 109

Number of villages fined: 27

Acquitted: 51

With the initial job of re-asserting British authority at Sialkot completed, Lawrence returned to Lahore a few days later. Lawrence' departure did not mark the end of the retribution, however, and once Monckton resumed office, the daily hangings and floggings continued—just as they did so many other places across northern India. One of Dr Graham's servants was among the locals who were later executed, and the Doctor's son, William Graham, described the scene after arriving in Sialkot at the end of July:

'I volunteered for Nicholson's force and got out but a few hours later, unfortunately not in time to have the governor's coachman and mate Benni shot. His [Dr Graham's] Mussalchee [torch-bearer] was hung here, he having rode out to Wuzeerabad for information for the mutineers as regarding the strength of Her majesty's 24th[,] artillery etc. His military career was a short one, and was polished off on his return. Only two servants stuck true, Causomat and Dirsie. All jewels etc. looted. House awfully destroyed, and everything nearly broken.'[25]

William's regret at having missed the execution of his father's servants is revealing of how the British generally regarded the issue of crime and punishment during the uprising. All Indian servants and soldiers who joined the uprising were considered simply as traitors and, regardless of their actual actions, considered equally guilty and deserving of the most severe punishment. The notion of betrayal was indeed central to the British understanding of the outbreak, and Cave-Browne's description of the killing of the British officer of the 26th BNI at Meean Meer in late July, provides a particularly evocative example of this:

> 'Unarmed as [Major Spencer] was, he went forward and endeavoured to reason with them: but in vain. A sepoy, stealing up behind, felled him with a blow from a hatchet, others rushed on him, and he who had grown up among them from boyhood—who had lived among them, and, it might be said, *for them*—and there were few who would have been said to be more beloved by their men—*he was hacked to pieces by his own BABAS** (* Literally *children*, a term of endearment which was commonly used by officers of sepoy regiments when speaking of or to their men. It is sad to reflect how such misplaced confidence, ay, and affection, have been requited.)'[26]

By evoking the paternalism of British rule, which saw 'natives' as children, the treachery of the *sepoys* was thus rendered doubly despicable. More importantly, however, resistance to British rule was, in and of itself, reduced to an act of betrayal and therefore morally and politically indefensible. The killing of British officers, women and children not only committed entire regiments to mutiny, it also condemned entire regiments and populations, to British retribution. All Indians who fought the British in 1857 were considered guilty of treason and betrayal and any previous bonds of friendship or loyalty were considered to have been disingenuous and deceitful. In this perceived struggle between good and evil, any form of retribution was implicitly justified and, to use the words of a later colonial officer, 'there could be no question of undue severity'.[27] Referring directly to the execution of the *Rissaldar* of the mounted police, Cooper praised the manner in which the 'hydra-headed disease' of mutiny had been defeated at Sialkot by British officials unflinching in their performance of duty:

> Had there been the faintest hesitation shown in bringing them to trial because they were Sikhs, or any tendency to relax the construction of the law, the effect would have been most dangerous. But the Judicial

Commissioner knew not what it was to swerve from the right line of action; and fearlessly did his delegate, Captain Lawrence, perform the stern duty of presiding over the trial, and of sentencing to death two of his own subordinates. Thus the impregnable stability of the State was acted upon throughout as a given axiom. No overtures have been made that were not in accordance with this line of policy, and in keeping with the tone of international communication with all civilised countries. No concessions have been made.'[28]

Cooper was expressing widely held sentiments concerning the efficacy of violence and its importance as the mainstay of colonial authority—more than anything else, it was the certainty of punishment that ultimately sustained British rule in India. The former commissioner of Delhi, Sir Charles Metcalfe, writing under the pseudonym of 'Indophilus,' made perhaps the most explicit formulation of the principles upon which British retribution were based:

'Human nature itself has to be vindicated; the feeling of the personal inviolability of the English race in India has to be restored, and the righteous indignation of our nation at the strange and horrible atrocities which have been perpetrated upon our women and children has to be appeased. These are indispensable conditions of success.'[29]

Metcalfe further illustrated his point with an apocryphal story about the notorious 'Thugs', or highway-robbers who strangled travellers:

'Before the operations which resulted in the suppression of Thugee commenced, a number of Thug leaders discussed in council whether they should exercise their profession upon Europeans, and they decided the question in the negative for three reasons: 1st, that Europeans generally carried arms; 2nd, that they seldom carried money; and 3rd, that if the Thugs strangled a single European they would never hear the last of it. The third reason was their real motive; and what we now have to do, is indelibly to impress the same opinion on the whole of India. On no other condition can a handful of foreigners bear rule over millions of natives.'[30]

Retribution was accordingly a product of weakness rather than strength, shaped by the peculiar circumstances of colonialism.[31] British punishment was deliberately excessive to mask the vulnerability of the colonial state, which had been so dramatically exposed by the uprising. In trying to justify the spectacle of mass-executions, one officer made the very same point:

'People may say that it was a cruel execution, but it was a necessity, and everyone felt that the sternest discipline was required to repress every and any attempt to rise on the part of so large a body of mutinous troops who had been coerced by a comparatively small number of Europeans, while any vacillation or weakness shown by our chiefs would have precipitated a rising.'[32]

* * *

While the use of gallows hill and gibbeting had long been abandoned in Britain, hangings and bodies left for public display were becoming a very common sight in northern India in 1857. In August, Gordon spent three days in the cantonment at Sialkot, during which time he witnessed five 'rebelliously inclined' locals being executed.[33] 'The sight of the gallows,' Gordon claimed, 'with a very moderate use of it, proved a most effective means of restoring order.'[34] There was however, nothing moderate about the British use of the gallows to exact retributive justice, as even the semi-official historian, John W. Kaye, admitted:

> 'Already our military officers were hunting down criminals of all kinds, and hanging them up with as little compunction as though they had been pariah-dogs, or jackals, or vermin of a baser kind. [...] Volunteer hanging parties went out into the districts, and amateur executioners were not wanting to the occasion. One gentleman boasted of the numbers he had finished off quite "in an artistic manner," with mango-trees for gibbets and elephants for drops, the victims of this wild justice being strung up, as though for pastime, in "the form of a figure of eight."'[35]

Who exactly the so-called 'criminals' were, was of course a moot point. Officers like Nicholson were attributed with the singular ability to distinguish between run-away *sepoys* and hapless villagers, to separate the guilty from the innocent. In reality, however, this was little more than a convenient myth and colonial retribution was largely indiscriminate. British officials acted as if the mutinies in the Bengal Army regiments, and the outbreak at various stations, had been personal attacks on themselves.[36] Accordingly, it was in many instances virtually impossible to draw a clear line between the military suppression of mutiny, legal punishment, or revenge and mindless slaughter. For the British, the horrors and moral threat of the uprising was embodied in the image of white women ravaged by Indian men. Indian rebels were accordingly dealt with as if they were each and every one a murderous rapist, and as if they all had the fresh blood of European children on their hands. The fate of the *sepoys* of the 26th BNI, who, as mentioned above, killed their officers at Mean Meer, is a case in point. The regiment, which had already been disarmed, consisted of about 600 men who fled from the Lahore area, and headed north-east, possibly towards Kashmir.[37] Pursued by local police and villagers, they were soon cornered at the Ravi River, where about 150 of them were either shot or driven into the water and drowned. Trapped on an island, much as the Sialkot rebels had been at Trimmu Ghat, the remaining 282 fugitives eventually surrendered to Deputy Commissioner Frederic Cooper, who had arrived from Amritsar, in charge of the local Sikh levies. Cooper had the prisoners marched back to a small town called Ajnala, where the hapless *sepoys* were locked up inside some old buildings for the night. At daybreak next morning, 1 August 1857, the prisoners were taken out in batches of ten to a nearby abandoned well that Cooper had discovered:

> 'Instantly a party of 10 Seikhs moved up within one yard, fired at their hearts, and in one moment they were launched into eternity. Bodies with the slightest signs of life in them were despatched by sowars and flung into the pit (Pandeys, Tewarrys, Brahmins and Mussulman) by the sweepers of the village.'[38]

Those who refused to walk to their executions, were dragged by ropes tied to their feet and shot on the ground.[39] This went on for several hours, and by 10am, after some of the Sikh levies who served as executioners had collapsed, 237 of the prisoners had been killed. When the last remaining prisoners refused to leave their temporary prison it was discovered that they had in fact died. As Cooper laconically noted: 'Forty-five were dragged out of their place of confinement, from combined hunger, fright, exhaustion, and their anticipated sentence. Their bodies were consigned to the sweepers to be cast into the pit...'[40] In the course of just forty-eight hours, Cooper later gloated, 'there fell by the law nearly 500 men.'[41] The well where the bodies had been disposed of was covered up and Cooper intended for it to serve as a deterrent against other outbreaks; he even had the audacity to claim that the local spectators to the slaughter at Ajnala 'marvelled at the clemency and the justice of the British.'[42] In reference to the well at Cawnpore, where the slaughtered European women and children had been dumped by Nana

Sahib's henchmen, Cooper proudly proclaimed that 'There is a well at Cawnpore, but there is also one at Ajnala!'[43]

Cooper's infamous line emphasised the deliberate mirroring of violence that took place during the uprising. Indian violence was not only seen to legitimise British retribution, it also shaped the forms and functions of colonial retributive violence.[44] When Cooper subsequently described the events at Ajnala in his memoirs, he did so with an unmistakable sense of achievement:

'The above account, written by the principal actor in the scene himself, might read strangely at home: a single Anglo-Saxon, supported by a section of Asiatics, undertaking so tremendous a responsibility, and coldly presiding over so memorable an execution, without the excitement of battle, or a sense of individual injury, to imbue the proceedings with the faintest hue of vindictiveness. The Governors of Punjab are of the true English stamp and mould, and knew that England expected every man to do his duty, and that duty done, thanks them warmly for doing it. The crime was mutiny, and had there even been no murders to darken the memory of these men, the law was exact. The punishment was death.'[45]

Conscious of the fact that his actions left him vulnerable to accusations that he had acted out of fear or revenge, Cooper presented an explicitly racialised portrayal, if not a caricature, of the embattled colonial officer carrying out his horrible duty in a dispassionate manner and without ever losing his head.[46] This was part of the narrative built around figures such as Nicholson, as a sort of Victorian myth of righteous vengeance, which allowed the British to glory in their own ability to inflict violence without emotion or hesitation. This was the proverbial 'stiff upper lip' at its most colonial and most brutal.[47]

Cooper furthermore invoked an absolute notion of 'the law', almost like Kipling later did in the *Jungle Book*, to justify what was in effect indiscriminate slaughter.[48] The British in India of course had a long history of enshrining exceptions and emergencies within the law; the legislation used to suppress the 'Thugs' during the 1830s, for instance, had been little more than the legalisation of the *ad hoc* measures already deployed outside the formal jurisdiction of the East India Company territories.[49] Martial law had been passed in several of the key regions of northern India in May 1857, and a spate of subsequent emergency acts had granted civilian officials almost unlimited powers to punish and execute rebels, on the spot and without legal process.[50] However, considering the *de facto* collapse of British authority in large parts of northern India in 1857, and the brutality and bitterness with which the conflict was being fought, this attempt at keeping reprisals within the bounds of law was in practice meaningless. Through their indiscriminate violence, British officials and civilians had already invoked the right to deploy such force, and the legislation did little more than provide a semblance of legality to unfettered retribution.[51] Although his superiors in the Punjab Administration supported Cooper's actions, he was pointedly ordered to refrain from any further executions: 'You have had slaughter enough.'[52]

By the end of the summer of 1857, various measures by the British authorities sought to reign in some of the most excessive violence, including the resolution to distinguish between degrees of culpability among mutineers, which earned the governor general the nickname of 'Clemency Canning'. Indiscriminate and summary punishment, however, was never simply replaced by due process and the rule of law. The trial of Bahadur Shah, for instance, took place within a strictly legal framework, even though the British were, technically speaking vassals of the Mughal Emperor.[53] Yet at the very same time that the Emperor was apprehended, his two eldest sons had simply been gunned down by their captor, Major Hodson, after they had surrendered. 'I am not cruel,' Hodson noted, 'but I confess I did rejoice at the opportunity of ridding the earth of these wretches.'[54] Formal executions and frenzied lynching often took place side by side and were in many instances quite indistinguishable—as Cooper's actions at Ajnala revealed.

The scale of the violence, and the ubiquity of death, was unlike anything any British had previously experienced and it left an indelible mark in contemporary accounts. One of these was Lieutenant V.D. Majendie's published narrative from, 1859, *Up Against the Pandies*, which included a remarkable passage touching on this very subject:

> 'It is rather startling when enjoying a quiet country ride to come suddenly upon a body writhing in its last agonies, or hanging lifeless before you—it somewhat abruptly breaks off your train of peaceful thought, and pleasant reveries of home—and I must plead guilty to something very like a revulsion of feeling, when, sauntering along one evening, and coming upon a moderately large green, which my truant fancy immediately metamor-

phosed into a village green in England, I became suddenly aware that there was swinging before me, not the signboard of the "Green Dragon" or "Marquis of Granby," but the pinioned lifeless corpse of a Sepoy, which a native policeman, tulwar in hand, was guarding. The man had not been dead long, and his face, over which there was no cap or covering, was as quiet as though he had been asleep; but the silence, and the absence of any mortal beings but my companion, the policeman, and myself—the dreary, listless way in which the body kept on swinging, and swaying, and turning to and fro—the arms—what deeds of wrong and murder may not those arms have done—now pinioned as if in mockery of the helplessness of death, made the scene a sombre one enough—sombre, and that was all; for no feeling of sorrow, pity, or remorse for the fiends who, falling into our hands after a bloody and treacherous career, meet the death which is so justly their due, can ever be roused, I should think, in an Englishman's breast. This very man now swinging before us may have dabbled those pinioned hands in women's blood, or the golden tresses of a child may have been wound round those fingers, while the other hand grasped the knife which was to sacrifice it: those eyes may have looked into the trusting blue eyes of a poor little baby, and seen it smile on him and on the sharp steel, in its innocence, and yet that smile may have failed to rouse his pity. Faugh! let us be off, such sort of reflections are not pleasant, but they are apt, my friends, to occur to one on such occasions.'[55]

In this small vignette, the author, almost unknowingly, reveals just how troubling it was for the British to justify their own violence. Any uncomfortable hints of empathy were shrugged off and briskly banished by the feverish invocation of the monstrous crimes ascribed to the hanged. The British could not allow themselves to recognise, even for a moment, any trace of humanity in the people they were killing by the hundreds and thousands every single day. Instead, they doubled down on the effort to pursue those rebels who had so far escaped colonial justice.

9

A PURSUING DESTINY

In his short story, 'The Lost Legion', first published in 1892, Rudyard Kipling described the tragic fate of a regiment of mutinous *sepoys* in 1857:

'When the Indian Mutiny broke out, and a little time before the siege of Delhi, a regiment of Native Irregular Horse was stationed at Peshawur on the frontier of India. That regiment caught what John Lawrence called at the time "the prevalent mania" and would have thrown in its lot with the mutineers, had it been allowed to do so. The chance never came, for, as the regiment swept off down south, it was headed off by a remnant of an English corps into the hills of Afghanistan, and there the tribesmen, newly conquered by the English, turned against it as wolves turn against buck. It was hunted for the sake of its arms and accoutrements from hill to hill, from ravine to ravine, up and down the dried beds of rivers and round the shoulders of bluffs, till it disappeared as water sinks in the sand—this officerless, rebel regiment.'[1]

The main inspiration for this story was John Nicholson's pursuit of the 55th BNI, which fled from Multan into the Swat region where they were annihilated by local tribesmen. If the 'Mutiny' was synonymous with the massacres of innocent Europeans, in the British imagination, its aftermath was encapsulated in the image of rebels mercilessly pursued into the mountains.[2] Hunting down these fugitives was not simply a matter of suppressing an uprising and reasserting colonial authority. Meek calls for restraint, or the insistence of proper trials, were met

161

with angry denouncements by those men on the spot who believed people back home had no true appreciation of the villainy of the rebels, as one missionary described it:

'I never saw or heard of men to whom, more appropriately or deservingly than to the Sepoys and their chief, could be applied the terrible character given by the Holy Spirit, when he so fully describes those whose profanity, crimes, and riot, exhibit them "as natural brute beasts, made to be taken and destroyed." 2 Peter ii, 12. They were men who neither knew nor showed mercy, any more than would be exhibited by the tigers of their own jungles.'[3]

Literally dehumanised, Indian rebels could be hunted and killed like wild beasts with complete impunity—and the blessing of the Bible. The rallying cry of 'Remember Cawnpore!', or stories such as those of the murder of Jane Hunter and her baby, imposed a moral obligation to bring the 'villains' to justice at any cost. As long as rebels 'lurked in the hills', the ignominy suffered by the British had not been righted, and the wound of the 'Mutiny' could not be healed. The 'Sepoy hunt' that ensued after Trimmu Ghat, was accordingly imbued with a strong sense of moral purpose.[4]

Once the situation at Sialkot had been brought under control, McMahon was despatched with some of the mounted police and Sikh levies to intercept any stragglers or mutineers who might double back after Nicholson had cut them off. The presence of troops south of Sialkot would furthermore send a signal to the local population who might have come to doubt the strength of British rule after more than a thousand rebels had passed through the area.[5] On his way to the Ravi River, McMahon, however, received the news of the final rout of the *sepoys* on 16 June, and he thus changed course and skirted along the Jammu border in the hope of intercepting any fugitives from Trimmu Ghat.[6] It soon turned out that a large group had sought refuge at Jasrota within the Jammu territory, and McMahon left his force behind and proceeded on his own with only a few *sowars* to accompany him.[7] Kashmir and Jammu were so-called princely states within India, which retained a degree of independence from British rule and which were technically outside of British jurisdiction. The *Diwan*, or local official, came out to meet McMahon and after some negotiation promised to hand over the rebels. The weakening of British authority, and the general chaos of the uprising, provided local rulers with some degree of leverage in their dealings with the colonial state and rebel fugitives thus became pawns in local negotiations. This had also been the case decades earlier when East India Company officials were hunting down gangs of 'Thugs', or highway robbers, who resided, or had taken refuge, outside British jurisdiction. If Indian rulers played their cards well, they could receive recognition for their support, thus improving their own status and power—but, on the other hand, they could also risk antagonising the British, and ultimately lose everything if they were seen to side with the rebels. At Jasrota, seventy-eight rebels were initially handed over to McMahon who had them all immediately shot, and smaller parties subsequently handed over shared the same fate.[8] Those who turned out to be camp-followers were sent to Sialkot under escort. A portion of the loot from Sialkot was also recovered, along with other valuables. In total, the *Diwan* handed over 1,989 rupees he had confiscated from the fugitives, 2,079 rupees were discovered on the persons of the mutineers when they were searched, and an additional 1,246 rupees were found to be in possession of the camp-followers. Jewellery worth 570 rupees was also recovered, along with 105 horses and 15 camels.[9] Considering that a *sepoy* made 84 rupees a year, while an NCO like Alum Bheg made 168, these were substantial sums of money, and they had all come from the treasury or private houses that had been plundered at Sialkot.

The breakdown of the fugitives handed over to McMahon at Jasrota is worth noting:

9th Light Cavalry	35th Native Infantry	46th Native Infantry
1 *Subadar*	1 *Subadar*	4 *Subadars*
2 *Havildars*	3 *Sepoys*	2 *Jemadars*
1 *Darogah*	—	7 *Havildars*
9 Troopers	—	9 *Naiks*
—	—	2 Drummers
—	—	100 *Sepoys*
13	4	124[10]

Although the *sowars* of the 9th had been on horseback and thus had a much greater chance of getting away, it appears their numbers had been completely annihilated during the first day of fighting at Trimmu Ghat; the four remaining men from the 35th must have deserted after their regiment was disarmed at Phillaur a month earlier. The ranks of the men of the 46th BNI, consisting of captains, lieutenants, sergeants, corporals, drummers and privates, respectively, indicate that an entire company had fled from the Ravi River as a unit. 'The arrival of my party on the border was opportune', McMahon later noted, 'as the mutineers at Jusrota were daily melting away and escaping to the hills, but after the interview with the Dewan this was stopped.'[11] It would seem that Alum Bheg along with other *sepoys* of the 46th BNI, were among those very fugitives who were 'melting away,' which would make it the second time in just a few days that he escaped capture in the nick of time.

Later on, smaller groups of Sialkot mutineers and camp-followers were apprehended in Chamba, near Dalhousie, and in the Kangra District, near Dharamsala.[12] Those *sepoys* who survived disarmament and the massacres and executions that took place all over Punjab during the second half of 1857 fled across the border, into the vast and mostly unmapped wilderness that made up the foothills of the Himalayas. This inaccessible and mountainous region became a rallying point and a safe haven for rebels—albeit a temporary one. The British kept pressuring local rulers to hand over fugitives, but these requests were largely ignored. As one colonial official described it:

> 'For many months past, fugitive sepoys, probably to the number of two hundred, mutineers of the 14th Native Infantry of Jhelum, the 46th of Sealkote, and 26th of Mean Meer, have been lurking about, more or less disguised, in the hill near Jummoo. Communications had been made with the Maharajah of Jummoo regarding the presence of these men, and his highness promised that they would be arrested, but this has not been effected.'[13]

By early 1858, the number of fugitives had dwindled to just a handful of the original *sepoys* who survived Trimmu Ghat, and had formed into small wandering bands, which included many of the camp-followers from Sialkot. Occasionally they were joined by fresh fugitives from regiments in Punjab, as well as other vagrants. They no longer had any firearms with them, and, according to a number of accounts, most were disguised as religious pilgrims or ascetics. Immediately after

Trimmu Ghat, for instance, fugitive rebels had been captured 'in disguise as Fakeers, Bunneahs, etc.'[14] *Banias* were common traders or moneylenders, and by adopting their identities the *sepoys* attempted to divest themselves of anything that would associate them with their former military profession. In effect, they sought to blend in with the kinds of pilgrims, mendicants and traders who commonly traversed the region and would be least likely to arouse the attention or suspicion of local authorities.

Even in the depth of the mountains, however, they were never completely safe from the British efforts to hunt down everyone remotely involved in the uprising. While travelling with William Hay, the Deputy commissioner of the Hill States, William Howard Russell had a chance encounter with two suspected fugitives in the mountains not far from the Kullu Valley. Russell, who was the correspondent for *The Times*, described the incident:

> 'Just as we were starting, the cry was raised that the sepoys had arrived, and some five of those wretched hill-men came up to our camp, dragging after them two tall men, bound hand and foot with ropes. They were brought up to Hay for examination. Their upright bearing at once denoted that they were soldiers. One was about six feet high, with a large ill-shapen nose, and a hideous mouth. He wore a dirty thin cotton cap on his head, and a few folds of country blanket round his body. His face and neck were smeared with whitish earth. His companion, a strongly-built and rather handsome man, was attired in the same way. When first questioned, they said they were fakirs from Cashmere; but Khoom Dass [one of Russell's servants], who was well-up in his religion, proceeded to examine them, and broke them down on cross-examination. The taller at last declared he was a *syce* [groom or grass-cutter] of the 46th Regiment of Native Infantry at Sealkote, but that he had nothing to do with the mutiny. One of our *syces* was at once sent for to examine him in the mysteries of his art; and as he completely failed to unravel them, he was driven to confess it was just possible that he might once have been a sepoy in that notorious regiment.'[15]

The two prisoners were accordingly despatched to Simla for further interrogation and Russell later learned that they 'underwent severe flogging and other punishments in prison.'[16]

While some of the fugitives still had loot remaining from Sialkot, most of the remaining rebels were barely surviving, scraping out a meagre existence while constantly being on the move and hiding out in the mountains.[17] They had little hope of ever making it back to Awadh but hunger and poverty eventually drove them from the hills, and by the spring of 1858, Alum Bheg and the others hatched a desperate plan. The closest town within British territory was Madhopur, located on the Ravi River at the head of the Bari Doab Canal. It was not a military station, but was home to 'a large number of native officials, artisans and workmen, nearly all of them from Hindoostan.'[18] There was also a sizeable bazaar, which made it a particularly attractive target for the fugitives. Two officers, *Havildar* Imam Bux of the 46th, and *Subadar* Ramadeen of the 4th N.I., were the masterminds who planned the raid, and they used a man named Ooree to establish contact with the 'Hindustani' labourers of Madhopur.[19] Ooree had been a *syce* at Sialkot, but escaped to Madhopur the previous winter, disguised as a mendicant *fakir*. It was he who ascertained that the 'Hindustani's' were willing to join the rebels in an attack on the bazaar. Imam Bux and Ramadeen would both later swim across the river to meet up with their co-conspirators in secret. One of the main obstacles was the fact that the rebels no longer had any weapons, so the 'Hindustanis' would have to gather those in preparation for the attack. An unsuccessful attempt was made in April 1858, when the fugitives were joined by a local *dacoit*, or robber, named Taroo. They initially managed to overpower the guards at the ferry at Bahari (Bhadrali), downriver from Madhopur. When they tried to cross the river, however, the ferry became stranded on a sandbank and the party waiting on the opposite bank panicked and fled. The whole affair was subsequently called off.

On 2 June, another attempt was made and this time, Alum Bheg and about thirty others successfully crossed the river on small rafts and inflated animal skins.[20] They were armed with *tulwars*, or swords, *lathis* (heavy iron-bound sticks), as well as a few matchlock guns they had acquired. The rest of the *sepoys* would cross over on the ferry once the first party had linked up with the 'Hindustanis' and seized control of the bazaar. Alum Bheg and his comrades approached the town using the cover afforded by the high banks of the river, cutting down a local watchman on the road and chasing away the guards at the entrance to the bazaar. As the party entered the bazaar, they were joined by some of the local labourers who began plundering the shops and setting fire to the buildings. The *sepoys* repeatedly asked for the whereabouts of the *'sahib logue'*, but were mistakenly directed to a house inhabited by several Eurasian clerks, which they then attacked. Two of the Eurasians managed to escape, but the third, Mr Middleton, was severely wounded, as were two of his children. His wife and a third child were killed by the attackers. At this point, a canal official appeared and wounded several of the *sepoys* with his revolver and after the Sikh guards opened fire, the party finally retreated. Alum Bheg and the others had completely miscalculated the support they would receive once they began their assault, anticipating that hundreds of 'Hindustanis' would side with them—some of the local labourers did so, but rather than take control of the station, they merely plundered the shops before running off. In the chaos of the burning bazaar, the attackers were driven back by the better-armed guards.[21] The British were now rallying and pursued the attackers to the river:

> 'Mr Kelly took a small party down along the bank of the river to try and cut off some of the sepoys, but owing to the difficult nature of the ground, having to go on foot he was in time only to get a few shots at the last of them as they were crossing towards the Jummoo territory on rafts and on skins. He hit one man but saw him struggle out of the water on hands and knees. Many Poorbeahs were drowned and about twenty bodies have been brought in for examination.'

The river was particularly deep at this spot, and the current swift. This was the second time that the Sialkot mutineers had been defeated by the Ravi.[22] A few straggling survivors managed to flee into the mountains on the other side of the river. Those who had the misfortune of being apprehended by the British were, in the words of one official, 'suitably disposed of.'[23]

In Punjab, where the local population had remained largely loyal to the British, the distinctions between friend and foe were drawn along regional lines, with 'Hindustanis' all being labelled as intrinsically disloyal. By December 1857, more than 2,500 'Hindustanis' in Government service had been deported from the province.[24] Following the attack on Madhopur, all remaining 'Hindustanis' were 'thoroughly purged' from Punjab, and 'a general weeding out of suspicious or idle characters' was advocated.[25] The events of 1857–58 accordingly had a profound impact on the ethnicity and composition of the colonial administration in the region. After the attack on Madhopur, a total of 995 'Hindustanis' were rounded up—mostly labourers on the canal, but also some of the Sialkot fugitives. More than 600 were subsequently released and deported, but eleven of those who were identified as having played an active part in the attack were hanged on the spot, under the provisions of Act XVI of 1857.[26] A few were given prison sentences and 155 were flogged. Amongst the prisoners at Madhopur, the authorities had identified one *sepoy* of the 35th, who was sentenced to transportation for life after he turned Queen's evidence and revealed all the details of the attack.[27] A *sepoy* of the 26th BNI, who had escaped Cooper's slaughter at Ajnala, was also among the prisoners and he was one of those hung at Madhopur. Another forty-one prisoners were sent to Sialkot for identification, among whom was Alum Bheg.[28] He narrowly avoided being executed then and there, but now found himself a prisoner of the British, and was marched back to the site of the outbreak, where it had all begun. The failed attack on Madhopur was little more than the final frenzy of a doomed rebellion, or, as one newspaper put it, 'a terrible, but not important event.'[29] For Alum Bheg, however, this marked the end of his desperate flight.

The attack on Madhopur had shown how groups of *sepoy* fugitives could still challenge the colonial state's attempts to re-establish law and order, especially when they combined with locals at outlying stations situated along the periphery of British control. The initial reports on the attack were furthermore highly exaggerated by local English newspapers. For instance, the Anglo-Indian newspaper, *Friend of India*, wrote:

> 'Some of the disbanded sepoys who have found a refuge in Cashmere have crossed the frontier and attacked Madhopore. They murdered fourteen Europeans, including several children, with circumstances of atrocious cruelty. When attacked by the Sikh guard of the treasury, they retreated with a quantity of plunder over the frontier. They appear to have had no motive except to gratify their thirst for European blood. Runbeer Singh, it is said, intends to surrender these men, but that personage has hitherto exhibited a reluctance to give up sepoys, which has called for the admonition from the Chief Commissioner.'[30]

This was of course a typically alarmist report, and once the true extent of the attack became clear, the *Friend of India* had to correct its initial account. By ascribing the attack to the fugitives' 'thirst for

European blood', however, they were perpetuating what had become standards tropes concerning rebel violence during the uprising. The incident nevertheless convinced the Maharaja of Jammu and Kashmir, Ranbir Singh, of 'the necessity of taking active measures to clear his territory of such lawless characters,' as one British official put it.[31] At the same time that Alum Bheg began his final journey back to Sialkot in chains, there was thus a 'general exodus' of the last survivors of the 46th BNI from Jammu and further into the Himalayas. Small groups were later reported near Leh, in Ladakh, heading east towards the Tibetan border, and another at Chini, near Simla, which might have been trying to undertake the impossible journey down to Nepal and then back into India. 'They may escape into Nepaul or into the deadly terai between the Himalayas and the plains,' one newspaper reported, and 'once they get among the people of Oude or Rohilcund they are quite safe.'[32] The wilderness of the Terai, along the border between British India and Nepal, was the very region that Nana Sahib had disappeared into and it was generally perceived as a haunt for fugitive rebels.

The truth was that the fugitives in Kashmir were desperate and had nowhere to run. The biggest group of refugees, some eighty-seven men and five women and children, made their way through the inhospitable mountain region to the Spiti Valley and, against all odds, crossed the Chinese border.[33] The Chinese authorities, however, maintained a strict policy of keeping out foreigners and refused to let them continue on their way. As a result, the fugitives were stuck, quite literally, in the middle of nowhere: a place known as Chuga, several days' march east of what is today Kaurik, located near 32nd latitude and 79th longitude, on the Chinese side of the border. With their journey onwards blocked, they could not turn back and risk running straight into the waiting arms of the British. Rumours of *sepoy* refugees having made it all the way to the Chinese border eventually reached the British authorities and the assistant commissioner of Kullu, Mr G. Knox, immediately set off in pursuit, along with fourteen Punjabi policemen and some local men despatched by the ruler of Spiti.[34] Chugra was a fourteen-day march from Kullu, through the Himalayas and across numerous rivers, where the local population was said to be 'in the lowest stage of civilisation.'[35] While Knox was closing in on the hapless fugitives, the newspapers in India got hold of the story and made much of the 'dreadful sepoys wandering about in the passes of the Himalayas.'[36] Some of the stories were particularly paranoid, combining the imperial rivalry with Czarist Russia and fears of the 'Great Game' power-struggles, with the ongoing conflict with China:

> 'There have been for some time back alarming reports that the Sepoys and the Chinese—"two such named mingled!"—had confederated in some arcana of the Himalayan range to make a conjoint attack on our protected Hill States, while the Russians and the Persians were to invade us from Cabul, and by some other curious routes.'[37]

Such baseless stories obviously had more in common with the kind of rumours that had circulated amongst the Indian population prior to May 1857, than any realistic reflection of global politics. The prospect of Indian rebels being in contact with foreign powers beyond the borders of British India, whether they be China or Nepal, nevertheless turned this minor incident into something much bigger.

Meanwhile, Knox was approaching the fugitives' encampment, which lay about a day's march inside China. Although he had received strict orders not to proceed beyond British territory, he ignored this and crossed the border. The local Spiti officials accompanying Knox went ahead and established communications with the Chinese officials watching the border. A plan of operations was prepared and, probably for the first time in history, British and Chinese officials collaborated in this part of the world. Because of the Second Opium War (1856–60) between Britain and China, the two powers were technically at war, yet in the middle of the Himalayas, this mattered little. In his official report, Knox described what happened next:

> 'I arrived at night and sent the Spiti men on ahead, that they might help in surrounding the Poorbeahs, but gave instructions that no attack should be made till my arrival on the spot. They went on in the night as the Poorbeahs would know they were going to be surrounded, and perhaps might attack them. The Chinese had for some days been posted on the heights above the accompanying ground of the Poorbeahs in order not to let them pass, the Spiti men were posted down below and surrounded the Poorbeahs. I went to the spot early in the morning, and immediately on seeing me at some distance off the Spiti men rushed with a shout at the Poorbeahs and by the time I came up the Poorbeahs had each of them their hands tied behind their backs. I must say that before this 2 of the Chinese and some 10 Spiti men [...] went to the Poorbeahs on pretence that they

would let them go on their road, demanded their arms; three cavalry pistols and two swords and their latties were thus given up, so when the Spiti people rushed on them, they had nothing to fear, as the Poorbeahs were disarmed.'[38]

Three of the fugitives who tried to run were shot and killed, leaving a total of eighty-four men and five women and children taken be into custody. After some final talks between Knox and the Chinese officials, with the Spiti men as interpreters, the assistant commissioner promised to pay the Chinese a reward for their help in securing the fugitives. The entire party then began the lengthy journey back through the mountains toward British India, where new iron shackles were just then being prepared to greet the prisoners.

This was the last, and biggest, seizure of fugitive rebels in Kashmir and both the authorities and the newspapers were jubilant. One official claimed that 'the successful capture of these ruffian mutineers, most of whom were probably engaged in the Sealkote mutiny and the Madhopore outrage, will have an excellent moral effect.'[39] As India officially became a Crown colony in August 1858, it was important for the British to be able to bring some closure to the turmoil of the uprising. Since the most infamous rebel leaders had thus far avoided capture, the apprehension of the fugitives in Kashmir made welcome news and allayed some of the lingering calls for retribution. *The Times'* correspondent wrote of the affair:

'The last of the fugitive mutineers who took refuge in the Himalayan regions are being picked up from time to time. The other day a party of 90, after extraordinary wanderings, were trying to escape by Thibet and Chinese territory. Fancy that world of glaciers and rocks and literally howling wilderness being traversed by Sepoys born in the hot and fertile plains of Hindostan! But a pursuing destiny awaited them. They were followed by a civil officer (Mr. Knox) and some 30 Sikhs and hill-men, and were captured in Chinese territory. That a single European with a few Punjabee followers, separated by some 20 marches over several mountain ranges from all European support, should be able to take so large a party in the remotest Himalayan uplands shows that British *prestige* still lives even in the rudest localities.'[40]

In the commitment to hunting down Indian rebels in the aftermath of the uprising, a new myth of British colonial mastery was established. The violent retribution and mass-executions had demonstrated the willingness of the British to go to any length in order to regain control over India, and to punish those rebels who dare challenge colonial rule.[41] With the relentless pursuit of rebel fugitives, the scope of colonial justice was extended beyond the political borders of British territory. Even when rebels evaded capture, the British fantasised about the divine justice they were certain would ultimately be meted out to their enemies. The figure of Nana Sahib, that was later displayed in London in Madame Tussauds' 'Chamber of Horrors,' accordingly depicted the arch-fiend 'in the winter costume of his country,' as a fugitive in the Himalayas. The placard next to the figure described him as the man who had made war 'against innocent women and children', and who brought 'desolation to India, and mourning to England'. Although Nana Sahib was never actually caught, and his fate remained unknown, the text provided a suitable resolution: although he escaped his earthly pursuers, 'a retributive Providence willed it that punishment was near. Nana was totally defeated whenever he attempted to make a stand, and becoming a wanderer in his native land, died, it is said, the coward's death, despised and forsaken.'[42] This was, in other words, a cathartic narrative, that brought closure and justice, albeit imagined, to the trauma of the 'Mutiny.'

One of the few exceptions to what had become a Victorian obsession with the hunt for Indian rebels, was the correspondent William Howard Russell, who was able to empathise with the plight of the fugitives. An editorial in *The Times* highlighted the sober tone struck by their correspondent in his most recent communication, where he described:

> 'the miserable fate of the Sealkote mutineers, wandering from province to province in the Himalayas, endeavouring to force their way into Thibet, and driven back into the hands of their masters. His anticipation of their fate, and his views on the disarmed regiments, are strangely corroborated by the miserable fate of the disarmed regiments at Mooltan, which, as if obeying an evil destiny, have broken loose, divided, and found everywhere the same utter destruction, so that not one survives.'[43]

Russell was here referring to the tragic end of the 55th BNI at Multan, which later served as the inspiration for Kipling's story. But the fate of the 55th was at the same time also the story of numerous other *sepoy* regiments, which like the 26th that was massacred by Cooper at Ajnala, or indeed the Sialkot brigade intercepted by

Nicholson at Trimmu Ghat, were all massacred. After Mr. Knox captured the last group refugees in the middle of the Himalayas, the men who had risen up at Sialkot almost a year before, had for all intents and purposes, been exterminated. By that point, however, Alum Bheg's fate had already been sealed. Captured at Madhopur, he was taken back to Sialkot so 'that a more formal and public example might be made,' and here he was promptly identified as belonging to the 46th BNI.[44] According to a British eyewitness, 'one of the prisoners showed a mark of a wound in the leg, which, according to his own statement, he received at "Trimmoo Ghat Putton," whilst engaged against Nicholson's movable column, just twelve months ago.'[45] Another prisoner, also a *havildar* of the 46th, was unexpectedly released when he was serendipitously recognised by one of the officers as having escorted his wife back to her house to retrieve her valuables during the outbreak.[46] For Alum Bheg, though, there was no reprieve—by virtue of being an officer, even if only an NCO, he was considered a ringleader in the mutiny and as guilty of the murders of the Hunters and others as if he had himself struck the fatal blows.

10

SHARP AND SHORT AS THE CANNONS ROAR

Along with a *sepoy* and two young musicians from his regiment, who had also been amongst the prisoners taken at Madhopur, Alum Bheg was sentenced to death after a brief court martial on 8 July 1858.[1] The musicians were only thirteen and sixteen years old, and in a much-reported act of mercy, the younger one was pardoned (the older one was not).[2] Following military custom, Alum Bheg and the two others were sentenced to be executed by being blown from a cannon two days later. The fear of British artillery was deeply ingrained in the minds of Indian troops and had led to mutiny on several occasions over the past decades. Furthermore, there seems to have been a blurring between British firing on *sepoys* with artillery, as happened at Barrackpore in 1824, and the use of the cannon in formal executions, as occurred on such a massive scale in 1857. Whatever the exact circumstances, the fact remained that the imagery of British artillery provoked a sense of dread among Indian *sepoys*.

To most of the British public, the spectacle of the execution of mutinous *sepoys* was by then a quite familiar one. If people had not personally witnessed Indians being blown from guns, they had certainly heard about such executions through personal letters, newspaper reports, or the numerous illustrations that were disseminated throughout the Empire. One particularly graphic account was published in *The Times* on 3 December 1857, under the prosaic title 'An Indian Execution'.[3]

The anonymous correspondent described how five *sepoys* were blown from the muzzle of cannons for conspiring to mutiny: 'There was a roar [...] a bank of white smoke, and a jet and shower of black fragments, sharp and clear, which leaped and bounded in the air; this and a fearful sound from the spectators, as if the reality so far exceeded all previous fancy that it was intolerable; then a dead stillness.' As the smoke cleared, the author proceeded to inspect the scene of the execution:

'I walked straight to the scattered and smoking floors before the guns. I came first to an arm, torn off above the elbow, the fist clinched, the bone projecting several inches, bare. Then the ground was sown with red grisly fragments, then a blackhaired head and the other arm still held together... [C]lose by lay the lower half of the body of the next, torn quite in two, and long coils of entrails twined on the ground. Then a long cloth in which one had been dressed rolled open like a floorcloth and on fire. One man lay in a complete and shattered heap, all but the arms; the legs were straddled wide apart, and the smashed body on the middle of them; the spine exposed; the head lay close by, too. The last body was that of a native officer, who was the arch fiend of the mutiny; he was a short man, with a cruel face. His head had been cut clean off, but the muscles of the neck had contracted round the throat like a frill. His face was half upturned and calm, the eyes shut. I saw no expression of pain on any of them. What had been his body lay on its face, the legs as usual not shattered, but all the flesh torn like cloth from a sharp angle in the hollow on the back, off and off, till it merged in one mangled heap. [...] The troops immediately marched off, and I rode home at speed, and when I dismounted the dogs came and licked my feet.'[4]

At a time when most modern states had long replaced the spectacle of the scaffold with penal institutions, the British in India still had recourse to exemplary punishment through singularly brutal rites of public executions.[5] The practice of execution by cannon was used by both the Marathas and the Mughals, and also appears to have been used as late as the early twentieth century in Iran and in Afghanistan.[6] The physical destruction of the body had a distinct religious function within the cultural context of the Indian sub-continent, since it effectively prevented the customary funereal rites of Muslims and Hindus alike. There was accordingly a deliberate cultural specificity to the punishment, which extended beyond death. Europeans first encountered this technique during the mid-1700s, and one of the earliest recorded instances of its colonial use was when the French-Irish Count Lally executed an Indian spy near Madras in South India in 1758.[7] Five years later, Major Hector Munro, who was soon to give the East India Company its first major victory in India at the Battle of Buxar, allegedly restored order amongst his Indian soldiers by blowing twenty-four mutinous *sepoys* from guns.[8] An attempt by the rival Maratha power to 'corrupt' *sepoys* at Bombay in 1780, similarly led to one of the ringleaders being executed by cannon by the British authorities, who emphasised the deterrent aims of the spectacle:

> 'We judged it highly necessary for the public safety in a case of such fatal tendency, to inflict the most exemplary punishment on the delinquent, and to make the example as striking as possible to deter others from the like attempts.'[9]

The use of the cannon was thus regarded as the ultimate tool of exemplary deterrence and it was in this capacity that it was deployed on such an overwhelming scale during the uprising in 1857.

The British in India conventionally favoured hangings when executing criminals or rebels. Controlling the symbolism of public executions, however, proved increasingly difficult within a colonial context, and the hanging of hundreds of 'Thugs' during the 1830s had fully exposed the porous nature of colonial rituals of power.[10] The 'Thugs' signally failed to conform to the expected pattern of behaviour of condemned facing execution: One British observer noted that the night before execution 'was passed by these men in displays of coarse and disgusting levity [...] they evinced neither penitence nor remorse', and on the way to the site of execution the following morning, the convicts continued singing their 'unhallowed carols.'[11] On the scaffold they did not confess to their crimes nor display a spirit of contrition as behoved repentant criminals facing justice. Instead the prisoners boldly climbed the scaffold and, rather than letting the low-caste executioners pollute them with their touch, tightened the noose around their own neck and then simply stepped off the platform—effectively taking command of the ritual that was intended to reflect their submission to the legal process of the colonial state.[12] British officials had to infer (rather wistfully) the deterrent efficacy of such executions:

> '...I may venture to say that four out of five [...] executed this season at Saugor have thrown themselves from the drop before it could be struck

and was among the very few who denounced the colonial violence he witnessed in India:

'All these kinds of vindictive, unchristian, Indian torture, such as sewing Mahomedans in pig-skins, smearing them with pork-fat before execution, and burning their bodies, and forcing Hindus to defile themselves, are disgraceful, and ultimately recoil on ourselves. They are spiritual and mental tortures to which we have no right to resort, and which we dare not perpetrate in the face of Europe.'[18]

Where such retribution would indeed have been unthinkable in conflicts against white people, the perceived need to reassert racial hierarchies during a time of crisis made such violence both permissible and seemingly indispensable.

The British ultimately assumed that violence was the only language Indians understood and the mass-executions by cannon enacted this particular logic in a highly systematic manner. The rebels were treated as an undifferentiated mass and the revenge of the British was defined by its indiscriminate and collective character.[19] The purely instrumental nature of the spectacle of violence as deterrent rather than punitive was made very clear by Sir John Lawrence prior to the execution of mutineers in Peshawar in June 1857:

'In respect to the mutineers of the 55th, they were taken fighting against us, and so far deserve little mercy. But, on full reflection, I would not put them all to death. I do not think that we should be justified in the eyes of the Almighty in doing so. A hundred and twenty men are a large number to put to death. Our object is to make an example to terrify others. I think this object would be effectually gained by destroying from a quarter to a third of them.'[20]

Similarly, when Cooper was told not to execute any more of his prisoners at Ajnala, Montgomery ordered him to send the rest to Lahore, adding that 'We want a few for the troops here.'[21] Irrespective of their alleged crimes, prisoners were accordingly reserved for execution where it was thought to have the biggest impact. The execution of mutineers was reduced to a spectacle of power—the identity and even guilt of the individual prisoners was less significant than the message their death conveyed and the performance of state power they were made to participate in.

Not everyone believed these spectacles reflected well on British rule in India and Russell was scathing in his newspaper reports for *The Times*, exposing the combination of fear and vengefulness that characterised the attitudes of many of his compatriots:

'...I have no sympathy with those who gloat over their death, and who in the press and elsewhere, fly into ecstasies of delight at the records of each act of necessary justice, and glory in the exhibition of a spirit as sanguinary and inhuman as that which prompted murderers, assassins, and mutilators to the commission of the crimes for which they have met their doom. The utterers of those sentiments have been so terribly frightened that they never can forgive those or the race of those who inflicted such terrible shocks to their nervous system. They see no safety, no absolute means of prevention to the recurrence of such alarms but in the annihilation of every Sepoy who mutinied, or who was likely to have done so if he could.'[22]

Such critical voices, however, had little impact on either official policies or public opinion, mainly due to the fact that the mass-executions were commonly believed to be the most effective, if not only, means of maintaining British control.[23] Descriptions of the reaction of Indian spectators invariably made reference to their changing skin-colour as a sure sign that the message had hit home: '...their faces grew ghastly pale as they gazed breathlessly at the awful spectacle.'[24]

In addition to their deterrent effect, these executions were perceived as uniquely effective in re-establishing colonial rule by bolstering the prestige of the British. In the semi-official history of the 'Mutiny', John W. Kaye described the impact of the executions at Peshawar:

'To our newly-raised levies and to the curious on-lookers from the country, the whole spectacle was a marvel and a mystery. It was a wonderful display of moral force, and it made a deep and abiding impression [...] Perhaps some of the most sagacious and astute of the spectators of that morning's work said to each other, or to themselves, as they turned their faces homeward, that the English had conquered because they were not afraid. [...] Among the rude people of the border the audacity thus displayed by the English in the face of pressing danger excited boundless admiration. They had no longer any misgivings with respect to the superiority of a race that could do such great things, calmly and coolly, and with all the formality of an inspection-parade. The confidence in our power, which the disbandment of the Native regiments had done so much to

revive, now struck deep root in the soil. Free offers of allegiance continued to come in from all tribes.'[25]

Deliberately leaving out the gory details, Kaye turned the executions into a celebratory demonstration of the virtues of the stalwart
British character that underpinned colonial rule and sustained the so-
called 'civilising mission'.[26] As previously noted, accounts of British
retribution served to emphasise the violence inflicted on European
men and women, rather than the violence of the executions themselves. The violence of Indian rebels was at times even blamed for having brutalised the British, as witness to an execution described in a
letter to a relative back in England: 'I am afraid we are all very blood-
thirsty, as almost everyone had a smile of gratified revenge on his lips.
We are all thinking of Cawnpore. [...] Those massacres have quite
changed me. I believe I could walk over a recently fought battle field
quite unmoved.'[27] The crucial point here is that the 'massacres' referred
to were those perpetrated by the Indian rebels and not the executions
witnessed by the author. British accounts of the executions of *sepoys* and
rebels were thus made morally palatable by consistently reminding the
public about those atrocities committed by Indian rebels; this was all
part of the retributive logic of colonial violence that relied on indigenous practice and was inspired by the alleged aggression ascribed to
Indians.[28] The prisoners tied to the mouths of guns were implicitly
depicted as the perpetrators of horrible crimes which not only justified
unrestrained retribution but also negated the brutality of colonial punishment.[29] Execution by cannon could thus be presented as both justified and civilised—or as Lord Roberts put it: 'Awe inspiring, certainly,
but probably the most humane, as being a sure and instantaneous mode
of execution.'[30]

Witnessing an execution became an established part of experiencing
the 'Mutiny' and the numerous accounts reproduced in newspapers or
anyone of the numerous memoirs published in the aftermath of the
uprising, often dwelled on the violence, in great and gory detail.
Describing the sensory aspects of the spectacle—the sound of the gun,
the smell of burnt flesh, the sight of the bouncing head and remains of
the corpse strewn on the ground in a bloody mess—satisfied a morbid
fascination with death and the voyeuristic impulse of an audience for
whom public executions were no longer a common sight.[31] Visual rep-

resentations of executions by cannon, disseminated through the press across the empire, furthermore provided an image of a carefully orchestrated military spectacle, indicative of the order that British rule imposed on Indian society.[32] Apart from the brute language of power and terror, colonial violence and its representation during 1857 thus conveyed a reassuring message to both an Anglo-Indian as well as a British audience.[33] This secondary function of colonial violence is clearly reflected in an eyewitness account of an execution in Bombay published in Charles Dickens' magazine *Household Words* in early 1858:

> 'Those who witnessed the impressive scene will never forget it. The Europeans were scarcely one to a thousand—in fact, they could hardly be seen amongst the myriads of Asiatics; but all appeared as cool and confident as if they had been at a review in Hyde Park. And yet there was scarcely a man present who had not been sleeping with a loaded revolver in his bedchamber for months…'[34]

The public execution was in fact described as a perfect reflection of the colonial situation itself: the British were isolated and outnumbered, yet ultimately triumphant thanks to their resolve and strength of character. In this sense, the executions served to sustain the 'bluff' that was colonialism, and shore up the self-confidence of the British in the crucible of rebellion.

The mass-executions were, nevertheless, messy affairs—both literally and symbolically—and it was only by sanitising the accounts of *sepoys* being blown from guns that they could be represented as orderly and unequivocally efficacious spectacles. Kaye's assessment of the executions of 10 June at Peshawar, for instance, was belied by the account of Lord Roberts who witnessed the affair:

> 'It was a terrible sight, and one likely to haunt the beholder for many a long day; but that was what was intended. I carefully watched the sepoys' faces to see how it affected them. They were evidently startled at the swift retribution which had overtaken their guilty comrades, but looked more crest-fallen than shocked or horrified, and we soon learnt that their determination to mutiny, and make the best of their way to Delhi, was in nowise changed by the scene they had witnessed.'[35]

This was not a controlled ritual and the 'stinking shower' of human remains was virtually impossible to instrumentalise. The *sepoy* regiments forced to watch the executions were deliberately positioned as near to the guns as possible, and various accounts describe how the prisoners had 'their intestines blown into the faces of their former comrades who stood watching the scene.'[36] Yet British spectators too were covered in 'minute blackened particles' of burned flesh while the gunners serving the cannon routinely demanded extra pay to have their white uniforms cleaned afterwards.[37] The artillerymen had no prior experience of this kind of work, and as one of them wryly remarked: 'this had not formed part of our *curriculum* at Woolwich'. Quite often the executions went terribly wrong, turning the carefully choreographed ceremony into the sort of grim farce described by one medical officer:

> 'One wretched fellow slipped from the rope by which he was tied to the guns just before the explosion, and his arm was nearly set on fire. Whilst hanging in his agony under the gun, a sergeant applied a pistol to his head, and three times the cap snapped, the man each time wincing from the expected shot. At last a rifle was fired into the bottom of his head, and the blood poured out of the nose and mouth like water from a briskly handled pump. This was the most horrible sight of all. I have seen death in all its forms, but never anything to equal this man's end.'[38]

While the British believed the public executions were effective in forcing Indians into submission and actually shored up their loyalty, these bloody spectacles could just as easily drive Indian troops, and the wider population, away from their colonial rulers. Some accounts clearly suggest that *sepoys* only deserted when the British lost trust in them, or when indiscriminate reprisals left wavering troops no other option but mutiny. The supposed efficacy of executions by cannon, however, was far too important for the British authorities to formally acknowledge their ambiguous symbolism and messy reality, let alone condemn the practice. In the House of Commons, Lord Stanley expressed this sentiment in no uncertain terms: 'Only by great exertions—by the employment of force, by making striking examples, and inspiring terror, could Sir J. Lawrence save the Punjab; and if the Punjab had been lost the whole of India would for the time have been lost with it.'[39] British rule in India, in other words, was sustained by the application of exemplary violence and this became one of the founding narratives of the colonial state in India post-1857.

The executions of 1857 were not spectacles of entertainment for the masses, nor were they lessons in citizenship—not least because

Indians did not enjoy the status of citizens within the colonial state.[40] Ruling through coercion rather than consent, the British could only ever hope to assert their power, rather than eliciting the approval of the crowd. And where the European ruler might fear that the crowd identified with the convict on the scaffold, the British in India could simply assume this to be the case; the mass-executions were never intended solely, or even primarily, for the attendant *sepoys*, but by extension for the entire Indian population. Accordingly, these spectacles became occasions for the British to reinforce racialised hierarchies in front of both *sepoy* regiments and locals who were forcefully gathered to witness the spectacle. The colonial execution was thus aimed (sometimes quite literally) at the Indian spectators, both in uniform and without, but operated within a structure of power from which they were specifically excluded. These spectacles furthermore marked the ultimate point of escalation in the application of brute force—beyond the cannon, there was no tool left in the armoury of the colonial state.

* * *

By July 1858, when Alum Bheg was sentenced to be 'cannonaded', the crisis of the 'Mutiny' was essentially over. The last fugitives of the 46th brought back as prisoners later that summer, were either branded with a 'D' for deserter, following military practice, or deported to the newly established penal settlement on the Andaman Islands in the Indian Ocean.[41] As an Indian officer, however, Alum Bheg was selected to be executed at Sialkot 'to make an impression'—although it was entirely unclear on whom that impression was to be made. There were no longer any *sepoy* regiments left to be forced to watch their comrades blown apart, nor any crowds of sullen villagers made to witness the spectacle at the point of the bayonet.[42] Accordingly, Alum Bheg was one of the very last rebels to be blown from a gun during the long aftermath of the 'Mutiny'—a gory leftover from an earlier and more anxious time.

9 July 1858 was the anniversary of the outbreak at Sialkot and Reverend Boyle held a special memorial service in the church.[43] Before sunrise the following morning, Alum Bheg was to be executed. An eyewitness account was published in the newspapers in India and later also back in Britain:

'On Saturday last, the 10th instant, all the troops in this station assembled on the plain in front of the sepoy lines, lately occupied by the 35th Bengal Native (Light) Infantry. Her Majesty's 52nd Light Infantry were on the right, next to them stood the regiment of Punjaub Infantry; the next in the line were the Battery of Artillery, which arrived here on the 5th instant. On the left were drawn up the 7th Dragoon Guards. The regiment deployed into line, the 7th Dragoon Guards wheeling up to the right, and H.M. 52d Light Infantry brought their right shoulders forward, thus forming three sides of a hollow square. The brigadier and his staff arrived on the ground at 4.30 A.M., and took up a prominent position in the interval of the square; four prisoners—sepoys belonging to the late 46th Bengal Native Infantry, who mutinied 12 months ago—were also marched into the interior of the square under an escort of H.M. 52d. [...] After the proceedings of the court martial had been read in the vernacular language, three guns were moved out to the front, clearing the right flank of the 52d and the left of the 7th Dragoon Guards.'[44]

Contemporary accounts of executions referred to the comrades of the condemned witnessing the spectacle, but Alum Bheg saw no friendly faces in the crowd of spectators as he was marched to the guns at sunrise on 10 July 1858. His entire regiment had been wiped out and the 'Hindustani' camp-followers were all gone or deported. By a bizarre coincidence, however, Gordon, along with the Indian convert Scott, happened to be present at Alum Bheg's execution, as the Reverend later described:

'It is believed that none of the Sialkot mutineers ever reached Delhi. I was occasionally invited by English officers to speak to little squads of them who were captured in the mountains and condemned to be banished, shot, or blown from the cannons' mouths; but whilst they besought me earnestly to save them from corporeal punishment, yet it was sad to see that they cared not a single word about the salvation of their souls. On one of these occasions particularly, accompanied by Mr. Scott, I was very solemnly and deeply impressed. Two regiments of English soldiers were drawn up front to front, separated by a little space. Between them stood three pieces of artillery loaded with blank cartridges. The three mutineers who were condemned to be executed were then brought out of prison under guard, and conducted down to the open space between the two regiments. Brother Scott walked along with them, and the group stood beside the loaded guns. A solemn and awe-inspiring stillness reigned among the uniformed spectators, whilst Mr. Scott spoke of the only Saviour of sinners to those who were about to enter the eternal world, assuring them that they would be safe if only they would put their trust in Him. But their rejection of the glad tidings was decided—nay, even bitter.'[45]

It never occurred to Gordon that if fears of conversion had originally triggered the outbreak, the words of missionaries were probably the last thing the condemned mutineers wanted to hear during their final moments. Indeed, the presence of missionaries at the execution might have actually confirmed every single suspicion Alum Bheg and the others harboured concerning the essentially Christian nature of British rule.

British accounts often focused on the demeanour of the prisoner about to be put to death, who, much like criminals in Europe, were expected to perform their part in the ritual of the execution. Ideally, a repentant prisoner stoically accepted his judgement and perhaps even addressed the crowd of spectators with a few edifying words of warning. The prisoner was thus expected to verbalise the deterrent logic of his own execution. Facing imminent death, few convicts, however, acted simply according to this script. During the suppression of the uprising in India, some rebels were indeed contrite, but others went to their death defiant and shouting obscenities, while others again were sullenly quiet and seemingly consigned to their fate. According to Cooper, who had ample opportunity to observe *sepoys* being put to death, 'every phase of deportment was manifested by the doomed men when inevitable death forced itself upon them—astonishment, shame, frantic rage, despair, the most stoic calmness, but no sign of contrition...'[46] The eyewitness accounts make no mention of how the three prisoners acted on 10 July 1858, and we can only imagine what Alum Bheg was feelings on this fateful morning. Alum Bheg was essentially executed as a proxy for Hurmat Khan. Having been swept up by events over which he had no control, he was about to be executed for murders he did not commit. Through the early morning haze he may have been able to make out the dusty-blue outline of the Himalayas, where he had been in hiding not so long ago. His home in Awadh, however, was thousands of miles away and he was never to see it again.

After Mr Scott withdrew, Alum Bheg's fetters were knocked off, and his arms and legs were tied to the wheels of the gun, with the mouth of the heavy barrel pressing against his chest.[47] The gun had been loaded with a half-charge of gunpowder and nothing else; with the body strapped to the cannon and the trunk in direct contact with the barrel, the burst of the blank charge alone would be more than sufficient to blow him to pieces. The hoarse yell of the command to 'fire' was given, echoing across the plain and across the lines of troops, and the fuses were lit. Seconds later the guns went off with a roar and Alum Bheg was 'instantaneously shivered to atoms.'[48] 'The body appears to swell and burst—like a shell,' a colonial photographer noted of another similar execution, and 'the pieces of flesh and bone are scattered all round and the head goes bounding in front.'[49] As the proceedings were completed, the troops marched back to their respective quarters.

One of the British soldiers who was present at the execution was a Corporal in the 52nd Regiment, who had been stationed with the 46th at Sialkot, and later fought them at Trimmu Ghat. In a letter to his father he described his thoughts of the spectacle he had witnessed:

'On the 10th of this month we [have] blown three from the guns at this station; it is a shocking sight to see, but what is that to the brutal murders which they have committed. I should like to have seen three hundred. Some of our young men who had lately come out from England did not like to see it, but they have not seen how they have brutally cut up our people. The three belonged to the 46th Regt. N.I. which we left in Sealkote…'[50]

The British troops present evidently had mixed reactions to the bloody spectacle but the atrocities indiscriminately ascribed to the rebels were yet again invoked to legitimise British retribution—and also as a coping mechanism to steady those forced to witness the sight of fellow human beings being blown apart. The execution nevertheless prompted the Corporal to reflect on his own mortality:

'Dear Father, I often think it is a great mercy that I am still spared, seeing that so many poor fellows have been taken off to that journey where they will never return. I may say I have seen hundreds taken from my side since I have been out in this country; and strange to say, all the ablest and strongest men are called away first, and many I dare say, not fit to meet their God.'[51]

Having witnessed the execution, Gordon simply observed that 'all that remained of the three wretched criminals was three limp, blackened sack-like inanimate objects, lying on the ground some considerable distance in front of the guns.'[52] What he did not mention, perhaps because he did not wait around after the brutal spectacle was over, was the fact that the heads of those executed remained quite intact even after the execution. The heads were thrown up in the air by the blast, but were otherwise the only identifiable body part left. Before the British troops marched off, one of them, Captain A. R. Costello of the 7th Dragoon Guards, picked up Alum Bheg's severed head and carried it away. It was at this point not yet a skull that could be handled with ease, but a recognisable human head, complete with facial features, hair, skin, flesh, muscle, tongue, teeth, brain matter, and, most likely, blood oozing from the torn neck. As the barren plain outside Sialkot was emptied of troops, all that remained of Alum Bheg's mangled corpse was removed by low-caste cleaners and disposed of as so much offal. Only his head was missing.

11

BUT FROM THE SKULLS OF THE SLAIN

Captain Costello left India just three months after he had witnessed Alum Bheg's execution and taken the head—just long enough for the head to have been skeletonised by insects and the intense heat of the summer.[1] The note found with Alum Bheg's skull is written on paper bearing the watermark of the Kildare Street Club in Dublin, which suggests that Costello brought the skull all the way back to Ireland when he returned from India in 1859. The note, however, also refers to Costello in the third person and describes him as being 'late' captain of the 7th Dragoon Guards.' It would thus appear that he got rid of the skull not too long after his return—perhaps when he got married in 1862, or when his new manor was built a few years later. While we will never know exactly what moved Costello to pick up the bloodied head of Alum Bheg, and go through the visceral process of defleshing the skull in order to bring this grisly trophy back home, it is nevertheless possible to make some educated inferences.[2]

For one thing, it is clear that Costello did not pick up Alum Bheg's head on a whim. Nor was this an unprecedented act. Costello might very well have heard of the many feats and inventive acts of violence attributed to his fellow Irishman, John Nicholson—including the story of how he kept the head of a man he had personally killed on his desk. The story involved a notorious 'freebooter' who was active on the frontier near Rawalpindi. A large reward had been offered for his capture, but when Nicholson realised that none of the locals were going to

191

turn the man in, he decided to take things in his own hands, as one of his fellow officer described:

> '"Saddle my horse," said Nicholson quietly. When the horse was brought, he mounted, and rode off alone to the freebooter's village, where, by some coincidence, the first person he met was the man he wanted. Nicholson ordered him to surrender, but he refused, and rushed at Nicholson, who thereupon cut him down. When the body was brought in, Nicholson had the head cut off and placed in Cutcherry[3] beside himself, and he contemptuously asked every Malik[4] who came to see him if he recognised to whom it belonged.'[5]

Displaying the head of an enemy was clearly not considered incompatible with the status and respectability of a gentlemanly colonial officer. On the contrary, it reflected a willingness to deploy 'savage' methods against savages, similar to the retributive logic so readily invoked by Cooper and others during the suppression of the Uprising. There was no pretence that the acquisition of the enemy's head served a purpose other than the intimidation of the enemy, but, like the executions by cannon, this momentary lapse in 'civilised' behaviour was excusable, even commendable, within a colonial context. An early twentieth-century biography of Nicholson acknowledged the moral predicament of this act, but found it easy to justify with reference to the efficacy of such culturally specific violence: 'It was a gruesome thing to do, perhaps, but it must be remembered that it was necessary to strike terror into the hearts of other evil-doers, to whom the freebooter in question had been something of a hero.'[6]

It was a well-established British practice to behead rebels and display their severed heads on pikes at the city-gates as a general warning—this had happened as recently as the suppression of the Irish Rebellion of 1798, and also in the Caribbean during the early nineteenth century, where the beheading of 'traitorous' slaves assumed a culturally specific significance.[7] It was accordingly not such an outlandish thing to do in 1857, as the British were fighting a new sort of rebels; the intended function of beheading was much as it had been in the case of Nicholson's 'freebooter'. Henry Dunlop, who fought with a volunteer cavalry unit in the region north of Delhi in 1857, described how they cut off the head of the local rebel leader, Shah Mall, and paraded it around the villages of the area:

'We carried a small silken union-jack as the banner of the Volunteers, and on this occasion an ensign also, in the shape of Shah Mull's gory head stuck on a long spear. This last was necessary, to prove to the country-people, who knew the sternly resolute features of the old ruffian well, that their leader was really dead.'[8]

Much like the spectacles of execution, the grisly display of the rebel leader's severed head was used to restore order and, in this instance, to compel the local population to pay taxes. As a bloody symbol of power, next to the Union Jack, the severed head signalled the end of the popular rebellion and the restoration of colonial authority. The use of the notion of 'necessity' is also noteworthy, implying that it was the recalcitrant nature of the rebels, and the irregular circumstances of the conflict, which forced the British to take recourse to such extreme measures. Yet again the savagery ascribed to the rebels was used to legitimise British violence. Similar to the practice of scalping in north America, where it was popularised by Europeans as proof of kills, slain enemies were also beheaded in India during 1857 by both sides in the conflict as a means of claiming rewards. The severed heads of Europeans, for instance, were sent in by rebels to several of the local rulers, including Bhadur Shah, Nana Sahib and the Begum at Lucknow.[9] When the noted rebel leader Maulvi Ahmadulah Shah was killed by a local raja in 1857, the Maulvi's head was cut off and despatched to the British authorities for identification and so that the Rs 50.000 reward could be claimed.[10]

* * *

Costello's decision to take Alum Bheg's head moreover took place during a period when there was a keen interest in the human skull as a key site of scientific inquiry. Racial differences, in particular, were studied and established in reference to the size and shapes of peoples' skulls, which were collected, measured and classified from all corners of the world. Exploration, conquest and collection went hand in hand within the European empires, and soldiers, medical personnel and colonial officials often doubled as amateur collectors and would-be scientists. In Europe, the posthumous dissection and the collection of body parts, had been reserved for executed criminals and the unclaimed corpses of the poor. In the imperial world, however, no such considerations

existed, and the scale of this practice assumed much greater propor-
tions. From the beginning of the nineteenth century onwards, indigenous graves were robbed, colonial battlefields and execution grounds
were scoured, while the trophies of 'savage' head-hunters were re-
appropriated to satisfy the demands of craniology and to populate the
medical collections and ethnographic museums of the Western World.

Costello was certainly not the first colonial officer to help himself
to the remains of the dead after an execution in colonial India. For
instance, following the hanging of 'Thugs', alluded to in the previous
chapter, a similar thing occured. Dr Henry Harpur Spry of the Bengal
Medical Service was present at the execution in 1832, and described
in a letter to his mother what happened after everyone else had left:

> 'After the murders were taken down from the scaffold I had the heads of
> half a dozen of them taken off and have them now in course of preparation
> intending to send them with a history of each to the London Phrenological
> Society, but the other day I got a request from the Chief Secretary to
> Government to allow him to have charge of any I might have to take home
> to Combe at Edinburgh.'[11]

Spry was evidently inspired by the craze for phrenology, which
emerged as one of the precursors to craniology and racial science during the late eighteenth and early nineteenth century in Europe and
America.[12] The central premise of phrenology was that the mind was
made up by a number of central faculties, such as 'Cautiousness' or
'Inquisitiveness', and their relative size and development effectively
determined a person's character. These faculties, it was further argued,
could accurately be mapped and measured by the shape, bumps and
dimensions of the skull, and the assumption was that an expert phre-
nologist could 'read' the personality of an individual—whether dead
or alive. In order to prove the validity of their theories, phrenologists
often relied on the skulls of criminals, since these would supposedly
exhibit more pronounced traits of, for instance, 'Secretiveness' and
'Destructiveness', untempered perhaps by sufficiently developed
'Benevolence'. Previously, the corpses of executed criminals had been
used for dissection, which was indeed part of the punishment, and the
availability of skulls of named murderers convicted for specific acts of
violence enabled phrenologists to trace the corresponding faculties in
the skull. As the craze for phrenology reached the outer reaches of the

Empire during the 1830s, it was almost inevitable that the Indian 'Thugs', who were considered to be hereditary criminals, should also be subjected to this newly developed 'science'.[13]

After removing the heads of the executed 'Thugs', it appears from Spry's own account that he simply left them outside to be macerated by insects and exposure to the elements. Once the skulls were defleshed and dry, they were sent to Edinburgh for phrenological examination. Despite its popularity, phrenology was not uncontested as a 'science', and it is worth noting that Spry did not have official permission to remove the heads of the executed 'Thugs'. The fact that he could do so with impunity, however, and later even publish his findings, reveals that the scientific framework within which the mutilation of the bodies took place mitigated, and implicitly legitimised, his actions.

Spry did not select the heads at random, and the seven skulls that were subsequently despatched to Scotland were supposedly those belonging to the most notorious 'Thugs', each of which accompanied by a detailed description of the individual and of the crimes for which he had been executed. Spry obtained this information from the trial-records, and when Robert Cox, an active member of the Phrenological Society of Edinburgh later examined the skulls, he referred back to these micro-biographies.[14] Considering his reliance on the information provided by Spry, Cox's conclusion was predictable: 'it may be confidently affirmed,' he claimed, 'that so far as our information extends, the heads and characters of these seven "Thugs" exactly correspond.'[15] This conclusion involved a significant sleight of hand, since phrenology was not an exact science, and without the accompanying biographies Cox's analysis would have been impossible. The skulls of criminals were so useful to phrenologists precisely because they would know what personal characteristics to look for—phrenology could elicit no information from a skull independently of the profile of the individual. Similar to the note found with Alum Bheg's skull, it was Spry's micro-biographies that gave meaning and value to the skulls of 'Thugs'.

If Spry had to contend himself with surreptitiously collecting the skulls of executed criminals in India, the battlefields at the peripheries of the Empire offered more fertile hunting grounds for the colonial head-hunter. In South Africa, the pervasive impact of racialised thinking meant that in many instances the indigenous population was considered simply as part of the natural fauna, meaning that their bodies could be treated like natural specimens.[16] The presence of white settlers and the bitterness and brutality of the conflicts fought on the frontiers further contributed to a perception of those who resisted colonisation as primitive savages who could be hunted as animals.[17] During the so-called Frontier Wars of South Africa, between 1779 and 1879, scientific collecting of human remains and the dehumanisation of non-white enemies in colonial warfare converged in the widespread practice of taking body parts as trophies.[18]

When the Xhosa chief Hintsa was shot and killed in 1836, for instance, the British soldiers and local settlers present not only pilfered the body for souvenirs—beads, ornaments and spear—but they also cut off and carried away his ears, teeth, testicles, as well as part of his beard.[19] While there was no pretence of a scientific rationale for the mutilation of Hintsa's body, any distinction between notions of loot, souvenirs, morbid mementos and ethnographic artefacts simply did not exist. One of Hintsa's ears was reportedly offered up for sale, demonstrating the commodification of this particularly grisly form of trophy.[20] A decade later, during the Seventh Xhosa War in 1847, a British soldier in the 91st Highlanders commented on the price demanded for the skulls of slain enemies in Cape Town: 'I have seen a [Xhosa] head for sale, I would have bought it but it was too dear so I shall wait till I can kill one myself.' When the soldier was deployed in Xhosa territory, he even thought of turning it into a business opportunity: 'I intend to make some money by selling [Xhosa] heads, which are very expensive in Cape Town.'[21]

These were not isolated cases, but common practices as British soldiers burned villages and indiscriminately killed or displaced the local populations. The Assistant Surgeon, and well-known anatomist, Robert Knox of the 72nd Highlanders, maintained a large collection of Xhosa skulls and when asked how he had required them, he responded wryly: 'Why, sir, there was no difficulty in Caffraria; I had but to walk out of my tent and shoot as many [Xhosa] as I wanted for scientific and ethnological purposes.'[22] Sadly, Knox was not bragging and another contemporary account describe the very process by which such 'scientific' collecting occurred:

> 'Doctor A…of the 60th had asked my men to procure for him a few native skulls of both sexes. This was a task easily accomplished. One morning

they brought back to camp about two dozen heads of various ages. As these were no supposed to be in a presentable state for the doctor's acceptance, the next night they turned my vat into a cauldron for the removal of superfluous flesh. And there these men sat, gravely smoking their pipes during the live-long night, and stirring round and round the heads in that seething boiler, as though they were cooking black-apple dumplings.'[23]

It was not simply that the scientific paradigm permitted the collection of human skulls for a higher cause, but also that the very nature of what became known as 'savage warfare' involved a process of completely dehumanising the indigenous population. Much as was the case in India during the Uprising of 1857, British violence in South Africa was inspired by rumours and exaggerated stories of how local warriors mutilated the bodies of white soldiers and settlers. The macabre irony, however, was that, during the nineteenth century, the British mutilated far more bodies than did the various local groups of so-called 'savages' they fought in South Africa and elsewhere in the Empire.

If the British did not themselves directly kill those whose heads they collected, they were only too happy to purloin already prepared skulls. In 1859, during his travels in what is today Tanzania, the famous explorer Richard Burton described 'passing though the poles decorated with skulls—a sort of negro Temple Bar—at the entrance Konduchi; they now grin in the London Royal College of Surgeons.'[24] The reference to Temple Bar, the gate in London from where the heads of traitors were exhibited up till the 18th century, implied that Africans were still engaged in practices which had long ceased in Britain itself. Crucially, the fact that Burton had the skulls sent to a medical collection in London, suggests that, as far as he was concerned, this was a much more fitting resting place.[25] The skulls may still have been grinning, but at least they were now being put to better use.

During the Lushai campaign of 1871–72, against so-called head-hunting tribes on the north-eastern frontier of British India, one officer noted the similarities between the British and their enemies' obsession with skulls:

'In fact all the medicos with us were quite as eager for Lushai skulls as any Lushai could have been for theirs; though, in the interests of civilisation, the Lushais' heads would have reposed in glass cases on velvet cushions probably, while those of our friends would have been elevated on poles exposed to the wind and the rain.'[26]

The analogy between British and Lushai headhunting was acknowledged, yet quickly dismissed: for all the similarities, any real comparison of 'civilised' and 'primitive' practices was inconceivable to Victorians. It was indeed one of the basic assumptions underpinning imperialism that British collecting practices were rational by definition, whereas those of their enemies were simply deemed irrational. The close alignment between imperialism and scientific collecting nevertheless reveal the comparison between the British and headhunting tribes to be an apt one. As a putative object of knowledge, the human skull was indeed fetishised within Victorian society; the skull of a 'Thug', a Xhosa, or an Indian rebel of the 'Mutiny', was accordingly as much of a trophy to the coloniser as the head of an enemy slain in battle might have been to the colonised. The violence intimately linked to the collecting of skulls by colonial officers and medical personnel furthermore make the notion of a purely scientific endeavour inherently unsustainable. Collecting the skulls and other body-parts of indigenous people was as much an expression of power and brute force as executions or massacres were.

During the Indian Uprising, body parts of rebels were collected mainly as souvenirs and as part of the widespread looting and pillaging carried out by British troops and their local allies. Souvenirs from the massacres of European civilians, including locks of hair and other items found at Cawnpore, were also collected by British troops in the Victorian tradition of *memento mori*.[27] Executions of rebels also produced souvenirs, as was the case when the famed rebel leader Tantia Tope was hanged in 1859:

> 'He struggled very slightly, and the mehters[28] were called to drag him straight. A sergeant of the 3rd Bengals acted as hangman. Thus finished the career of the rebel chief, Tantia Topee, with all due solemnities of British military routine. When the suspended body became motionless, the troops were all marched off, and the body remained hanging for the remainder of the evening. After the troops left, a great scramble was made by officers and others to get a lock of his hair, &c.'[29]

These types of souvenirs were not so different from those that spectators at public executions might collect in Europe, or even the more macabre mementos kept by collectors, including books bound in the skin of a murderer, or the death-masks of the famous and infamous alike.[30]

There was certainly no shortage of skulls belonging to Indian rebels available for the thousands of British troops who fought during the 'Mutiny'. Photographic evidence shows skulls and bones spread out in the courtyard of the 'Secundra Bagh' at Lucknow, while William Henry Russell noted the 'heaps of human bones' found on the banks of the river near Satichaura Ghat at Cawnpore.[31] One Englishman who was in Delhi just after the assault, described walking along the Jamuna river just outside the city, with the traces of the recent conflict everywhere:

> 'dead horses and camels, and occasionally human remains, with portions of exploded shells, might be seen. The "Brahminee hawks" and vultures were still hovering around. I took up a human skull; it was that of a Sepoy for the marks of the pawn were still on the front teeth. A round shot or sword-cut had taken off the top of the head; death must have been instantaneous. I thought of the classic poet as I thus looked upon the most vivid realisation of them I ever saw, or ever expect to see:
>
> "The wrath which hurled to Pluto's gloomy reign
> The souls of mighty chiefs untimely slain;
> Whose limbs, unburied on the naked shore,
> Devouring dogs and hungry vultures tore!"'[32]

Elsewhere, at the village of Doondea-Kheyra, which was about to be demolished, a British officer inspected a temple where some of the survivors from Cawnpore had taken refuge months earlier. The temple was 'pitted with bullet-marks and blackened by fire; and, sad reminiscence of the tragedy enacted, a human skull, lying, with a terrible significance, among the dust and rubbish of the deserted buildings.'[33] A uniquely Victorian aesthetic, almost gothic in nature, seems to have influenced the way that the British interacted with human remains on the battlefields of India, and it is interesting to note how skulls elicited far more emotional responses than did the corpses of dead rebels encountered with such frightful frequency.

Costello was furthermore not the only soldier serving in the 'Mutiny' who brought a skull back home. Reporting on the return of the soldiers of the 42nd Highlanders from service in India, one newspaper noted in passing that 'one of them has brought, as a trophy of the Indian war, the skull of a Sepoy, which had been perforated by bullets.'[34] This skull was, apparently, simply that of 'a Sepoy' but derived its value from the bullet-holes which testified to the intensity of combat as well as, of course,

British victory. It was at times a rather banal wish to acquire a souvenir that led British soldiers to collect body-parts from dead Indians, as one 'Mutiny'-veteran recounted half a century later:

> 'Our officers had told us not to go near an out-lying part because dead bodies were putrefying there. But one of our fellows sneaked out without telling anybody and brought back a black man's skull to make a box for his pipeclay. He thought p'raps it would be a sort of souvenir. Well, it was. It brought the cholera, and between Saturday and Monday we left 300 of our poor chaps behind. It was terrible.'[35]

While it remains unclear whether it was indeed the rotting head that was the source of cholera, the story gives some indication of just how disgusting the taking of a head could be. As opposed to skulls picked up from a battlefield months and years after their owner died, the collection of a 'fresh' head entailed careful defleshing. Later accounts of trophy-skulls describe the stench they exuded, and some turned green and grew mould when not preserved properly.[36] Surrounded by death and decay, British troops during the uprising grew accustomed to such sights and smells, as Henry Dunlop of the Volunteer Cavalry described:

> 'Numerous dead bodies of Sepoys lay along the road by the Serai. Exposure to the sun had distended and bloated every limb; the corpse looked as though blown full of air. We had read and heard of the murderers of our women and children, so looked on with grim satisfaction on the distorted features of the dead around, limiting our pity to the case of an unfortunate pariah dog, which some stray shot had killed amidst the Sepoys, and whose body was also bloated out and distended, almost a ludicrous caricature of the human mortality around.'[37]

If British soldiers were not actively encouraged to mutilate the bodies of Indian rebels, they were certainly not given any reason to view them with anything but indifference or disdain. Anyone who was in India during those years could thus with ease have acquired the skull of a *sepoy* should he have wished to do so. The circumstances surrounding Captain Costello's involvement in the 'Mutiny' were, however, somewhat unusual.

* * *

Captain Costello and the 7th Dragoon Guards were only despatched to India towards the end of 1857 and arrived too late to participate in any of the actual fighting. The 'Mutiny' was accordingly not included in the regiment's battle-honours and none of the troopers received the Mutiny Medal. Costello himself went back to Ireland where he resigned his commission altogether; he never involved himself again with either the military or with India. Costello had, in other words, participated in one of the most celebrated colonial wars of the nineteenth century with nothing to show for it. To grasp the full significance of this, it is important to remember that scores of Victorian heroes were forged in the crucible of the 'Mutiny'—including more than thirty recipients of the Victoria Cross from other cavalry units who saw action during the uprising. The most exciting part of Costello's brief sojourn in India, by contrast, was probably the execution of Alum Bheg and the compulsion to acquire a war-trophy may thus have been much greater. It is also worth noting that Costello's regiment had served in South Africa during the Seventh Xhosa War 1846–7, just a few years before he joined. There may thus very well have been stories and tales involving the taking of trophy-skulls circulating amongst the veterans of the regiment. To bring back the skull of a murderous mutineer, and one who had moreover been executed by cannon, might thus have gone some way towards soothing Costello's sense of 'losing out' by making up for some of the glory of which he and his comrades had been cheated.

There is nothing to suggest that Costello had a phrenological interest or that Alum Bheg's skull was ever intended for scientific examination. Nevertheless, Costello would undoubtedly have been aware of scientific practices of collecting skulls at the time—practices which opened up a space for such actions as socially permissible and morally sanctioned. There was moreover an element of opportunism to Costello's action, since he did not single-handedly defeat Alum Bheg and behead him as proof of his status and masculinity. Costello simply happened to be present at an execution, which 'produced' a head that could be collected and preserved. Taking possession of Alum Bheg's head nonetheless constituted a very deliberate assertion of dominance on the part of Costello.

In the mid-nineteenth century, when Costello acquired Alum Bheg's head, a skull could mean a range of different things. A skull could be akin to a hunting-trophy, testifying to the martial prowess of the 'barbarian gentleman', but it could also be a memento of the 'Mutiny' or a souvenir from an execution witnessed.[38] In Costello's case it was probably a combination of all three, although it appears that he did not want just any old skull and that the story of the murder of Dr Graham and the Hunters was part of the intrinsic value attached to Alum Bheg's head. The description of Alum Bheg that Costello provided on the small note—as a 'principal leader in the mutiny' who intercepted fleeing Europeans and personally killed them—was really much closer to Hurmat Khan's role during the outbreak at Sialkot. But Hurmat Khan had gotten away, and the fugitives from the 46th who were brought back to Sialkot for punishment were indiscriminately executed for the murder of Dr Graham and the Hunters as well as all the other victims. We know that the officers of the 7th Dragoon Guards dined with Reverend Boyle while at Sialkot, and moreover messed with the officers of the 52nd, and it is likely that Costello's knowledge of the outbreak at Sialkot was based on such encounters.[39] Skulls were, as we have seen, easily available in India in 1858, but their meaning and value as trophies was derived entirely from the stories attached to them. The greater the infamy of the living person, the greater the worth of his skull. Costello thus turned the insignificant Alum Bheg into a 'principal leader', transforming his skull into a far more interesting trophy. And while the story Costello attached to the trophy testified to the violence and treachery of Indian rebels, the skull itself became the proof of British victory.

A photograph taken in 1857 of Captain Thomas B. Ray of the Volunteer Cavalry provides another hint of what a trophy-skull might have meant to a British officer who served in the 'Mutiny'. The portrait shows Ray in his uniform and with the revolver he carried in India and carefully arranged like a colonial still-life on the table next to him is a human skull and a pith-helmet. In this portrait, the dapper and moustachioed Ray accordingly presents himself as a colonial gentleman officer with the tools of his trade, and the skull is as much a prop in his self-fashioning as is the *tulwar*, or Indian sword, resting by his side. Like a hunter posing with a tiger-skin or the mounted head of a deer, the trophy-skull in the photograph is proudly displayed as a reflection of Ray's martial status without any indication of shame or embarrassment. Because Ray served in the Volunteer Cavalry like Dunlop, it is likely that the skull was actually that of Shah Mall, which, having served its purpose as a tool of intimidation, was apparently kept as a personal trophy. There are several later examples of colonial officers who kept human trophy-skulls proudly exhibited on their desk or mantelpiece; in some instances, this was combined with a sense of respect, and even affection, for the defeated enemy. By displaying the skull of a 'savage' within the confines of one's home, the threat once posed by this individual was effectively neutralised and the savagery domesticated.

The pride that Costello might have derived from possessing Alum Bheg's skull could not, however, be taken for granted. Human remains are symbolically tricky objects, and can invoke horror and disgust just as easily as they inspire respect for the 'barbarian gentleman'.[40] The fact is that, over time, the skull itself became a troublesome trophy: it embodied the violence of Empire, both Indian and British, making it a les-than-appropriate morbid memento during the aftermath of the 'Mutiny', when calls for retribution and bloody vengeance were gradually replaced by a more restrained Victorian form of commemoration. The many stories and reports of the rape of European women by Indian rebels, which had so occupied the British press during the uprising, were thus officially denied by the Government in an explicit attempt to control public sentiments and facilitate a new era of peaceful co-existence between rulers and ruled.[41] Narratives of atrocities carried out by mutineers, as detailed in the note accompanying Alum Bheg's skull, had initially served to rally the British forces during the suppression of the uprising, but once the dust had settled, and peace supposedly restored, they proved merely to be painful and disruptive.[42]

Attitudes to the Empire, and to colonial violence more generally, also underwent significant changes within Britain during these years. The Morant Bay Rebellion in Jamaica in 1865, for instance, was brutally suppressed by the British authorities and hundreds of former slaves were either executed or flogged.[43] The incident caused an outcry and the Governor, E.J. Eyre, was eventually recalled and dismissed, though the debate concerning the morality and legality of the violence raged for decades.[44] A few years later, in 1872, a small group of Sikhs, belonging to the Kuka sect, attacked several villages belonging to Muslims in Punjab, and a local British official panicked and promptly executed sixty-eight of them by blowing them from cannon.[45] The response was much as it had been over the Eyre affair, not least because such blatantly excessive violence belied the ideals of the civilising mission and made imperialism so hard to defend.

Like the brutality of the British repression of the 'Mutiny', the taking of Alum Bheg's skull would accordingly have been difficult to justify once the moral hangover of colonial violence kicked in during the decades following 1857. Possessing a trophy-skull might have been personally rewarding for Costello, yet the violence that the skull symbolised was morally incompatible with the rhetoric of liberal imperialism which shaped British imperialist project during the second half of the nineteenth century. The skull of Alum Bheg was, in a sense, a permanent relic of a passing madness and would have seemed increasingly out of place in an era where people perceived themselves as rational and enlightened. Phrenology, too, had fallen out of favour and the 'Thug' skulls in Edinburgh were later re-classified as racially significant specimens and subjected to another type of examination within the field of craniology. This also goes some way towards explaining why, having gone through all the trouble of preserving the skull and taking it back home, Costello appears to have gotten rid of it so quickly.

* * *

It is not that the obsession with skulls went away, or that the collecting practices of human remains within the European empires ceased in the second half of the nineteenth century—quite the opposite, in fact. In Africa, the colonial practice of collecting skulls was so prevalent and conspicuous that it was noticed and commented on among the local population. A Muslim who had accompanied Richard Burton on the expedition in 1859, referred to above, later told the famous journalist and explorer, Henry Morton Stanley, that Burton was 'one of the wickedest white men born, because he saw him pick up men's skulls and put them in sacks, as if he was about to prepare a horrible medicine with them.'[46] Two decades later, in Southern Africa, Zulu warriors fighting the British asked a Dutch trader 'Why did the Whites cut off the heads of those who had fallen, and put them in their wagons? What did they do with these heads? Or was it to let the Queen see how they had fought?'[47] The very people whom the British considered as savage and un-civilised, it turns out, were troubled by the white man's propensity for head-hunting. During the Zulu War 1879–80, in particular, skulls were being collected on a large scale and when the first batches were received at the Royal College of Surgeons it was even reported in the press:

> 'The skulls possess all the characteristics which are typical of the negro races. It is to be hoped that additions will be made to those Zulu skulls now received, and that also some of the officials connected with the British army in Afghanistan will follow the good example, and send home some skulls and skeletons of the inhabitants of that country.'[48]

The Zulu War and the Second Afghan War were taking place at the same time, and the intimate relationship between military campaigns and the scientific collection of body parts within the Empire was accordingly quite explicit.

Apart from ending up in various collections, Zulu skulls were furthermore also being sold quite openly in the imperial metropole during the immediate aftermath of the war. These commercial skulls, however, were sold, not as scientific specimens, but as household objects intended for the gentlemen's smoking room.[49] Never known for its squeamishness, the satirical *Punch* magazine took issue with the crass commodification of human remains in a piece entitled 'Skulls for Cigar-Holders':

> 'There have lately been displayed in Piccadilly, in the shop-window of Mr. Ward, the famous Taxidermist and Naturalist, numerous specimens of human skulls, neatly mounted and fitted up as cigar-cases and tobacco-holders. In the former character, the *cranium* is pierced with holes, through which the cigars stand out, "like quills upon the fretful porcupine." We know nothing of the locus a quo of these ghastly relics of mortality. Probably they may be Zulu crania—war-trophies brought back by some of our young bloods, fresh from South-African warfare, and with some taint of its practices. We know that savage warriors—Maori, Dyak, and Fan—are found of turning the heads of their slaughtered enemies to account as ornaments and symbols of prowess, if not as cigar-boxes. But this appropriation of foemen's skulls to purposes at once of use and ornament among ourselves, marks a distinct move in civilisation, and establishes another tie of fellow-feeling and common usage between us and our savage dependencies.'[50]

Undermining the distinction between civilised and un-civilised, which after all was the foundation of imperialism, Ward had simply gone too far. A later newspaper report described Ward's shop, with its room full of Zulu skulls, as 'a perfect Golgotha', referring to the site where Jesus was crucified, the name of which meant 'place of the skull'.[51] Golgotha, however, was also the epithet used for the execution grounds and sacrificial groves of the West-African kingdoms, against which the British waged several major campaigns. In 1874, Stanley accompanied the British force that invaded Ashanti, and he provided an evocative description of the scene they encountered as they entered the capital of Kumasi:

'We came to a grove, whence the terrible effluvia issued which caused all men in Coomassie to describe the place as a vast charnel-house. The grove, which was but a continuation of the tall forest we had travelled through, penetrated as far as the great market-place. A narrow footpath led into this grove, and now the foul smells became so suffocating that we were glad to produce our handkerchiefs to prevent the intolerable and almost palpable odour from mounting into the brain and overpowering us. After some thirty paces we arrived before the dreadful scene, but it was almost impossible to stop longer than to take a general view of the great Golgotha. We saw some thirty or forty decapitated bodies in the last stages of corruption, and countless skulls which lay piled in heaps and scattered over a wide extent. The stoutest heart and the most stoical mind might have been appalled.'[52]

Where Richard Burton had found a Temple Bar in Africa, people were now finding a Golgotha in Ward's shop in the heart of London, and they were duly appalled. Attitudes were gradually changing, and heads and skulls could no longer be acquired and treated with quite the same ease and lack of circumspection that had characterised the endeavours of a Spry or a Knox, in India or in Africa, decades before. Not without provoking a public outcry, at least.

During the 1890's, several cases involving the acquisition of skulls under dubious circumstances, reached the headlines and sparked public debate in the imperial metropole and beyond. In 1890, disturbing rumours emerged that the Scottish naturalist, James S. Jameson, who was with the rear column of Stanley's Emin Pasha Relief Expedition to what is today Uganda, had paid local cannibals to kill and eat a young girl in order to satisfy his curiosity concerning this 'barbarous' practice. The story caused a sensation and while Jameson himself died of fever while still in Africa, Stanley and several other members publicly denounced this horrible act, which brought the entire expedition into disrepute. It furthermore turned out that before he died, Jameson had sent the head of an African man home to his wife. William Bonny, who had been a member of the expedition, later confirmed the story in an interview with *The Times*:

'It is perfectly true that Mr. Jameson did procure the head and neck of a native, which he sent to England to be embalmed. I have myself seen this head in a glass case at the house of Mrs Jameson in London. It is not a mere skull, but a preserved head, with the skin and hair upon it.[53] The facts in connexion with this incident are these: A native with whom we were all well acquainted was shot and killed by an Arab. Mr. Jameson sent some soldiers to get the body and bring it into camp. This was done, and Mr. Jameson then had the head cut off, packed in salt, boxed, and shipped to London. When it arrived here it was handed over to Messrs. Rowland Ward and Co., of Piccadilly, who dressed the head for Mr. Jameson's representatives. While at the house of Mrs. Jameson upon one occasion she showed me the curiosity, asking me as she did so "Do you know this gentleman?" I replied "Yes, I know him well. I have shaken hands with him many times." [...] It will thus be seen that Mr. Jameson was inclined to carry his scientific researches to an unusual point, and this fact will to a great extent explain the cannibal incident.'[54]

Considering how common the collecting of heads from Africa was, it is evident that it was the 'cannibal incident' that sowed doubts about the unhealthy and obsessive nature of Jameson's so-called 'scientific researches'. The involvement of Ward's taxidermist business is also noteworthy and may very well have served to further undermine any pretence that Jameson had been acting under a genuine impulse of rational inquiry. Jameson's fully-preserved head was not, however, as unusual as might be assumed and similar specimens were until recently held in both Dutch and Portuguese collections. The skeleton and body cast of Sarah Baartman, the so-called 'Hottentot Venus', who was exhibited both before and after her death as a sort of ethnographic freak show, was also on display in a museum in France right up the 1970s. It is not known what eventually happened with the head Jameson sent his wife, but given that she complained about its smell it is quite possible she did not keep it for long.

A few years after the Jameson scandal, a somewhat similar case occurred in South Africa, following the suppression of the Bechuana

War of 1897. Luka Jantje, a Tswana chief and one of the leaders of the rebellion, was killed and when his body was later disinterred so that his wives could identify him, a British officer present supposedly said 'I'd like that fellow's skull', and offered a private soldier money to retrieve it.[55] Soon after local newspapers reported on the story:

> 'Early next morning some Volunteers were out for a stroll, when they discovered that the grave had been opened afresh, and a private in one of the Cape town corps was engaged in severing Luka's head from the trunk. He had no proper scientific appliance, and the reader may be spared the details of how he devoted himself to the task. Suffice it to say that the Volunteers saw him dislocate the head and carry it away. They expressed to him their disgust, and he replied that he was acting "under orders," and would receive £5 from an officer for the trophy.'[56]

With its unwholesome element of grave-robbing, in addition to trophy-taking, the incident caused a scandal in Cape Town where 'people remembered the shudder with which the white people of South Africa heard of the mutilation of bodies of men, women and children by the Mashones and Matabele.'[57] Rather than the act itself, it was accordingly the way that a white man's actions reminded people of atrocities ascribed to the enemy in the recently-concluded rebellion that gave cause for concern. An official inquiry, however, failed to identify the officer responsible for the theft of the head and the case was eventually dropped. The commentary in the newspapers of the time is nevertheless noteworthy, as it gives some indication of a more qualified acceptance of the collecting of body parts within the Empire:

> 'The only gleam of satisfaction to be derived from this unhappy business is that there has been very little disposition in any quarter to treat it lightly. A few years ago it might have been different. During the first Matabele war the jawbone of a native chief who was shot while attempting to escape from custody was exhibited at a large drapery establishment here without exciting the slightest protest. I fancy the public failed to realise what this gruesome relic really implied, and certainly the idea that it could only have been obtained by the mutilation of the dead did not readily suggest itself to them, or more might have been heard of it. The practice of collecting heads for scientific purposes has, of course, been very common in Africa. Stanley relates that Schweinfurth boiled the heads of the slain at Mombuttu to prepare skulls for the British Museum. Emin Pasha proposed once to do the same on the coastward march with Stanley, and when the latter pro-

tested, he smilingly retorted, "All for science." In the case of Luka Jantje's head no such excuse can be pleaded; and the effect of this incident is from every point of view to be deplored.'[58]

Without the justification of scientific inquiry, however perfunctory, the furtive theft of a head was clearly beyond the pale, especially in a settler colony where such acts would recoil on the European population. The officer who took the head was never formally identified, but rumours had it that when he was later recommended for a Victoria Cross, following his service in the South African War, the story of the head came back to haunt him, and the medal was never conferred. Years later, when the officer had been forced to find work as a shift boss in a mine, the skull of Luka Jantje was allegedly still adorning the wall of his room.[59]

In 1898, the Sudan Campaign reached its bloody climax with Lord Kitchener's crushing victory over the Dervishes at the Battle of Omdurman. Afterwards, the tomb of the Mahdi was deliberately destroyed and the body of the Muslim religious leader thrown into the Nile. In 1885, the Mahdi had killed and beheaded Charles Gordon, the Victorian imperial hero *par excellence*, and Kitchener's victory was thus regarded as a righteous act of retribution. The campaign had been covered extensively by embedded journalists, including a young Winston Churchill, and for the first time since Russell's reportage from the 'Mutiny', the conduct of the British military came under close and critical scrutiny. In one particularly devastating article, the journalist Ernest N. Bennett claimed that the wounded Dervishes on the battlefield of Omdurman had either been killed or left to die, while civilians in the vicinity had been indiscriminately fired on by artillery. The most striking accusation, however, was Bennett's description of Kitchener's destruction of the Mahdi's tomb:

'Yet at the close of the nineteenth century a British commander, not content with desecrating a tomb, actually orders a dead man's body to be torn out of its grave! The embalmed body of the Mahdi was dug up, the head wrenched off, and the trunk cast into the Nile. It is almost incredible that the disinterment and mutilation of a dead body which had lain in the grave for more than ten years should have been possible under a General whom "Christian" England is now delighting to honour! The act is nothing more or less than a return to the barbarism of the Middle Ages.'[60]

There had earlier been rumours that the skull of the Mahdi was on its way to the Royal College of Surgeons, and George Bernard Shaw had even decried this as an example of 'Tartar-like savagery'.[61] The skull, however, never materialised and the British press was occupied by celebrating Kitchener's victory and commenting on the inter-imperial rivalry that manifested itself in the Fashoda Incident soon thereafter in 1898. Bennett's claims nevertheless re-ignited public interest in the actions of Kitchener and the accusations caused a sensation in Britain in early 1899. For months discussions of Kitchener's conduct permeated both the press and the Government. The liberal politician John Morley made the memorable comment: 'You send your soldiers to civilise savages. Take care the savages do not barbarise your soldiers.'[62] *The Manchester Guardian* newspaper made a very similar point:

> 'It is, we believe, quite "exceptional" for a British general to insult a dead body. These things are done by savages, but they hardly form a suitable beginning for the lessons in civilisation which we are to teach the Soudanese. Indeed it may be doubted whether, after all that has been said about our civilising mission, public opinion in this country has yet been educated up to calm acquiescence in such a measure.'[63]

Kitchener eventually ended up having to explain himself personally to Queen Victoria in a highly contrite letter in March 1899. 'When I returned to Fashoda', he claimed, 'the Mahdi's skull, in a box, was brought to me, and I did not know what to do with it. I had thought of sending it to the College of Surgeons where, I believe, such things are kept. It has now been buried in a Moslem cemetery.'[64] The Queen accepted Kitchener's profuse apologies and even concurred with the decision to destroy the Mahdi's tomb, lest it should become a pilgrimage site and inspire another outburst of 'fanaticism'. As for the treatment of his body, however, it 'savours in the Queen's opinion, too much of the Middle Ages.'[65]

For all intents and purposes, the Queen's reply should have signalled the end of the matter. Some two decades later, however, the British poet and writer, Wilfrid Scawen Blunt, published his diaries in which a very different version of events emerged. Blunt noted in his diary entry for April 1899 that he had met an officer, referred to only as D——, who provided the details:

'The mutilation of the body seems all to have come of a mere bit of rowdy nonsense on the part of certain young English officers. [D——] says it has long been a custom with the members of White's Club who are in the army to bring back trophies from any wars they may be engaged in and present them to the club. He, D——, had jokingly proposed to E——W——to bring back the Mahdi's toenails from the coming campaign. Kitchener, on this hint, seems to have fancied having the Mahdi's head for himself to make an inkstand of, and gave Gordon the order to dig the body up and keep the head for him. This accordingly was done, and at the same time fingernails were taken by some of the young officers, but they got to talking about it at Cairo and hence the trouble.'[66]

This was, in Blunt's opinion, 'revolting—a piece of military revenge for the death of Gordon,' and the poet even questioned whether the skull had in fact been buried at Wadi Halfa, as Kitchener claimed. A newspaper report from February 1899 actually asserted that the Mahdi's skull had been exhibited at a gathering in London of the conservative Primrose League, 'amid the frantic applause of the knights and dames of the Tory organisation.'[67] Considering this, it is quite difficult to say with any certitude where the Mahdi's skull actually ended up.

For all the controversy and royal involvement, Kitchener's purloining of the Mahdi's skull would not have become an issue purely on its own merits. It came, however, right on the tail of extensive accusations of various atrocities, including the killing of wounded enemies and civilians, in addition to the destruction of the Mahdi's tomb, all of which Kitchener's numerous political enemies were only too happy to exploit. In the debacle concerning the Mahdi's skull, the intimate relationship between the racialised logic of colonial warfare and the treatment of the enemy's body nevertheless became particularly explicit. At a time when the rules of war were being codified for conflict between 'civilised' nations, 'uncivilised' people were explicitly excluded from the protection provided by law. As a wartime correspondent, Winston Churchill participated in the Battle of Omdurman, and he later confirmed the reports that British soldiers had indeed killed many of the enemy wounded afterwards. Churchill was neither sentimental nor particularly critical of the Empire, and his explanation for the atrocities is noteworthy—namely the way British troops perceived their enemies:

'The unmeasured terms in which the Dervishes had been described in the newspapers, and the idea which had been laborious circulated, of "avenging Gordon," had inflamed their passions, and had led them to believe that it was quite correct to regard their enemy as vermin—unfit to live. The result was that there were many wounded Dervishes killed.'[68]

The matter of the Mahdi's skull was raised again following the final battle of the 1906 uprising in South Africa, when it was rumoured that not only had wounded Zulus been killed, but the body of their leader, Bambhata, had also been decapitated by colonial forces. Much as had been the case at Omdurman, any atrocities were blamed on local auxiliaries rather than regular British soldiers. The military authorities, however, did confirm that the head of Bambhata had indeed been cut off:

> 'It was intimated to the officer commanding the troops that the dead body of Bambaata was lying at the bottom of a gorge about 2000 feet below the camp, and as it was most essential that it should be ascertained definitely whether Bambaata was really killed or not, Major Platt, Native Medical Corps, with a number of natives, was sent down to bring up the body for the purpose of identification. On reaching the spot where the body lay it was found to be in an advanced stage of decomposition., and as the natives refused to carry it to camp decapitation was absolutely necessary to ensure definite identification by responsible persons acquainted with Bambaata. The head was not exhibited, but was kept covered and in privacy under an armed guard, and was only shown to persons who stated that they knew Bambaata intimately and would be able to recognise him.'[69]

When the report was read out in the House of Commons, the Irish MP William Redmond posed the obvious question: namely whether it was 'conceivable for a single moment that if it had been a white foe his body would have been so treated?' Churchill, who had since become a politician after his days as a wartime correspondent, caused a slight shock with his pugnacious contribution to the debate: 'Mr. Churchill said he was afraid that the British Government were not in the best position with regard to the decapitation. Hon. members would remember that under the late Administration after the battle of Omdurman the body of the Mahdi was treated most shamefully.'[70] The political agenda behind Churchill's intervention was an obvious jab at his political opponents, and the affair of the Mahdi's skull had evidently not been forgotten and could still be used to great effect in debates in Parliament. Churchill's final salvo was received with cheers: 'I do not consider the steps taken by the officer in Natal were half so discreditable to civilisation as the steps taken in regard to the Mahdi.'[71] The political debates nevertheless obscured the fact that there was little real concern about the fate of Bambatha's head. Later photographic evidence suggests that the head was, in fact, kept as a trophy, and there are also indications that British officers had also taken cuttings of the chief's hair as souvenirs.[72]

* * *

Almost a century after Europeans first began hunting for skulls in South Africa, little had changed within the British Empire. Duane Spencer Hatch, who later became secretary of the YMCA, described his experience during the Waziristan Campaign on the Northwest Frontier in 1917, with his friend Sherman:

> 'We passed the remains of the twenty-seven stalwart Mahsuds who had been killed by the Londoners in the first skirmish. We camped about eight miles beyond there that night. Sherman was all excited. Besides being a clergyman, he had one year of medical school and it was his desire to go back to college and finish his medical course. Every doctor, he told me, always wanted to have a mounted skull in his office. Now these giant Mahsuds had the finest heads anyone had ever seen in all the world. He wanted one of those skulls, as I suppose every medical officer who passes them did. But not one of the others would entertain the indiscretion of touching one.'[73]

Sherman asked for permission from his superiors and when this was denied, he secretly left the camp on a bicycle early next morning, as Hatch recounted it:

> 'About ten o'clock he returned sweating like a horse, a sizable gunnysack bundle tied on the handle bars. He went straight to his bed-roll and wrapped the bundle in it. He could hardly wait to tell me, "I had great luck; but I'm going to be a bit selfish with you as one of the two heads has the skull cracked in a bit, but you're not a medic and won't mind. I cut off some other rare bones, too, very important for medical demonstration."'[74]

The racialisation of non-white people was accordingly not invariably negative and the warlike tribesmen of India's frontier regions, for instance, were positively constructed as 'martial races' and considered well-suited for military service, much as high-caste Brahmins had been prior to 1857. The valorisation of some indigenous people, however, did not prevent their bodies from being mutilated in the name of 'science' or simply as souvenirs. As long as those who resisted imperialism were not white, and were not recognised as 'civilised', their bodies were not protected by the conventional observances regarding the respect and treatment of enemy dead.

During the numerous military campaigns within the British Empire that lasted well into the 1960s, the mutilation of the bodies of the enemy also continued unabated. During the 1931 Saya San Rebellion in Burma, the heads of rebels were cut off so that they could be identified—much as had been the case with Bambhata in 1906.[75] This procedure, either improvised or formalised, was repeated during the bloody conflicts of decolonisation, including the Malaya Emergency 1948–60 and the suppression of the Mau Mau in Kenya 1952–60.[76] Such practices were by no means limited to British colonial forces: Soldiers from the Spanish Foreign Legion, for instance, collected both heads and ears as trophies during the Rif War in Morocco in the early 1920s, and as late as the 1970s, the Portuguese routinely decapitated the bodies of insurgents.[77] During the war in the Pacific War, American soldiers collected skulls and other trophies from Japanese bodies on an unprecedented scale, and skulls taken during that conflict, as well as the Korean War and the Vietnam War, are to this day kept in private homes and various institutions in the US.[78] As events in places like Iraq and Afghanistan within recent decades have shown, the humiliation and desecration of the body of the enemy, whether dead or alive, is hardly a thing of the past—even though trophies today are more likely to be taken in the form of digital photos or video footage rather than physical souvenirs.[79] In the twenty-first century, we would nevertheless do well to question self-righteous assertions of cultural superiority when the savagery we ascribe to others so often serves simply as a pretext for a savagery of our own.

* * *

By the time Joseph Conrad wrote *Heart of Darkness* in 1899, the skulls of slain enemies, stuck on poles outside Mr Kurtz' compound, had become morbid markers, not of African savagery, but of the violence and moral decrepitude of Western imperialism. Yet little more than a decade before, the famous artist, designer and, less famously, socialist, William Morris, had invoked an equally poignant inversion of the symbolism of the skull. In a withering piece of political satire, Morris skewered the self-congratulatory sentimentality of late-Victorian imperialism by listing some of the items that he felt had been left out of the 1886 Indian and Colonial Exhibition in London:

'Examples of the last remains of the art of India which our commercialism has destroyed have been made to do duty as a kind of gilding for the sordidness of the rest of the show, and are a sorry sight indeed to one who knows anything of what the art of the East has been. But let that pass. There are perhaps, certain exhibits of examples of the glory of the Empire which have been, I think, forgotten. We might begin at the entrance with two pyramids, *à la Timour*, of the skulls of Zulus, Arabs, Burmese, New Zealanders, etc., etc., slain in wicked resistance to the benevolence of British commerce. A specimen of the wire whips used for softening the minds of rebellious Jamaica negroes under the paternal sway of Governor Eyre might be shown, together with a selection of other such historical mementoes, from the blankets infected with small-pox sent to unfriendly tribes of Red-Skins in the latter eighteenth century down to the rope with which Louis Riel was hanged last year, for resisting a particularly gross form of land-stealing. The daily rations of an Indigo ryot and of his master under one glass case, with a certificate of the amount of nourishment in each, furnished by Professor Huxley. The glory of the British arms gained in various successful battles against barbarians and savages, the same enclosed in the right eye of a louse. The mercy of Colonists towards native populations; a strong magnifying-glass to see the same by. An allegorical picture of the emigrant's hope (*a*) on leaving England; (*b*), after six months in the Colonies. A pair of crimson plush breeches with my Lord Tennyson's "Ode" on the opening of the Exhibition, embroidered in gold, on the seat thereof. A great many other exhibits of a similar nature could be found suitable to the exposition of the Honour, Glory, and Usefulness of the British Empire.'[80]

At first glance, the story of Alum Bheg's skull may seem like little more than a curious anecdote with little bearing on the broader history of either the Indian Uprising, or of the British Empire and its legacies more generally. Yet the violence that produced Alum Bheg's skull, and which was made explicit in the accompanying note, serves as a poignant reminder of the otherwise hidden violence implicit to the collecting, and exhibiting, of the human remains of indigenous people since the nineteenth century. There was nothing intrinsically interesting about Alum Bheg's skull, and without the cursory trial and subsequent execution, the skull would not have been that of a rebel and a murderer and would have been of no appeal to Costello. Without the execution, it would moreover not have been possible for Costello to collect in the first place. It was accordingly the very process by which a skull had become 'available' for collecting that made it worthwhile as a collectable object—the basic fact that a skull could be collected is also the reason why it was collected. The story of the provenance, or microbiography, of a skull thus served a crucially constitutive role in turning it into an object of significance and in this respect, there was much less difference between practices of so-called scientific collecting and the taking of war-trophies than is usually assumed. This raises a further question regarding the commonly perceived dichotomy between scientific collection and the taking of war-trophies as 'rational' and 'irrational' practices respectively.

In the case of Alum Bheg, the taking of his head cannot be regarded as an isolated act pertaining only to the corpse of an executed enemy. If the execution by cannon was a culturally specific measure, the act of turning Alum Bheg's skull into a trophy was merely a slight improvisation, and logical extension, of the formally authorised mutilation of his body. Deeply entangled with the forms and functions of colonial violence, Costello's treatment of Alum Bheg was thus informed by the racialised logic that underpinned the imperial project. The fate that befell Alum Bheg was shared by thousands of indigenous people in Asia, Africa, Australia and the Americas. And that story is not inconsequential to our understanding of the encounter between the West and the non-Western world in a more general sense.

EPILOGUE

THE DEAD BODIES OF THY SERVANTS

The outbreak at Sialkot cast long shadows and had an indelible impact on the lives of survivors and relatives alike. Sarah Graham quickly left India, never to return. She was reported to have been so grief-stricken that she remained in her cabin throughout the voyage home, and she was dressed in mourning when she arrived at Southampton along with many other 'refugees' from the Uprising.[1] Robert Hunter, the brother of Thomas, was also a missionary in India, and it was he who had originally encouraged Thomas to take up a career as a missionary. The death of his brother, however, deeply troubled Robert, and shortly afterwards he abandoned his divine calling. He had not given up the commitment to proselytising in India, he explained:

'But I felt that, with my peculiarities of mental constitution, I could not hope again to be an effective labourer in the East. Nearly every object I beheld would call up the scene of the murders, and it would be in the last degree harrowing to my feelings to listen to panegyrics on the rebel party, by whom so many of those dearest to me had been barbarously murdered. If exposed to these influences there was imminent risk, either that I should be driven to an abatement of that strong love for the heathen, without which a missionary is useless, or that in the effort to resist this temptation, my mind would sink into a hopelessly morbid state. Could it have been assumed that the call of duty still summoned me to the East, it would have been a distrust of Divine grace to suppose that strength would not be afforded; but, believing the effects produced on my mind, by the terrible bereavement, to be such as wholly to disqualify me for labouring effectively in India, I viewed this as a providential intimation that my work there was over, and should have regarded it as presumption and not faith to go forward. There was thus no course open to me but the very painful one of resigning my office as a missionary.'[2]

The traumatic experience of losing his brother at the hands of the 'rebel party' had evidently not given Robert Hunter much cause for reflection as to exactly why a rebellion had taken place—nor what role missionaries may have played in fomenting such animosity. Andrew Gordon, too, felt vindicated rather than responsible following the outbreak at Sialkot:

'We have no idea that England will give up India as long as she has any soldiers to send here, and we do not think she should, for the people are not prepared to govern themselves as they were in America. The petty kings here would only try to kill one another. Yet God has sent, for some reason, a terrible judgement on the ruling as well as the rebellious power. One thing is certain: they cannot blame it on missionaries. I hope they will attribute it to their indifference to Christianity and favour towards idolatry.'[3]

Dr Graham's nephew, James, however, harboured an intense dislike of the missionaries and did indeed blame them for much of what had taken place. Shortly after he was informed of his uncle's death, James wrote from India to his sister back in Ireland, describing what he perceived to be the main causes for the uprising:

'It is also owing greatly to missionaries: poor illiterate country parsons who have never travelled twenty miles in their lifetimes, and whose minds are as narrow as their travels, come out here, and without the slightest respect for the religion of people who in their own words and deeds are infinitely their superiors, commencing preaching Christianity, not by showing in their acts, not displaying that charity to others which is its vital principle, but with the wildest abuse of all other sects and denominations. They inflame the minds of the people against us. These narrow minded padres never think that they are inciting the minds of 150 millions of people. They think only of their own pockets, and of how they will be able to cook up their next home report, which is a mass of fiction. Yes, my dear Sarah, know yourself and let all your friends know that by your subscriptions to missionaries you are purchasing the murders of your friends and relations...'[4]

James was not alone in this assessment. In the aftermath of the Uprising, the British were forced to acknowledge that the 'Mutiny' had been, in part at least, provoked by their own interference in local religious beliefs and practices. In 1858, control of India was transferred from the East India Company to the British Crown, and a policy of strict non-interference was maintained (in principle if not always in practice). One of the guiding principles of British rule in India was accordingly that the Government could never again be seen to interfere in religious matters, lest they alienate the local population. When Gordon and the American missionaries in 1858 sought to secure permission to build a church near the city in Sialkot, they ran afoul of this new policy. Their church was to be built on land next to the spot where a *tahsil*, or official revenue office was being constructed, and the fear was that, as Gordon put it, 'the natives would be liable to suspect that the government was itself erecting a mission church, contrary to the recently-announced government policy of neutrality in religious matters.'[5] After much bureaucratic wrangling, the Americans eventually got their permission, yet it was clear that the days when the interests of state and church might converge were well and truly over.

While Dr Graham's nephew was largely despondent, claiming that 'India will never be the same to me again,' Dr Graham's son, William, was seething with hate. 'I can never have revenge sufficient to satiate my thirst,' he wrote, 'and it's a thing I can't and won't do again, command black men of any sort.'[6] As a captain in the cavalry, he was present at the taking of Delhi in September 1857, and shortly afterwards visited the imprisoned Mughal emperor, Bahadur Shah. He described the meeting in a letter to a relative:

> 'I saw the King of Delhi, and abused him like a pick-pocket, and treated him anything but as the Great Mogul. I saw his three sons also after they were killed, lying at the Kotwali, where the Europeans were treating their remains with every indignity.'[7]

Although Bahadur Shah had nothing to do with events in Sialkot, and had been no more than a figurehead at Delhi, he was considered the principal leader of the Uprising and thus became the target for much abuse.[8] Brigadier Brind's brother, Major James Brind, was also present at the taking of Delhi and he took a far bloodier revenge in the neighbourhood known as Kucha Chelan, where he personally oversaw the killing of as many as 200 locals who had been 'identified' as rebels. Those who were not bayoneted on the spot, were forced to clean the latrines in the British camp before they too were executed. The Indian poet Zahir Dehlavi described the slaughter, which included many Delhi luminaries:

> 'Some were arrested and taken through the Rajghat gate to the river side and there were shot. The bodies were all thrown into the river. Meanwhile many of their women were so disturbed by what they saw that they left their homes with their children and jumped into the wells of Kucha Chelan were stacked with dead bodies. My pen refuses to describe this further.'[9]

Even from the distance of several years, the official historian of the 'Mutiny', John W. Kaye, nevertheless still found it possible to defend Brind's actions:

> 'There was not a kinder-hearted, as there was not a braver man in the Delhi army than James Brind; but he was a man of an excitable temperament, and he had been working day and night in the batteries, under a fierce sun, seldom or never sleeping all the time. And he had ever before him the memory of the fact that his brother had been killed at Sealkote by the treacherous connivance of his own servants.'[10]

While the violence of Indians was perceived as innate and treacherous, British brutality could be explained and even justified with reference to the climate, physical exhaustion and, ultimately, the savagery ascribed to their Indian victims. A few days before, John Nicholson, the scourge of the Sialkot rebels, personally led one of the columns during the final assault on Delhi. During the intense street-fighting that followed, he was shot in the chest and fatally wounded. Initially abandoned by the coolies who were supposed to take him to the hospital, Nicholson was eventually taken back to the British camp where he died in agony nine days later.[11] His death came as a hard blow to the British, 'in the hour of victory' at Delhi. Herbert Edwardes telegraphed the news to Nicholson's former colleagues in Punjab, gushing about the man's greatness:

> 'How grand, how glorious a piece of handiwork he was! It was a pleasure even to behold him. And then his nature was so equal to his frame! So undaunted, so noble, so tender, so good, so stern to evil, so single-minded, so generous, so heroic, yet so modest. I never saw another like him, and never expect to do so. And to have had him for a brother, and now to lose him in the prime of life. It is an inexpressible and irreparably grief. Nicholson was the soul of truth.'[12]

One can only guess, but it seems unlikely that those Indians at the receiving end of Nicholson's so-called 'tenderness' would be able to recognise him in this eulogy. His death on the battlefield, and subsequent beatification, however, allowed Nicholson's callous brutality to be conveniently glossed over and he became an instant Victorian hero, glorified in children's books and commemorated in statues.

At Sialkot, the death of Thomas and Jane Hunter was commemorated with the Hunter Memorial Church, which was completed in 1865. Today, Sialkot today has a sizable local Christian community, and it is only because of the Scottish missionaries that the events of 1857 are at all remembered. Locals will point to the bridge crossing the Nullah where Thomas and Jane were killed, right next to the jail and court-house which are still located where they were during the Uprising. In general, however, there are few traces of the outbreak, and only a single bastion of the old fort still stands, crumbing and overgrown by vines. The ruins of Monckton's grand house west of the cantonments are barely discernible amidst shrubs and bushes and will have disappeared in a few years.

Dr Graham's nephew had originally wanted to move his uncle's body to the cemetery in the cantonment and rebury him in a proper casket. He was nevertheless advised against this as Dr Graham's body had apparently been highly decomposed at the time of its burial and none of the other bodies were moved either. The temporary burial site of Dr Graham, Thomas Hunter, Jane Hunter and the baby, in the small enclosure next to the fort, became their permanent resting place. The inscriptions on the graves read:

'To the memory of James Graham Esquire, M.D., Superintending Surgeon One of the victims who fell by the hands of the native soldiery on the 9th July 1857, when they broke out into Mutiny and rebelled at this station

In memory of Revd. Thomas Hunter, M.A., Missionary of the Church of Scotland 9th July 1857
"Faithful unto Death"

In memory of Jane Scott and Thomas, wife and son of Revd. Thomas Hunter 9th July 1857
"In their death—not divided"'[13]

The graves were still intact by 1983, when some of the Christian community in Sialkot took photographs of the small enclosure.[14] Since then, however, the surrounding buildings have been expanded onto the small plot of the cemetery, and the gravestones themselves destroyed. While I was able to locate the site of the graves in 2017, I was not allowed to inspect them any further, as the local residents worried that the Christian community might reclaim the land that has been illegally encroached upon. Whatever remains of the graves of Dr Graham and the Hunters is today buried under trash in someone's backyard.

When I visited the Hunter Memorial church in 2017, the old care-taker, who had been working there for almost 60 years, told me that he had heard stories about the man who killed the Hunters when he was a child: how the murderer had fled to Jammu, and how, when he was caught, his arms and legs were cut off. This was, as I found out, actually the true story of what ultimately happened to Hurmat Khan.[15] The man who was responsible for the murders for which Alum Bheg was exe-cuted, had fled from Sialkot on 9 July 1857, and despite the Rs 1,000 reward offered for his capture, went into hiding just across the border in Kashmir. In 1862, a stranger was spotted in a small village on the British side of the border; he claimed to have been sent by one 'Hurmat Shah' to fetch the wife of a man named Fazla. Local officials had long been on the lookout for Hurmat Khan and knew that the wife of Fazla was the very woman with whom Hurmat Khan had quarrelled over with a court clerk, which had led to Hurmat Khan's subsequent dis-missal. The British at Sialkot were accordingly informed and with the assistance of the local authorities of Jammu, it was ascertained that this 'Hurmat Shah' lived in a hut near the city gate of the Jammu fort. A spy even managed to enter the hut, and when it was reported that 'Hurmat Shah' had a sword hanging on the wall, it was seen to prove that he was indeed the fugitive, Hurmat Khan.

Due to the reward, Hurmat Khan was nevertheless known to be extremely cautious and he had on previous occasions taken to the hills at the slightest alarm. According to Gordon, a scheme worthy of Kipling was devised to capture the fugitive murderer:

'An English gentleman at Sialkot organised a sham marriage procession. Armed men were dressed as peasants would dress for a wedding, and were packed in *yakkas* (one-horse vehicles) in genuine marriage procession style. The Englishman played the part of the dainty bride, secluded from vulgar gaze in a covered and closely curtained ox-cart, as a native bride ought to be. The bells jingled merrily; the bridal party wended their way along the road leading to the murderer's hut, amid noisy talking and laughter, without exciting any suspicion. Suddenly the wedding guests were transformed into a [164] body of armed men, who, headed by the bearded bride, surrounded the hut. Hurmat Khan, drawing his sword, stood at his doorway. Knowing his fate if captured, he made a desperate defence, holding forty men at bay for three hours, which was doubtless owing to the desire of his assailants to capture him alive if possible; but all their efforts to accomplish this failed. Finally, they all closed in upon him in a body, and he received a sword-cut in the loins which put an end to his life. His body was sent to Sialkot and identified on oath—in fact the whole city recognised it.'[16]

And so it turned out that the murder of Thomas and Jane Hunter and their baby was avenged after all. By that time, however, Alum Bheg was long dead and his skull somewhere in Britain. Between the time that Costello picked up the still-bleeding head on 10 June 1858, and its discovery as an old skull in a pub in 1963, we know nothing of the whereabouts of Alum Bheg. The pub, which opened in the early 1860s, was named The Lord Clyde after Sir Colin Campbell and his association with the Indian Uprising might explain why the skull ended up there in the first place. In the early twentieth century one of the proprietors of the pub was furthermore named Monckton and he may have been related to Henry Monckton, the Deputy Commissioner of Sialkot in 1858.[17]

After all these years, however, it is high time for Alum Bheg to return home. What he knew as home, of course, no longer exists, and while he was probably born in what is today India, he was executed in what is now Pakistan. The Uprising of 1857 also does not hold the same significance in Pakistan, as it does in India, where the commemoration of so-called 'freedom-fighters' is a fraught issue and thoroughly politicised. When the bodies of the 282 *sepoys* massacred by Cooper at Ajnala were discovered in 2014, the Indian Government showed no interest whatsoever, and it was locals who eventually excavated the bodies and cremated them.[18] A Sikh shrine has since been built at the site next to the well, known as Kallianwala Ku or 'black man's well', and it is still possible to see human bones, including pieces of skull with bullet-holes. Neither a murderer, nor a martyr, Alum Bheg nevertheless deserves better than to end up in a display case, or to be pressed into the service of some political agenda that he himself would not have recognised.

Repatriation is, however, a complex and bureaucratic process and can only take place between institutions, which means that I cannot legally return the skull as a private individual. Unlike repatriation to indigenous communities in South Africa, New Zealand or Australia, there are no South Asian activists calling for the return of human remains from Western museums and collections. I hope with this book to have at least made people aware of the existence of these issues.

It is worth bearing in mind that the manner of Alum Bheg's execution was deliberately intended to deny him his funeral rites and, for what it is worth, I think the peaceful site of the Battle of Trimmu Ghat, on the island in the Ravi River, which today marks the border between India and Pakistan, would be a fitting place to bury him. Ultimately, that is not for me to decide, but whatever happens the final chapter of Alum Bheg's story has yet to be written.

> 'That skull had a tongue in it, and could sing once:
> how the knave jowls it to the ground, as if it were
> Cain's jaw-bone, that did the first murder!'
> Shakespeare, *Hamlet*, Act 5, Scene 1.

NOTES

INTRODUCTION

1. Joseph Conrad, *Heart of Darkness*, orig. 1899, Norton Critical Edition, 3rd edition; New York: Norton, 1988, pp. 57–8.
2. See Frances Larson, *Severed: A History of Heads Lost and Found*, London: Granta, 2015.
3. Ricardo Roque, 'Stories, Skulls, and Colonial Collections, *Configurations*, 19, 1 (Winter 2011), pp. 1–23, 18.
4. I am much indebted to Dr Heather Bonney for being so generous with her time and expertise.
5. Costly DNA tests would not have been helpful without a sample to match with the results.
6. See for instance Saul David, *The Indian Mutiny*, London: Viking, 2002, pp. 277–8.
7. The encyclopaedic work of Kaye and Malleson provides a more detailed account, see John Kaye and GB. Malleson (ed.), *Kaye's and Malleson's History of the Indian Mutiny, I-VI*, London: Allen, 1888–9, II, pp. 471–5. For more recent references to the outbreak at Sialkot, see Frances Robinson, *Angels of Albion: Women of the Indian Mutiny*, London: Viking, 1996, pp. 179–83; and Nile Green, *Islam and the Army in Colonial India: Sepoy Religion in the Service of Empire*, Cambridge: Cambridge University Press, 2009, pp. 40 & 84–5.
8. Report by Brevet Colonel G. Farquharson, 11 July 1857, in 'Report regarding the mutinees of the 14th and 46th Regiment Native Infantry at Jhelum and Sealkote', National Archives of India (NAI), Military Department, 15 July 1857, 83 A.
9. F. G. Cardew, *A Sketch of the Services of the Bengal Army*, Calcutta: Office of the Superintendent of Government Printing, 1909, p. 444. See also G.H.D. Gimlette, *A Postscript to the Records of the Indian Mutiny*, London: H.F. & G. Witherby, 1927, pp. 157–9.

10. See for instance 'Chancery', *Dublin Evening Post*, 14 Sept. 1833; and Information provided by the Royal Dragoon Guards Museum, with thanks to Daniel Greenhough.

11. See 'Diary of William B. Armstrong 4th Dragoon Guards and 7th (Princess Royal) Dragoons'; and 'Diary of 7th Dragoon Guards 1851–1859', Royal Dragoon Guards Museum.

12. 'Queen's Troops', *Allen's India Mail*, 4 Oct. 1858, p. 808.

13. 'Passengers Departed', *Allen's India Mail*, 6 Nov. 1858, pp. 885 and 890.

14. Information provided by the Royal Dragoon Guards Museum. See also 'Mayo Assizes', *Mayo Constitution*, 13 March 1866.

15. See for instance 'Landed Estates Court: In the Matter of the Estate of Arthur Robert Costello, Owner and Petitioner', *Mayo Constitution*, 1 July 1862; 'The Allegation Against Mr Murrough O'brien', *Irish Times*, 30 Nov. 1883; 'The Land Commission', *Dublin Daily Express*, 1 Aug. 1884; and 'Common Pleas Division', Jan. 26' *Dublin Daily Express*, 27 Jan. 1885.

16. http://skehana.galwaycommunityheritage.org/content/people/sample-page-1-article-images—last accessed 2 Aug. 2017.

17. 'The Overland Mail', *The Morning Post*, 4 Sept. 1858.

18. 'Diary of William B. Armstrong', entry for 10 July 1858.

19. 'A Ghastly Memento—A Protest', *The Sphere*, 4 Feb. 1911. Nothing further is known about this skull, and its whereabouts today remain unknown. The disapproving tenor of the piece in *The Sphere* is indicative of the fact that the collecting of such mementos was a contentious issue, even during the high-point of British imperialism. This is further discussed in the final chapter.

20. No. 3365: 'Skull', *Official Catalogue of the Royal United Service Museum*, London: J.J. Keliher & Co., 1914, 'Additions to Museum Catalogue', p. 1. The murder of an English Lady, i.e. Jane Hunter, is explicitly mentioned. See also 'Diary of William B. Armstrong', entry for 14 Aug. 1858.

21. A.T. Harrison (ed.) *The Graham Indian Mutiny Papers*, Belfast: Public Record Office of Northern Ireland, 1980. A selection of Thomas Hunter's letters are reproduced in John F. W. Youngson, *Forty Years of the Panjab Mission of the Church of Scotland, 1855–1895*, Edinburgh: R. & R. Clark, 1896.

22. Andrew Gordon, *Our India Mission: A Thirty Years' History of the India Mission of the United Presbyterian Church of North America*, Philadelphia: Andrew Gordon, 1886. The original letters from Gordon and the other American missionaries to their church in the United States are reproduced in *Evangelical Repository*, 16 (1857), pp. 29–505.

23. The only published account focusing specifically on Sialkot is Gregory Rich, *The Mutiny in Sialkot—With a brief description of the Cantonment from 1852 to 1857*, Sialkot,1924, and it relies overwhelmingly on Gordon's account in *Our India Mission*.

24. The reference here is obviously Ann Laura Stoler, *Along the Archival Grain: Epistemic Anxieties and Colonial Common Sense*, Princeton; Oxford: Princeton University Press, 2009.

25. See for instance Carlo Ginzburg, *The Cheese and the Worms*, Baltimore: Johns Hopkins University Press, 1980; Natalie Zemon Davis, *The Return of Martin Guerre*, Cambridge, Mass,: Harvard University Press, 1983; and Robert Darnton, *The Great Cat Massacre and Other Episodes in French Cultural History*, New York: Basic Books, 1984.

26. Syud Ahmed Khan, *The Causes of the Indian Revolt*, orig. 1858, Benares: Medical Hall Press, 1873; 'A few words relating to the late Mutiny of the Bengal Army, and the Rebellion in the Bengal Presidency, by Shaik Hedayut Ali, Subadar and Sirdar Bahadoor, Bengal Sikh Police Battalion, commanded by Captain T. Rattray, who has translated this paper from the original Ooroo', Kaye Papers, H/727(a), 759–66, APAC, referred to in the following as 'Shaik Hedayut Ali' with the pagination as found in the online version: https://books.google.com/books?id=xoQIAA AAQAAJ&pg=PA1&lpg=PA1&dq=shaik+hedayut&source=bl&ots=3 AiK8Rf6sa&sig=DvqXTvX7F6mKgYnGAi_z6ytmDI8&hl=en&sa=X& ved=0ahUKEwjmguet37zVAhUBzmMKHc5xAk4Q6AEIQzAI#v=one page&q=shaik%20hedayut&f=false—last accessed 4 Aug. 2017.

27. See Alison Safadi, '*From Sepoy to Subadar/Khvab-o-Khayal* and Douglas Craven Phillott', *The Annual of Urdu Studies*, 25 (2010), pp. 42–65; and Gajendra Singh, 'Finding Those Men with Guts: The Ascription and Re-Ascription of Martial Identities in India after the Uprising', in Crispin Bates and Gavin Rand (eds.), *Mutiny at the Margins: New Perspectives on the Indian Uprising of 1857, Vol. 4: Military Aspects of the Indian Uprising*, London and New Delhi: Sage, 2013, pp. 113–34.

28. Kim A. Wagner, '"In Unrestrained Conversation": Approvers and the Colonial Ethnography of Crime in nineteenth-century India', in Roque, Ricardo and Kim A. Wagner (eds.), *Engaging Colonial Knowledge: Reading European Archives in World History*, Cambridge Imperial and Post-Colonial Studies Series, Basingstoke: Palgrave, 2011, pp. 135–62.

29. See also Kim A. Wagner, *The Great Fear of 1857: Rumours, Conspiracies and the Making of the Indian Uprising*, Oxford: Peter Lang Oxford, 2010.

30. See also Gajendra Singh, *The Testimonies of Indian Soldiers and the Two World Wars: Between Self and Sepoy*, London and New York: Bloomsbury, 2014; and Clare Anderson, *Subaltern Lives: Biographies of Colonialism in*

the Indian Ocean World, 1790–1920, Cambridge: Cambridge University Press, 2012.

31. Eric Stokes (C. A. Bayly ed.), The Peasant Armed: The Indian Rebellion of 1857, Oxford: Clarendon Press, 1986; Tapti Roy, 'Visions of the Rebels: A study of 1857 in Bundelkhand', Modern Asian Studies, 27, 1, (Feb. 1993), pp. 205–228; Tapti Roy, The Politics of a Popular Uprising: Bundelkhand in 1857, Delhi: Oxford University Press, 1994; Rudrangshu Mukherjee, Awadh in Revolt 1857–1858: A Study of popular Resistance, New Delhi: Permanent Black, 2001; and Ranajit Guha, 'The Prose of Counterinsurgency', Subaltern Studies II. Delhi, 1983, pp. 1–42. Reprint: Guha, Ranajit and Spivak, G.C.(eds.), Selected Subaltern Studies, New York: 1988, pp. 45–88, which I personally much prefer to his better-known book, Elementary Aspects of Peasant Insurgency in Colonial India, Delhi: Oxford University Press, 1983.

32. See Conrad, Heart of Darkness, p. 13.

33. Niall Ferguson, Empire: How Britain Made the Modern World, London: Penguin, 2003; Andrew Roberts, A History of the English-Speaking Peoples since 1900, London: Weidenfeld & Nicolson, 2006; Richard Gott, Britain's Empire: Resistance, Repression and Revolt, London: Verso, 2011.

34. Shashi Tharoor, Inglorious Empire: What the British Did to India, London: Hurst, 2017.

1. THE HOT WIND OF AN INDIAN MAY

1. Gordon, Our India Mission, p. 129.

2. Youngson, Forty Years, p. 86.

3. Ibid, 87.

4. R. Kipling, Kim, orig. 1901, Norton Critical Edition, New York: Norton, 2002, p. 57.

5. A. Brandreth to G.F. Edmonstone, 10 July 1857, Government Records, Vol. 7:1—Punjab: Mutiny Records (Correspondence), Lahore: Punjab Government Press, 1911, p. 200. Hereafter referred to as Mutiny Records 7:1.

6. Denzil Ibbetson (ed.), Gazetteer of the Sialkot District, 1883–4, Lahore: Civil and Military Press, 1884, pp. 100–102. See also Rich, The Mutiny in Sialkot, p. 14.

7. Rich, The Mutiny in Sialkot, pp. 2–7.

8. A.A. Roberts to R. Montgomery, 20 March 1858, Government Records, Vol. 8:1—Punjab: Mutiny Records (Reports), Lahore: Punjab Government Press, 1911, p. 226. Hereafter referred to as Mutiny Records 8:1.

9. Gazetteer of the Sialkot District, 104; and G. Dodd, The History of the Indian Revolt and of the Expeditions to Persia, China, and Japan, 1856–7–8, London: W. and R. Chambers, 1859, p. 202.

10. H. Monckton to A.A. Roberts, 2 Feb. 1858, *Mutiny Records 8:1*, p. 278.
11. 'The Indian Revolt', *The Derby Mercury*, 21 Oct. 1857.
12. Ibid. See also H. Monckton to A.A. Roberts, 2 Feb. 1858, *Mutiny Records 8:1*, p. 278.
13. Kaushik Roy (ed.), *1857 Uprising: A Tale of an Indian Warrior (Translated from Durgadas Bandopadhyay's Amar Jivancharit)*, Delhi: Anthem Press, 2008, p. 45.
14. Christopher Wilkinson-Latham, *The Indian Mutiny: Men-at-Arms Series 67*, London: Osprey Publishing, 1977; Ian Knight, *Queen Victoria's Enemies (3): India: Men-at-Arms Series 219*, London: Osprey Publishing, 1990; Michael Barthorp, *The British Troops in the Indian Mutiny 1857– 59: Men-at-Arms Series 268*, London: Osprey Publishing, 1994.
15. A.A. Roberts to R. Montgomery, 20 March 1858, *Mutiny Records 8:1*, p. 226.
16. Roy (ed.), *1857 Uprising*, p. 43.
17. Gimlette, *A Postscript to the Records of the Indian Mutiny*, pp. 157–159.
18. Dirk H. A. Kolff, *Naukar, Rajput and Sepoy: The Ethno-history of the Military Labour Market in Hindustan, 1450–1850*, Cambridge: Cambridge University Press, 1990; Seema Alavi, *The Sepoys and the Company: Tradition and Transition in Northern India 1770–1830*, Delhi: Oxford University Press, 1995.
19. W.H. Sleeman, *On the Spirit of Military Discipline in our Native Indian Army*, Calcutta: Bishop's College Press, 1841, pp. 22–23.
20. Ibid., p. 71.
21. Ibid., pp. 5–6.
22. Ibid., p. 40.
23. For a recent overview, see Jon Wilson, *India Conquered: Britain's Raj and the Chaos of Empire*, London: Simon & Schuster, 2016.
24. Kolff, *Naukar, Rajput and Sepoy*.
25. Alavi, *The Sepoys and the Company*; and Douglas M. Peers, '"The Habitual Nobility of Being": British Officers and the Social Construction of the Bengal Army in the Early Nineteenth Century', *Modern Asian Studies*, 25, 3 (Jul., 1991), pp. 545–569, 551.
26. Gavin Rand and Kim A. Wagner, '"Recruiting the 'Martial Races": Identities and Military Service in Colonial India', *Patterns of Prejudice*, 46, 3–4 (2012), pp. 232–54.
27. Muslim recruits from places such as Rohilkhand, on the other hand, aspired towards the Mughal ideal of the warrior gentleman, and consequently came to dominate cavalry recruitment, see Alavi, *The Sepoys and the Company*.
28. Alavi, *The Sepoys and the Company*; and Green, *Islam and the Army in Colonial India*.

29. See also Sabyasachi Dasgupta, *In Defence of Honour and Justice: Sepoy Rebellions in the Nineteenth Century*, New Delhi: Primus Books, 2015.
30. Peers, "'The Habitual Nobility of Being'".
31. E. Martineau to J. Becher, 5 May 1857, Kaye Papers, H/725(2),1057, APAC.
32. See Crispin Bates, 'Some Thoughts on the Representation and Misrepresentation of the Colonial South Asian Labour Diaspora', *South Asian Studies*, 33 (2017), pp. 7–22.
33. Alavi, *The Sepoys and the Company*, pp. 77–78.
34. Thanks to Crispin Bates, Dilip Menon and Katherine Schofield for suggestions and input on this subject.
35. Peers, "'The Habitual Nobility of Being'", p. 553.
36. The most detailed account of this affair is in P. Bandyopadhay, *Tulsi Leaves and the Ganges Water: The Slogan of the First Sepoy Mutiny at Barrackpore 1824*, Kolkata: K. P. Bagchi and Co., 2003.
37. Peers, "'The Habitual Nobility of Being'", p. 547.
38. Cited in Bandyopadhay, *Tulsi Leaves and the Ganges Water*, p. 101.
39. Peers, "'The Habitual Nobility of Being'", pp. 547–8.
40. Ibid.
41. See David, *The Indian Mutiny*, pp. 23–24. Gurkha battalions had already been established after the Company's war with Nepal in 1814–16, and following the Sikh Wars of 1845–6 and 1848–9, both Sikhs and Muslims from Punjab entered the Bengal Army in increasing numbers.
42. Ibid.
43. 'Shaik Hedayut Ali', pp. 6–7.
44. Ibid., pp. 15–17.
45. Sleeman, *On the Spirit of Military Discipline*, p. 18. Italics and parenthesis in original.
46. Roy, *The Politics of a Popular Uprising*, pp. 24–25.
47. *Kaye's and Malleson's History*, I p. 310.
48. Ibid., pp. 312 and 313–15.
49. See also Roy, *The Politics of a Popular Uprising*, pp. 25.
50. See also Mukherjee, *Awadh in Revolt*, pp. 1–63.
51. 'Shaik Hedayut Ali', p. 5.
52. Ibid., p. 6.
53. Mainodin Hassan Khan, in C. T. Metcalfe (trans.), *Two Native Narratives of the Mutiny in Delhi*, Westminster: A. Constable and Co., 1898, p. 37.
54. Ibid., pp. 37–8.
55. 'Shaik Hedayut Ali', p. 2.
56. Gordon, *Our India Mission*, p. 129.
57. Dr Graham to J. Graham, 8 May 1857, *The Graham Indian Mutiny Papers*, p. 17.

58. Gordon, *Our India Mission*, p. 135; and letter by A. Gordon, 16 July 1857, *Evangelical Depository*, p. 314.
59. Gordon, *Our India Mission*, p. 135.
60. Dr Graham to J. Graham, 8 May 1857, *The Graham Indian Mutiny Papers*, p. 17.
61. Ibid.
62. See Youngson, *Forty Years*, pp. 70–7.
63. Letter from T. Hunter, 2 April 1856, Youngson, *Forty Years*, pp. 78–79.
64. Ibid., p. 78.
65. Ibid., p. 89.
66. Gordon, *Our India Mission*, pp. 89–90.
67. Ibid., p. 128.
68. Ibid., pp. 128–9.
69. Letter from T. Hunter, 24 Jan. 1857, Youngson, *Forty Years*, pp. 92–93.
70. Ibid., p. 93.
71. Letter from T. Hunter, 28 Feb. 1857, ibid., p. 94.
72. Gordon, *Our India Mission*, p. 129
73. Ibid., pp. 129–30.
74. Ibid.
75. Edward Vibart, *The Sepoy Mutiny; as seen by a Subaltern from Delhi to Lucknow*, London: Smith Elder and Co., 1898, p. 262. For the story of Delhi during the Indian Uprising, see William Dalrymple, *The Last Mughal: The Fall of Delhi 1857*, London: Bloomsbury, 2006.
76. Gordon, *Our India Mission*, pp. 130–1.
77. Ibid.
78. Ibid.
79. The allusion is to the elders of the Presbyterian church.
80. Ibid., p. 132.
81. Ibid.
82. Ibid.
83. Ibid.
84. Ibid., p. 133.
85. Letter from A. Gordon, 15 May 1857, *Evangelical Depository*, p. 210.
86. Ibid., p. 209.
87. Khan, *The Causes of the Indian Revolt*, p. 53
88. Mainodin Hassan Khan, in Metcalfe, *Two Native Narratives*, p. 38.
89. Gordon, *Our India Mission*, p. 129.

2. A RELIGIOUS QUESTION FROM WHICH AROSE OUR DREAD

1. For a more detailed account of the introduction of the Enfield Rifle, see Wagner, *The Great Fear*, pp. 27–44.

2. 'Depots for Training Officers, &c., in the Use of the Rifle Musket', *Allen's India Mail*, 30 Jan. 1857, p. 83.

3. 'The Punjab School of Musketry', *Allen's India Mail*, 17 March 1857, p. 171.

4. Report by Brevet Colonel G. Farquharson, 11 July 1857, in 'Report regarding the mutinees of the 14th and 46th Regiment Native Infantry at Jhelum and Sealkote', National Archives of India (NAI), Military Department, 15 July 1857, 83 A.

5. Rifle companies in the Bengal Army were already armed with the 1838 Brunswick Rifle, see Wagner, *The Great Fear*, p. 27.

6. See examination of Lieut. M.E. Currie, in George W. Forrest (ed.), *Selections from the Letters, Despatches and Other State Papers Preserved in the Military Department of the Government of India, 1857–58*, 4 vols, Calcutta Military Department Press, 1893, I, Appendix D, p. lxv.

7. 'The School of Musketry at Sealkote', *Allen's India Mail*, 15 April 1857, p. 240.

8. In this context 'Hindostanee' refers to a *sepoy* in the Bengal Army.

9. Traditionally *Chamars* were tanners and therefore untouchable.

10. *Subadar*, or captain.

11. Nund Singh to Nehal Singh, 10 June, cited in J.W. Kaye, *A History of the Sepoy War in India 1857–1858, 3 vols*, London: W.H. Allen & Co., 1876–80, I, pp. 651–2.

12. *The Delhi Gazette*, 26 Feb. 1857.

13. See examination of M.E. Currie, in Forrest, *Selections*, I, Appendix D, p. lxv.

14. J. Abbott to R. Birch, 29 Jan. 1857, HC PP, 1857, Session 2 [2254], p. 7.

15. Examination of E. Martineau during the trial of Bahadur Shah, P.K. Nayar (ed.), *The Trial of Bahadur Shah*, Hyderabad, Orient Longman, 2007, p. 84; and examination of M.E. Currie, in Forrest, *Selections*, I, Appendix D, lxii.

16. Examination of Byjonath Pandy, in Forrest, *Selections*, I, p. 8. The English transliteration of Indian names could be quite atrocious.

17. Examination of Ajoodiah Singh, ibid., p. 12.

18. A later cross-examination revealed that the word used had been *bharosa* or 'trust', ibid., Appendix D, p. lxxiv.

19. Examination of Sewbuccus Sing, ibid., pp. lxix-lxx.

20. Metcalfe, *Two Native Narratives*, p. 38.

21. Wagner, *The Great Fear*, pp. 54–9.

22. Petition cited in W. Mitchell to A.H. Ross, 27 Feb. 1857, in Forrest, *Selections*, I, pp. 46.

23. General order by Governor-General, 27 March 1857, in Forrest, *Selections*, I, pp. 94–7.

24. See Wagner, *The Great Fear*, pp. 79–97.

25. Examination of Shaik Pultoo, in Forrest, *Selections*, I, p. 124.

26. *The Delhi Gazette*, 18 April 1857.

27. Khan, *The Causes of the Indian Revolt*, pp. 51–2.

28. Deposition of Sheo Churrun Das, *Depositions taken at Cawnpore under the directions of Lieut-Colonel G. W. Williams*, (Allahabad, 1858), no. 17.

29. 'Shaik Hedayut Ali', p. 7.

30. *The Delhi Gazette*, 7 May 1857.

31. Ibid.

32. Metcalfe, *Two Native Narratives*, p. 38.

33. N.A. Chick (ed.), *Annals of the Indian Rebellion*, Calcutta: Sanders, Cones and Co., 1859, p. 76.

34. Nund Singh to Nehal Singh, 10 June, Kaye, *A History of the Sepoy War*, I, p. 653.

35. E. Martineau to J.W. Kaye, 20 Oct. 1864, Kaye Papers, H/725(2), 1019, APAC. This letter is a fragment and some words have to be inferred from the context.

36. Examination of E. Martineau, Nayar, *Trial of Bahadur Shah*, p. 84.

37. *Kaye's and Malleson's History of the Indian Mutiny*, I, pp. 416–17.

38. Examination of E. Martineau, Nayar, *Trial of Bahadur Shah*, p. 83.

39. E. Martineau to J.W. Kaye, 20 Oct. 1864, Kaye Papers, H/725(2), 1027, APAC.

40. John Cave-Browne, *The Punjab and Delhi in 1857: Being a Narrative of the Measures by which the Punjab was Saved and Delhi Recovered during the Indian Mutiny*, London: W. Blackwood and Sons, 1861, I, p. 42.

41. E. Martineau to A. Becher, 20 March 1857, Martineau Letters, Mss. Eur. C571, APAC.

42. Ibid.

43. Ibid.

44. Ibid.

45. Ibid., 23 March 1857.

46. Ibid.

47. See Ian Copland, 'Christianity as an Arm of Empire: The Ambiguous Case of India under the Company, c. 1813–1858', *The Historical Journal* (2006), pp. 1025–54.

48. S. Wheler to J.B. Hearsey, 4 April 1857, in S. A. A. Rizvi and M. L. Bhargava (eds.), *Freedom Struggle in Uttar Pradesh*, Lucknow: Publications Bureau, 1957–61, I, p. 297.

49. Letter from E.A. Stevenson and R.A. Hill, 12 Feb. 1857, *Evangelical Repository*, pp. 29–30.

50. Letter from T. Hunter, 24 Jan. 1857, Youngson, *Forty Years*, pp. 93–94.

51. Letter from A. Gordon, n.d., *Evangelical Repository*, 53.

52. Khan, *The Causes of the Indian Revolt*, p. 18.
53. 'New Church in the Punjab', *Illustrated London News*, 29 April 1854; and Rich, *The Mutiny in Sialkot*, p. 3.
54. The sacred thread worn by Brahmins.
55. 'Shaik Hedayut Ali', pp. 4–5
56. See Andrea Major, *Sovereignty and Social Reform in India: British Colonialism and the Campaign Against Sati, 1830–60*, Abingdon: Routledge, 2010.
57. Khan, *The Causes of the Indian Revolt*, p. 20. See also 'Shaik Hedayut Ali', pp. 3–4.
58. Khan, *The Causes of the Indian Revolt*, p. 16.
59. 'Shaik Hedayut Ali', p. 5.
60. See James W. Hoover, *Men Without Hats: Dialogue, Discipline, and Discontent in the Madras Army 1806–1807*, Delhi: Manohar, 2007.
61. 'Shaik Hedayut Ali', pp. 1–2.
62. Ibid.
63. Interview with Mahoobalee, Sleeman, *On the Spirit of Military Discipline*, pp. 11–12.
64. See Kaye, *A History of the Sepoy War*, I, pp. 195–9; and Clare Anderson, *The Indian Uprising of 1857–8: Prisons, Prisoners and Rebellion*, London: Anthem, 2007, pp. 27–55.
65. 'Shaik Hedayut Ali', p. 4.
66. Anand A. Yang, 'Disciplining "Natives": Prisons and Prisoners in Early Nineteenth Century India, *South Asia*, 10, 2 (1987), 29–46.
67. 'Shaik Hedayut Ali', p. 3.
68. Ibid., p. 4.
69. Alavi, *The Sepoys and the Company*, p. 31.
70. Anonymous petition to Major Matthews, March 1857, Kaye, *A History of the Sepoy War*, I, pp. 639–41.
71. Khan, *The Causes of the Indian Revolt*, p. 14.
72. See Wagner, *The Great Fear*, pp. 107–123.
73. Defence of Mattadin Havildar, in Forrest, *Selections*, I, pp. cxliv-cxlv.
74. Ibid.
75. Khan, *The Causes of the Indian Revolt*, p. 52.
76. Wagner, *The Great Fear*, pp. 131–88.
77. Examination of Ahsan Ulla Khan, in Nayar, *Trial of Bahadur Shah*, p. 60.
78. Jewan Lal, in Metcalfe, *Two Native Narratives*, p. 235.
79. J. Lawrence to C. Canning, 4 May 1857, quoted in *Kaye's and Malleson's History*, I pp. 427–8.
80. Ibid.
81. Dr Graham to J. Graham, 8 May 1857, *The Graham Indian Mutiny Papers*, p. 17.

82. Report by Lieut. Col. A. Campbell, 11 July 1857, in 'Report regarding the mutinees of the 14th and 46th Regiment Native Infantry at Jhelum and Sealkote', National Archives of India (NAI), Military Department, 15 July 1857, 83 A.

83. Letter by Mrs Campbell, 12 July 1857, 'Letter from India', *Glasgow Herald*, 11 Sept. 1857. See also letter by Mr. Jones, 13 July 1857, 'Letter from a gentleman in the civil service, dated Sealkote, July 13', *The Times*, 2 Sept. 1857.

84. R.G. Wilberforce, *An Unrecorded Chapter of the Indian Mutiny*, London: John Murray, 1894, p. 13. See also W.S. Moorsom, *Historical Record of the Fifty-Second Regiment (Oxfordshire Light Infantry) from the year 1755 to the year 1858*, London: Richard Bentley, 1860, p. 392.

3. COMMON FAME IS BUT A LYING STRUMPET

1. Letter by Mr. Jones, 13 July 1857, *The Times*, 2 Sept. 1857.
2. Wilberforce, *An Unrecorded Chapter*, p. 14.
3. Ibid., pp. 14–15.
4. Letter from A. Gordon, 15 May 1857, *Evangelical Repository*, p. 209.
5. Dr Graham to J. Graham, 23 May, *The Graham Indian Mutiny Papers*, p. 21.
6. Letter from A. Duff, 16 June 1857, *Evangelical Repository*, p. 291.
7. See Jenny Sharpe, *Allegories of Empire: The Figure of Woman in the Colonial Text*, Minneapolis: University of Minneapolis Press, 1993; and Nancy L. Paxton, *Writing Under the Raj: Gender, Race and Rape in the British Colonial Imagination, 1830–1947*, New Brunswick: Rutgers U.P., 1999; and Alison Blunt, 'Embodying war: British women and domestic defilement in the Indian 'Mutiny', 1857–8', *Journal of Historical Geography*, 26, 3 (2000), pp. 403–28.
8. Letter from R.A. Hill, 26 May 1857, *Evangelical Repository*, p. 227.
9. Cited in *Kaye's and Malleson's History*, II, p. 342.
10. H.R. James to R. Montgomery, 19 May 1857, *Mutiny Records 7:1*, p. 45; and A.A. Roberts to R. Montgomery, 20 March 1858, *Mutiny Records 8:1*, pp. 235–6.
11. G. Bourchier, *Eight Month's Campaign Against the Bengal Sepoy Army, During the Mutiny of 1857*, London: Smith, Elder and Co., 1858, n. p. 6.
12. Letter by Mr. Jones, 13 July 1857, *The Times*, 2 Sept. 1857.
13. A.A. Roberts to R. Montgomery, 20 March 1858, *Mutiny Records 8:1*, p. 236.
14. H.R. James to R. Montgomery, 21 May 1857, *Mutiny Records 7:1*, p. 51.

15. See also Thomas Dixon, *Weeping Britannia: Portrait of a Nation in Tears*, Oxford: Oxford University Press, 2015.
16. Gordon, *Our India Mission*, p. 134.
17. A.A. Roberts to R. Montgomery, 20 March 1858, *Mutiny Records 8:1*, p. 231.
18. Letter by Mr. Jones, 13 July 1857, *The Times*, 2 Sept. 1857.
19. H.R. James to R. Montgomery, 19 May 1857, *Mutiny Records 7:1*, p. 45.
20. A.A. Roberts to R. Montgomery, 20 March 1858, *Mutiny Records 8:1*, pp. 236–7.
21. Ibid., p. 278.
22. Letter from R.A. Hill, 17 July 1857, *Evangelical Repository*, p. 317.
23. Gordon, *Our India Mission*, p. 135. Italics in original.
24. G. Ousely to E. Thornton, 25 Jan. 1858, *Mutiny Records 8:1*, p. 393.
25. Ibid.
26. Dr Graham to J. Graham, 18 May 1857, *The Graham Indian Mutiny Papers*, p. 17.
27. Gordon, *Our India Mission*, p. 136.
28. Letter by Mr. Jones, 13 July 1857, *The Times*, 2 Sept. 1857.
29. Ibid.
30. Letter from A. Gordon, 15 May 1857, *Evangelical Repository*, p. 210.
31. Letter from E.H. Stevenson, 29 May 1857, ibid., pp. 213–14.
32. Letter from A. Gordon, 1 June 1857, ibid., p. 212.
33. Ibid.
34. Ibid., 15 June 1857, ibid., pp. 287.
35. Gordon, *Our India Mission*, p. 136.
36. Letter from E.H. Stevenson, 29 May 1857, *Evangelical Repository*, p. 214
37. See for instance Dr Graham to J. Graham, 23 May, *The Graham Indian Mutiny Papers*, p. 21.
38. Gordon, *Our India Mission*, pp. 136–7.
39. See Anand Yang, 'A Conversation of Rumours: The Language of Popular "Mentalitès" in Late Nineteenth-Century Colonial India', *Journal of Social History*, 20, 3 (Spring 1987), pp. 485–505; and Guha, *Elementary Aspects*, especially chapter 6: 'Transmission', pp. 220–277. See also Wagner, *The Great Fear*; and Wagner, '"Treading Upon Fires"'.
40. Address of Judge Advocate General Major F.J. Harriott, Nayar, *Trial of Bahadur Shah*, pp. 163–4.
41. Reproduced in Rizvi, *Freedom Struggle*, I, pp. 353–4.
42. 'Translation of an urzee in urdu from Taj-Ood-Deen to the King of Dehlee, 29 May 1857', *Mutiny Records 7:2*, p. 206.
43. Report by Captain Mackenzie, *Mutiny Records 8:1*, pp. 388–9.

44. W.H. Sleeman to W.H. Macnaghten, 29 March 1838, Thagi & Dakaiti, G5, Sept 1836–April 1839, 102, NAI.
45. There is little evidence to suggest that mendicants were involved in the dissemination of sedition in 1857, but see C.A. Bayly, *Empire and Information: Intelligence Gathering and Social Communication in India 1780–1870*, Cambridge: Cambridge University Press, 1996, pp. 318–19. See also Wagner, '"Treading Upon Fires"'.
46. R.E. Egerton to A.A. Roberts, 9 Feb. 1858, *Mutiny Records 8:1*, p. 262.
47. Wilberforce, *An Unrecorded Chapter*, pp. 34–35. Nicholson would furthermore tap the telegraph wires to keep himself up to date with all messages being passed along the line, ibid.
48. G. Ousely to E. Thornton, 25 Jan. 1858, *Mutiny Records 8:1*, p. 392.
49. Bourchier, *Eight Month's Campaign*, p. 11.
50. Ibid., p. 10. See also D.K.L. Choudhury, 'Sinews of Panic and the Nerves of Empire: The Imagined State's Entanglement with Information Panic, India 1880–1912', *Modern Asian Studies*, 38, 4 (Oct. 2004), pp. 965–1002; R. Peckham (ed.), *Empires of Panic: Epidemics and Colonial Anxieties*, Hong Kong: Hong Kong University Press, 2015; and Harald Fischer-Tiné (ed.), *Anxieties, Fear and Panic in Colonial Settings: Empires on the Verge of a Nervous Breakdown*, Cham, Switzerland: Palgrave Macmillan, 2016.
51. Reproduced in Chick, *Annals of the Indian Rebellion*, Appendix, pp. vi–viii. See also Dalrymple, *The Last Mughal*, p. 220. The letter formed part of the evidence against Bahadur Shah, during his trial, see Nayar, *Trial of Bahadur Shah*, pp. 102–104.
52. This sentence hints at the different ways the Hindu and Muslim *sepoys* reacted to the rumours of the greased cartridges.
53. The reliance on European artillery during the unrest at Berhampore is here conflated with the use of guns to execute *sepoys*; it may also be noted that Mangal Pandey was hanged, and not blown away.
54. Chick, *Annals of the Indian Rebellion*, Appendix, p. vii.
55. See also Tapti Roy, 'Rereading the Texts: Rebel Writings in 1857–58', in Sabyasachi Bhattacharya (ed.), *Rethinking 1857*, New Delhi: Orient Longman, 2007, pp. 221–36; and Nupur Chaudhuri and Rajat Kanta Ray, '1857: Historical Works and Proclamations', in Crispin Bates (ed.), *Mutiny at the Margins: New Perspectives on the Indian Uprising of 1857 Volume VI: Perception, Narration and Reinvention: The Pedagogy and Historiography of the Indian Uprising*, London and New Delhi: Sage, 2014, pp. 19–30.
56. Chick, *Annals of the Indian Rebellion*, Appendix, p. viii.
57. See Faisal Devji, 'The Mutiny to Come', *New Literary History*, 40, 2, India and the West (Spring 2009), pp. 411–430.
58. See Rajat Kanta Ray, *The Felt Community: Commonality and mentality before*

the emergence of Indian Nationalism, Oxford, Oxford University Press, 2003.

59. 'Translation of a Proclamation addressed to the Native Soldiers of the regiments of Infantry, Cavalry and Artillery, Etc., cantoned at Lahore', translated 20 March 1858, *Mutiny Records 8:1*, pp. 258–9.

60. This is a distinctly Hindu greeting.

61. The salary of a *sepoy* in the Bengal Army at the time was Rs 7.

62. 'Translation of a Proclamation', *Mutiny Records 8:1*, pp. 258–9. For another example of a similar letter, sent from Delhi to Punjab, see 'Proclamation from Delhi published by Lahore Chronicle', *Aberdeen Journal*, Sept. 2 1857. It is worth remembering that the extant copies of these letters and proclamations are translations of the originals.

63. Mainodin, in Metcalfe, *Two Native Narratives*, p. 37.

64. 'Translation of an inflammatory placard discovered on a Garden Gate at Sealkote', translated 20 March 1858, *Mutiny Records 8:1*, pp. 259–60.

65. Dr Graham to J. Graham, 14 June 1857, *The Graham Indian Mutiny Papers*, p. 29; and 'Letter from India', *Glasgow Herald*, 11 Sept. 1857.

66. 'Petitions of native officers and men of the 39th Reg Bengal NI expressing loyalty: Translation of a petition of the native Commissioned and Non-Commissioned Officers and Sepoys of the 39th Regiment of Native Infantry to the Right Hon Governor Gen of India', IOL/F/4/2699, APAC.

67. Dr Graham to J. Graham, 19 June 1857, *The Graham Indian Mutiny Papers*, p. 31.

4. ESCAPE AT ONCE FROM THIS HORRIBLE PLACE

1. Proclamation found at Sialkot', translated by A. A. Roberts, 31 Aug. 1857, *Mutiny Records 7:2*, p. 12.

2. Gordon, *Our India Mission*, p. 137.

3. Ibid.

4. Ibid., p. 138.

5. Letter from A. Gordon, 15 June 1857, *Evangelical Repository*, p. 286.

6. Gordon, *Our India Mission*, p. 139. Emphasis in original

7. Letter from A. Gordon, 16 July 1857, *Evangelical Repository*, p. 315.

8. Letter from T. Hunter, 9 June 1857, in Youngson, *Forty Years*, p. 99.

9. Dr Graham to J. Graham, 7 June 1857, *The Graham Indian Mutiny Papers*, p. 25.

10. This was the wife of Dr James Graham, the assistant surgeon of the 46th BNI, and no relation of Sarah or Dr Graham.

11. S. Graham to J. Graham, 10 June 1857, *The Graham Indian Mutiny Papers*, pp. 26–7.
12. Ibid., p. 27.
13. Ibid.
14. Dr Graham to J. Graham, 30 May 1857, *The Graham Indian Mutiny Papers*, p. 22.
15. Dr Graham to J. Graham, 7 June 1857, *The Graham Indian Mutiny Papers*, p. 25.
16. Bourchier, *Eight Month's Campaign*, pp. 7–8.
17. See Dalrymple, *The Last Mughal*, pp. xix and 284.
18. Wilberforce, *An Unrecorded Chapter*, p. 31; *Kaye's and Malleson's History*, II, p. 301.
19. Wilberforce, *An Unrecorded Chapter*, p. 32.
20. Dr Graham to J. Graham, 6 June 1857, *The Graham Indian Mutiny Papers*, p. 24.
21. Boyle would have sent a letter to Jhelum, via Gujrat, which was then telegraphed to Lahore.
22. S. Graham to J. Graham 10 June 1857, *The Graham Indian Mutiny Papers*, p. 27. Italics in original.
23. Dr Graham to J. Graham, 13 June 1857, *The Graham Indian Mutiny Papers*, p. 28. For a broader discussion of this attitude in the colonial context, see Mark Condos, *The Insecurity State: Punjab and the Making of Colonial Power in British India*, Cambridge: Cambridge University Press, 2017.
24. Dr Graham to J. Graham, 29 June 1857, *The Graham Indian Mutiny Papers*, p. 36.
25. Letter from T. Hunter, 9 June 1857, Youngson, *Forty Years*, p. 98.
26. Letter from A. Hill, 17 July 1857, *Evangelical Repository*, p. 317.
27. Ibid.
28. Rich, *The Mutiny in Sialkot*, p. 19.
29. Ibid., p. 20.
30. Dr Graham to J. Graham, 8 July 1857, *The Graham Indian Mutiny Papers*, p. 42.
31. Ibid.
32. Ibid.
33. Ibid.
34. Chick, *Annals of the Indian Rebellion*, p. 742.
35. A. Brandreth to R. Montgomery, 18 July 1857, Mutiny Records 7:1, p. 218.
36. Letter by Rev. Boyle, 14 July 1857, 'Letter written by a clergyman', *The Times*, 8 Sept. 1857.
37. Ibid.

38. Ibid.
39. Boyle's account has a strong teleological slant.
40. Ibid.
41. Gordon, *Our India Mission*, p. 146.
42. Ibid.
43. Rich, *The Mutiny in Sialkot*, pp. 59–60.
44. Letter by Mr. Jones, 13 July 1857, *The Times*, 2 Sept. 1857.
45. Account from *Courrier de Lyon*, *The Morning Chronicle*, 23 Sept 1857.
46. Letter written by A.H. Princep, 14 July, 1857, 'The Mutiny at Sealkote,' *The Times*, 1 Sept. 1857.

5. TENANTS OF PANDEMONIUM

1. Letter by Mr. Jones, 13 July 1857, *The Times*, 2 Sept. 1857.
2. Letter by Officer in 52nd, 'The Indian Revolt', *The Derby Mercury*, 21 Oct. 1857.
3. Ibid.
4. Letter by Mr. Jones, 13 July 1857, *The Times*, 2 Sept. 1857.
5. Cave-Browne, *The Punjab and Delhi in 1857*, II, 60. See also Frederic Cooper, *The Crisis in Punjab, from the 10th of May until the Fall of Delhi*, London: Smith, Elders and Co., 1858, p. 137.
6. Report by Lieut. Col. A. Campbell, 11 July 1857, in 'Report regarding the mutinees of the 14th and 46th Regiment Native Infantry at Jhelum and Sealkote', National Archives of India (NAI), Military Department, 15 July 1857, 83 A.
7. Dodd, *The History of the Indian Revolt*, p. 203.
8. Khan, *The Causes of the Indian Revolt*, p. 53.
9. J.G. Medley, *A Year's Campaigning in India, from March, 1857, to March, 1858*, London: W. Thacker and Co., 1858, p. 34.
10. Report by Lieut. Col. A. Campbell, 11 July 1857, in 'Report regarding the mutinees of the 14th and 46th Regiment Native Infantry at Jhelum and Sealkote', National Archives of India (NAI), Military Department, 15 July 1857, 83 A.
11. 'Letter from a Lady in the Punjab', *Isle of Wight Observer*, 31 Oct. 1857. It was common for private letters to be anonymised when they were published in the press, but the lady in question is undoubtedly Mrs Caulfield.
12. Literally: 'English infidels'.
13. Cooper, *The Crisis in Punjab*, pp. 137–8.
14. Cave-Browne, *The Punjab and Delhi in 1857*, II, p. 60; and 'The Roman Catholic Residents in India, *The Standard*, 22 Oct. 1857.
15. Cave-Browne, *The Punjab and Delhi in 1857*, II, p. 60.

16. Letter from Officer of 46th BNI, 'The Mutiny at Sealkote', *The Times*, 1 Sept. 1857.
17. Mainodin, in Metcalfe, *Two Native Narratives*, p. 60.
18. Roy, 'Visions of the Rebels', p. 209.
19. Letter from Officer of 46th BNI, *The Times*, 1 Sept. 1857.
20. R.C. Lawrence to R. Montgomery, 18 July 1857, *Mutiny Records 7:1*, pp. 234–235.
21. 366 prisoners were released from the jail at Sialkot, of whom 153 were recaptured, see 'Gaols', *The Homeward Mail*, 8 March 1859.
22. Wagner, *The Great Fear*, p. 146.
23. Luke 9:1.
24. Gordon, *Our India Mission*, p. 148.
25. 'As per Return furnished by the Deputy Commissioner of Sealkote', *The London Gazette*, 6 May 1858, p. 2245.
26. Gordon, *Our India Mission*, p. 148.
27. Ibid.
28. Wagner, *The Great Fear*, pp. 172–3, and 180.
29. Andrew Ward, *Our Bones are Scattered: the Cawnpore Massacre and the Mutiny of 1857*, London: John Murray, 1996, pp. 416–17.
30. Gordon, *Our India Mission*, p. 154.
31. Letter from Captain Montgomerie, 13 July 1857, 'The Mutiny at Sealkote', *The Times*, 2 Sept. 1857.
32. 'The Mutiny at Sealkote,' *The Times*, 1 Sept. 1857.
33. Rich, *The Mutiny in Sialkot*, p. 38–39.
34. 'The Mutiny at Sealkote', *The Times*, 2 Sept. 1857.
35. Ibid.
36. Ibid.
37. 'The Mutiny at Sealkote,' *The Times*, 1 Sept. 1857.
38. Ibid.
39. Report by Brevet Colonel G. Farquharson, 11 July 1857, in 'Report regarding the mutinees of the 14th and 46th Regiment Native Infantry at Jhelum and Sealkote', National Archives of India (NAI), Military Department, 15 July 1857, 83 A.
40. 'The Mutiny at Sealkote', *The Times*, 2 Sept. 1857.
41. Letter from Officer of 46th BNI, *The Times*, 1 Sept. 1857.
42. The *cote* is the bell-of-arms, a small structure where arms are kept. The *Kote Havildar* was the Indian NCO responsible for handing out and locking up firearms and ammunition.
43. 'Letter from a Lady in the Punjab', *Isle of Wight Observer*, 31 Oct. 1857.
44. Rich, *The Mutiny in Sialkot*, p. 53.
45. Ibid.
46. Ibid.

25. Elsewhere the aims of sepoys, peasants and landowners converged to a far greater degree, see Roy, *The Politics of a Popular Uprising*; and Mukherjee, *Awadh in Revolt*.

26. This was the wife of the civil surgeon, who was not related to Dr Graham.

27. 'Letter from India', *Glasgow Herald*, 11 Sept. 1857.

28. Horse-drawn carriage.

29. Gordon, *Our India Mission*, p. 155.

30. *The London Gazette*, 6 May 1858, p. 2243.

31. 'Letter from a Lady in the Punjab', *Isle of Wight Observer*, 31 Oct. 1857.

32. McMahon cited in Rich, *The Mutiny in Sialkot*, p. 63.

33. *The London Gazette*, 6 May 1858, p. 2243. This was the wife of the other Dr Graham.

34. 'The Indian Revolt', *The Derby Mercury*, 21 Oct. 1857.

35. Gordon, *Our India Mission*, p. 156.

36. Sealkote', *The Times*, 7 Sept. 1857.

37. 'Letter from India', *Glasgow Herald*, 11 Sept. 1857.

38. Youngson, *Forty Years*, pp. 109–110.

39. 'The Indian Revolt', *The Derby Mercury*, 21 Oct. 1857.

40. 'The Roman Catholic Residents in India, *The Standard*, 22 Oct. 1857.

41. McMahon cited in Rich, *The Mutiny in Sialkot*, p. 61.

42. Alexander Duff, *The Indian Rebellion: Its Causes and Results—In a Series of Letters*, London: s.n., 1858, pp. 54–5.

43. See for instance Letter from A. Gordon, 30 June 1857, *Evangelical Repository*, pp. 310–313.

44. Dodd, *The History of the Indian Revolt*, p. 203.

45. 'The Mutiny at Sealkote,' *The Times*, 1 Sept. 1857.

46. Cooper, *The Crisis in Punjab*, p. 136.

47. Cooper, *The Crisis in Punjab*, p. 137.

48. See Edward Leckey, *Fictions Connected with the Indian Outbreak of 1857 Exposed*, Bombay: Chesson and Woodhall, 1859.

49. 'Simla', *The Times*, 9 Oct. 1857.

50. 'Sepoy atrocities', *The Morning Chronicle*, 3 Oct. 1857.

51. Gordon, *Our India Mission*, p. 156.

52. Account from *Courrier de Lyon*, *The Morning Chronicle*, 23 Sept 1857.

53. Gordon, *Our India Mission*, p. 156.

54. Report by Brevet Colonel G. Farquharson, 11 July 1857, in 'Report regarding the mutinees of the 14th and 46th Regiment Native Infantry at Jhelum and Sealkote', National Archives of India (NAI), Military Department, 15 July 1857, 83 A.

55. 'The Mutiny at Sealkote', *The Times*, 2 Sept. 1857; and 'The Mutiny at Sealkote,' *The Times*, 1 Sept. 1857. No single regiment in the Bengal

Army was one hundred percent homogenous in terms of caste and religion of the soldiers and there was evidently a few Hindus in the 9th BLC.

56. Report by Lieut. Col. A. Campbell, 11 July 1857, in 'Report regarding the mutinees of the 14th and 46th Regiment Native Infantry at Jhelum and Sealkote', National Archives of India (NAI), Military Department, 15 July 1857, 83 A.

57. M.A. Sherring, *The Indian Church During the Great Rebellion*, London: James Nisbet and Co., 1859, p. 326.

58. A Brandreth to G.F. Edmonstone, 23 July 1857, *Mutiny Records 7:1*, p. 225.

59. Gordon, *Our India Mission*, p. 147.

7. GORGING VULTURES AND HOWLING JACKALS

1. Roy, 'Visions of the Rebels', p. 210.
2. Khan, *The Causes of the Indian Revolt*, pp. 47–8.
3. This happened on numerous occasions, see Dalrymple, *The Last Mughal*.
4. Report by John Nicholson, 19 July 1857, 'India', *The Belfast Newsletter*, 8 Dec. 1857; Cave-Browne, *The Punjab and Delhi in 1857*, II, p. 68; and Cooper, *The Crisis in Punjab*, p. 143.
5. A.A. Roberts to R. Montgomery, 7 Aug. 1857, *Mutiny Records 7:1*, p. 345.
6. Cave-Browne, *The Punjab and Delhi in 1857*, II, 74, n.; and Dalrymple, *The Last Mughal*, p. 307. See also Moorsom, *Historical Record of the Fifty-Second*, p. 395.
7. Bourchier, *Eight Month's Campaign*, p. 16; and Wilberforce, *An Unrecorded Chapter*, p. 10. This was obviously a nickname given by British officers.
8. Roy (ed.), *1857 Uprising*, p. 43.
9. 'The 52nd Regiment', *The Times*, 11 Dec. 1857.
10. 'India', *The Belfast Newsletter*, 8 Dec. 1857
11. Ibid.
12. Moorsom, *Historical Record of the Fifty-Second*, p. 396.
13. Wilberforce, *An Unrecorded Chapter*, p. 57.
14. Bourchier, *Eight Month's Campaign*, p. 13; and Cave-Browne, *The Punjab and Delhi in 1857*, II, pp. 72–73.
15. Bourchier, *Eight Month's Campaign*, p. 14.
16. Wilberforce, *An Unrecorded Chapter*, p. 22.
17. Cave-Browne, *The Punjab and Delhi in 1857*, II, p. 73.
18. Wilberforce, *An Unrecorded Chapter*, pp. 53–54.
19. Moorsom, *Historical Record of the Fifty-Second*, p. 394.
20. Wilberforce, *An Unrecorded Chapter*, p. 54.

21. Moorsom, *Historical Record of the Fifty-Second*, p. 397.
22. 'The 52nd Regiment', *The Times*, 11 Dec. 1857.
23. Bourchier, *Eight Month's Campaign*, p. 18.
24. Moorsom, *Historical Record of the Fifty-Second*, pp. 397–398.
25. Bourchier, *Eight Month's Campaign*, p. 18.
26. Cave-Browne, *The Punjab and Delhi in 1857*, II, p. 75.
27. A Brandreth to G.F. Edmonstone, 23 July 1857, *Mutiny Records 7:1*, pp. 225–6.
28. Cooper, *The Crisis in Punjab*, p. 148.
29. Wilberforce, *An Unrecorded Chapter*, p. 57.
30. Ibid., pp. 58–59. There is probably some embellishment in this anecdote.
31. Moorsom, *Historical Record of the Fifty-Second*, p. 397.
32. Bourchier, *Eight Month's Campaign*, p. 18.
33. Thanks to Gajendra Singh for his expert input.
34. Bourchier, *Eight Month's Campaign*, p. 18.
35. Wilberforce, *An Unrecorded Chapter*, p. 59.
36. Ibid., p. 60.
37. Bourchier, *Eight Month's Campaign*, p. 18.
38. 'The 52nd Regiment', *The Times*, 11 Dec. 1857.
39. Moorsom, *Historical Record of the Fifty-Second*, p. 397.
40. Bourchier, *Eight Month's Campaign*, p. 19.
41. Ibid.
42. 'The Indian Mutiny', *Glasgow Herald*, 9 Nov. 1857.
43. Cooper, *The Crisis in Punjab*, pp. 148–149.
44. *The Times*, 11 Dec 1857.
45. Moorsom, *Historical Record of the Fifty-Second* Moorsom, 397.
46. Cooper, *The Crisis in Punjab*, Cooper 148.
47. Glasgow Herald 9 Nov 1857.
48. W. Leeke, *The History of Lord Seaton's Regiment (The 52nd Light Infantry)*, London: Hatchard and Co., 1866, II, p. 395; Wilberforce, *An Unrecorded Chapter*, p. 61. See also Moorsom, *Historical Record of the Fifty-Second*, p. 398.
49. 'The 52nd Regiment', *The Times*, 11 Dec. 1857.
50. Cave-Browne, *The Punjab and Delhi in 1857*, II, p. 77.
51. Wilberforce, *An Unrecorded Chapter*, p. 67.
52. Moorsom, *Historical Record of the Fifty-Second*, p. 398.
53. Wilberforce, *An Unrecorded Chapter*, pp. 64–5.
54. Diaries of Col. E.L. Ommaney, vol. A, pt 6, entry for July 1857, Umritsur, NAM, 6301/143, p. 91. Thanks to Jacob Smith for help getting this account.
55. Wilberforce, *An Unrecorded Chapter*, p. 65.
56. Bourchier, *Eight Month's Campaign*, p. 21.

57. Wilberforce, *An Unrecorded Chapter*, pp. 70–71.

58. Cooper, *The Crisis in Punjab*, p. 148; and Rich, *The Mutiny in Sialkot*, p. 69.

59. Moorsom, *Historical Record of the Fifty-Second*, p. 399.

60. Cave-Browne, *The Punjab and Delhi in 1857*, II, p. 78.

61. Bourchier, *Eight Month's Campaign*, p. 22.

62. Cave-Browne, *The Punjab and Delhi in 1857*, II, p. 79. See also Bourchier, *Eight Month's Campaign*, p. 22.

63. Wilberforce, *An Unrecorded Chapter*, p. 73.

64. Ibid., p. 72.

65. Leeke, *The History of Lord Seaton's Regiment*, II, p. 396.

66. Wilberforce, *An Unrecorded Chapter*, pp. 71–2.

67. Ibid.

68. S.S. Thorburn, *The Punjab in Peace and War*, Edinburgh: William Blackwood and Sons, 1904, p. 217.

69. 'London, Monday, Sept.14, 1857', *The Morning Post*, 14 Sept. 1857.

70. Moorsom, *Historical Record of the Fifty-Second*, p. 398.

8. JUSTICE SO PROMPT AND VIGOROUS

1. Gordon, *Our India Mission*, p. 142. Italics in original.

2. Ibid.

3. 'Letter from India', *Glasgow Herald*, 11 Sept. 1857; and *The London Gazette*, 6 May 1858, p. 2244.

4. Rich, *The Mutiny in Sialkot*, pp. 79–80.

5. Gordon, *Our India Mission*, p. 156. According to Rich two more Englishmen died in the days following the outbreak, Captain J.E. Sharpe, and Hospital Sergeant Nully. They were both buried next to the fort, see Rich, *The Mutiny in Sialkot*, p. 79. We do not know anything about these men, nor how they died.

6. R.C. Lawrence to R. Montgomery, 18 July 1857, *Mutiny Records 7:1*, p. 233.

7. 'The Mutiny at Sealkote,' *The Times*, 1 Sept. 1857. Considering the absolute destruction of Indian cities such as Delhi or Lucknow at the hands of the British later on, there is more than a little hyperbole in this statement.

8. Letter from A. Gordon, 4 Aug. 1857, *Evangelical Repository*, p. 384.

9. Ibid.

10. Ibid., p. 385.

11. Gordon, *Our India Mission*, p. 143.

12. Letter from A. Gordon, 4 Aug. 1857, *Evangelical Repository*, p. 385.

13. Ibid.
14. Ibid.
15. R.C. Lawrence to R. Montgomery, 18 July 1857, *Mutiny Records* 7:1, p. 234.
16. Gordon, *Our India Mission*, p. 159.
17. R.C. Lawrence to R. Montgomery, 18 July 1857, *Mutiny Records* 7:1, p. 233.
18. Ibid., p. 234.
19. Ibid., pp. 234–5.
20. Ibid., p. 235.
21. Ibid., p. 234.
22. 'An Execution at Sealkote', *The Sheffield & Rotherham Independent*, 26 Sept. 1857.
23. Ibid.
24. R.C. Lawrence to R. Montgomery, 18 July 1857, *Mutiny Records* 7:1, p. 238.
25. W. Graham to J. Graham, 27 July 1857, *The Graham Indian Mutiny Papers*, p. 45.
26. Cave-Browne, *The Punjab and Delhi in 1857*, II, pp. 98–99.
27. Brigadier-General R. E. H. Dyer to the General Staff, 25 Aug. 1919, in *Disorders Inquiry Committee, 1919–1920: Evidence, III: Amritsar* (Calcutta, 1920), p. 203.
28. Cooper, *The Crisis in Punjab*, p. 149.
29. 'Retribution—Delhi', *The Letters of Indophilus to "The Times"—with additional notes*, London: Longman, Brown, Green, Longman's, and Roberts [1858], pp. 5–6.
30. Ibid.
31. See E.J. Thompson, *The Other Side of the Medal*, London: The Hogarth Press, 1925; Thomas Metcalf, *The Aftermath of the Revolt: India 1857–1870*, London: Oxford University Press, 1965; Wagner, 'Treading Upon Fires' and 'Calculated to Strike Terror'; and Condos, *The Insecurity State*.
32. C.E. Stewart, *Through Persia in Disguise: With Reminiscences of the Indian Mutiny*, London: George Routledge & Sons, 1911, p. 11.
33. Gordon, *Our India Mission*, p. 161.
34. Ibid., p. 159.
35. *Kaye's and Malleson's History*, II, p. 177.
36. See Amy Louise Wood, *Lynching and Spectacle: Witnessing Racial Violence in America, 1890–1940*, Chapel Hill: The University of North Carolina Press, 2009, p. 22.
37. Cooper, *The Crisis in Punjab*, p. 154.

38. F.H. Cooper to A.A. Roberts, 5 Aug. 1857, Mutiny Records 7:1, pp. 393–4.

39. Ibid., p. 394.

40. Ibid.

41. Cooper, *The Crisis in Punjab*, p. 163.

42. Ibid., p. 164.

43. Ibid., p. 167.

44. The work of Michael Taussig is obviously significant to this argument, see especially *Shamanism, Colonialism, and the Wild Man: A Study in Terror and Healing*, Chicago, IL: University of Chicago Press, 1987. This is further discussed in the penultimate chapter.

45. Cooper, *The Crisis in Punjab*, p. 164.

46. If this sounds familiar, it is because a very similar narrative emerged following the Amritsar Massacre in 1919, see Kim A. Wagner, 'Seeing Like a Soldier: The Amritsar Massacre and the Politics of Military History', in Martin Thomas and Gareth Curless (ed.), *Decolonization and Conflict: Colonial Comparisons and Legacies*, London: Bloomsbury, 2017, pp. 23–37.

47. See Dixon, *Weeping Britannia*.

48. Don Randall, 'Post-Mutiny Allegories of Empire in Rudyard Kipling's Jungle Books', *Texas Studies in Literature and Language*, 40, 1 (Spring, 1998), pp. 97–120.

49. Radhika Singha, *A Despotism of Law: Crime and Justice in Early Colonial India*, New Delhi: Oxford University Press, 1998; and Naser Hussain, *The Jurisprudence of Emergency: Colonialism and the Rule of Law*, Ann Arbor, MI: University of Michigan Press, 2003.

50. See Charles Ball, *The History of the Indian Mutiny*, 2 vols, London: London Printing & Publishing Co., 1858, II, pp. 395–396. See also Wagner, *The Great Fear*, pp. 173–174.

51. For a more detailed discussion of British reprisals, and the attempts at restoring order, see Jacob Ramsay Smith, 'Imperial Retribution: The hunt for Nana Sahib and rebel leaders in the aftermath of the Indian "Mutiny" of 1857', unpublished PhD thesis, Queen Mary, University of London, 2017.

52. Cooper, *The Crisis in Punjab*, p. 168.

53. See Dalrymple, *The Last Mughal*, pp. 431–43; and Wagner, *The Great Fear*, pp. 228–34.

54. G.H. Hodson (ed.), *Hodson of Hodson's Horse; or Twelve Years of a Soldier's Life in India*, London: Kegan Paul, Trench, & Co., 1883, p. 224. See also Dalrymple, *The Last Mughal*, pp. 396–9.

55. V.D. Majendie, *Up Among the Pandies; or, A Year's Service in India*, London, 1859, pp. 101–2.

9. A PURSUING DESTINY

1. R. Kipling, 'The Lost Legion', *The Strand*, May, 1892, p. 476.
2. See Smith, 'Imperial Retribution'.
3. W. Butler, *Land of the Veda*, New York: Hunt & Eaton, 1895, p. 448.
4. 'The Indian Mutinies', *The Times*, 26 October 1857.
5. W.R. Eliott to A.A. Roberts, 15 Feb. 1858, *Mutiny Records 8:1*, p. 286.
6. C.A. McMahon to A.A. Roberts, 4 Feb. 1858, ibid., p. 281.
7. Ibid. See also A. Brandreth to G.F. Edmonstone, 23 July 1857, *Mutiny Records 7:1*, p. 224.
8. C.A. McMahon to A.A. Roberts, 4 Feb. 1858, *Mutiny Records 8:1*, p. 281.
9. Ibid., p. 282.
10. Ibid. See also A. Brandreth to G.F. Edmonstone, 30 July 1857, *Mutiny Records 7:1*, p. 271.
11. C.A. McMahon to A.A. Roberts, 4 Feb. 1858, *Mutiny Records 8:1*, p. 282.
12. E.J. Lake to R. Montgomery, 5 Jan. 1858, *Mutiny Records 8.1*, p. 158.
13. R. Temple to G.F. Edmonstone, 14 June 1858, NAI, Foreign Political, 27 Aug. 1858, 7–10 S.C.
14. 'Official News from Lahore', *The Morning Chronicle*, 17 Sept. 1857.
15. W.H. Russell, *My Diary in India, in the year 1858–9*, 2 vols, London: Routledge, Warne, and Routledge, 1860, II, pp. 184–5.
16. Ibid.
17. G. Knox to R.G. Taylor, 27 Aug. 1858, NAI, Political Proceedings, 23 Sept. 1859, no. 102.
18. R. Temple to G.F. Edmonstone, 14 June 1858, NAI, Foreign Political, 27 Aug. 1858, 7–10 S.C.
19. This reconstruction is based mainly on J. Naesmith to R. Temple, 9 July 1858, NAI, Foreign Political, 31 Dec. 1858, 3288–3300 F.C.
20. J.H. Dyas to R. Lawrence, 2 June 1857, NAI, Foreign Political, 27 Aug. 1858, 7–10 S.C.
21. Ibid.
22. J. Naesmith to R. Temple, 9 July 1858, NAI, Foreign Political, 31 Dec. 1858, 3288–3300 F.C.
23. Ibid.
24. A.A. Roberts to R. Montgomery, 20 March 1858, *Mutiny Records 8:1*, pp. 250–1.
25. J. Naesmith to R. Temple, 9 July 1858, NAI, Foreign Political, 31 Dec. 1858, 3288–3300 F.C.
26. J. Naesmith to R. Temple, 3 June 1858, NAI, Foreign Political, 27 Aug. 1858, 7–10 S.C.; and J. Naesmith to R. Temple, 9 July 1858, NAI, Foreign Political, 31 Dec. 1858, 3288–3300 F.C.

27. J. Naesmith to R. Temple, 9 July 1858, NAI, Foreign Political, 31 Dec. 1858, 3288–3300 F.C.
28. Ibid.
29. 'The Punjaub', *The Homeward Mail*, 27 July 1858.
30. Ibid.
31. E. Lake to E. Thornton, 8 Sept. 1858, NAI, Political Proceedings, 23 Sept. 1859, no. 100.
32. 'India', *Dublin Evening Mail*, 6 Oct. 1858.
33. G. Knox to R.G. Taylor, 27 Aug. 1858, NAI, Political Proceedings, 23 Sept. 1859, no. 102.
34. Ibid.
35. E. Lake to E. Thornton, 8 Sept. 1858, NAI, Political Proceedings, 23 Sept. 1859, no. 100.
36. 'India', *Dublin Evening Mail*, 6 Oct. 1858.
37. 'China and India', *The Times*, 16 Sept. 1858.
38. G. Knox to R.G. Taylor, 27 Aug. 1858, NAI, Political Proceedings, 23 Sept. 1859, no. 102.
39. R. Temple to G.F. Edmonstone, 20 Sept. 1858, NAI, Political Proceedings, 23 Sept. 1859, no. 98.
40. 'Correspondent, Lahore', *The Times*, 9 Nov. 1858.
41. See Smith, 'Imperial Retribution'.
42. *Biographical and descriptive Sketches of the Distinguished Characters which compose the Unrivalled Exhibition and Historical gallery of Madame Tussaud and Sons*, London: W.S. Johnson, 1866, p. 36, no. 261. There was no evidence that Nana Sahib had in fact committed suicide—'the coward's death' alluded to.
43. 'London, Saturday, October 23, 1858', *The Times*, 23 Oct. 1858.
44. 'The Mutinies in India', *The Times*, 21 Sept. 1857.
45. 'The Overland Mail', *The Morning Post*, 4 Sept. 1858.
46. Rich, *The Mutiny in Sialkot*, p. 53.

10. SHARP AND SHORT AS THE CANNONS ROAR

1. See Diary of Capt W B Armstrong Diary 7DG-1, entry for 8 July and 10 July.
2. 'The English Raj in India', *The Times*, 7 Oct. 1858; 'The Overland Mail', *The Morning Post*, 4 Sept. 1858; and 'Sealkot', *Allen's India Mail*, 15 Sept. 1858, p. 775.
3. 'An Execution in India', *The Times*, 3 Dec. 1857.
4. Ibid. This morbid curiosity appears to have been common amongst British spectators at executions, see F.C. Maude *Memories of the Mutiny*, London and Sydney: Remington and Company Limited, 1894, I, p. 277.

5. Michel Foucault, *Discipline and Punish: The Birth of the Prison*, London: Allen Lane, 1977. For a more recent work on executions within a non-European context, see Stacey Hynd, *Imperial Gallows: Capital Punishment, Violence and Colonial Rule in Britain's African Territories c. 1903–1968*, Oxford: Oxford University Press, 2007.

6. See Sumit Guha, 'An Indian Penal Regime: Maharashtra in the Eighteenth Century', *Past & Present*, 147 (May 1995), pp. 101–26.

7. M. Wilks, *Historical Sketches of the South of India, in an Attempt to Trace the History of Mysoor*, London: Longman, Hurst, Rees, Orme, and Brown, 1810, I: p. 397.

8. R. Montgomery Martin, *The Indian Empire: With a Full Account of the Mutiny of the Bengal Army*, London: London Printing and Publishing Co., 1861, II, pp. 99–100. Thanks to Vijay Pinch for sharing his current work on this particular incident.

9. 'Extract of the General letter from Bombay,' 30 April 1780; APAC, IOR, Home Misc., H/149 (5): 111.

10. See Kim A. Wagner, *Thuggee: Banditry and the British in Nineteenth-Century India*, Basingstoke: Palgrave, 2007.

11. H.H. Spry, *Modern India: with Illustrations of the resources and Capabilities of Hindustan*, 2 vols, London: Whittaker & Co., 1837, I, p. 165.

12. Ibid., pp. 166–168. Executioners often came from the caste of *Chamars* or tanners and shoemakers, who traditionally worked with leather and therefore were untouchable.

13. W.H. Sleeman to F.C. Smith, 15 Aug. 1832, APAC, BC, F/4/1406/55521.

14. Lieutenant-Colonel [G.A.] Fitzclarence, *Journal of a Route across India, through Egypt, to* England, London: John Murray, 1819, p. 157.

15. 'Blowing from Guns at Peshawur', *Daily News*, 5 Nov. 1857.

16. Maude, *Memories of the Mutiny*, I, p. 71. Elsewhere Neill explicitly stated that 'The task will be made *as revolting to his feelings as possible...*' [italics in original], ibid., II, p. 526. See also H. W. Norman, *Delhi—1857: The Siege, Assault, and Capture*, London and Edinburgh: W. & R. Chambers, 1902, p. 252.

17. *The Letters of Indophilus*, p. 8.

18. Russell, *My Diary in India*, II, p. 43.

19. See also Rudrangshu Mukherjee, '"Satan Let Loose upon Earth": The Kanpur Massacres in India in the Revolt of 1857', *Past and Present*, 128 (Aug. 1990), pp. 92–116.

20. Quoted in *Kaye's and Malleson's History*, II, p. 367.

21. Cooper, *The Crisis in Punjab*, p. 168.

22. 'The British Army in India', *The Times*, 19 July 1858.

23. See Christopher Herbert, *War of No Pity: The Indian Mutiny and Victorian Trauma*, Princeton, NJ: Princeton University Press, 2008.

24. 'Blowing from Guns at Peshawur', *Daily News*, 5 Nov. 1857.

25. *Kaye's and Malleson's History*, II, pp. 369–70. See also T. R. Holmes, *A History of the Indian Mutiny*, London: Macmillan & Co., 1883, p. 338, fn.

26. *Kaye's and Malleson's History*, II, p. 369, fn.

27. 'The Mutiny at Jubbulpore', *Daily News*, 3 Nov. 1857.

28. Michael Taussig, *Shamanism, Colonialism, and the Wild Man: A Study in Terror and Healing*, Chicago: University of Chicago Press, 1987.

29. It became something of a recurrent feature in popular literary depictions of the 'Mutiny' to have the roles reversed, with the British protagonists strapped to a cannon by cruel Indians, see for instance Jules Verne, *The Steam House, part I: The Demon of Cawnpore* & *The Steam House, part II: Tigers and Traitors*, New York: Charles Scribner's Sons, 1881; and Percival Lancaster, *Chaloner of the Bengal Cavalry*, London: Blackie and sons Limited, 1915. In George Macdonald Fraser's *Flashman and the Great Game*, London: Barrie and Jenkins, 1975, the eponymous anti-hero is almost blown from a cannon by British troops who mistake him for an Indian rebel, thus re-inverting the moral thrust of the colonial execution-narratives.

30. Lord [F.S.] Roberts, *Forty-One Years in India: From Subaltern to Commander-in-Chief*, London: Macmillan and Co., 1897, p. 68, fn.

31. See also Wood, *Lynching and Spectacle*.

32. See for instance 'Execution of mutinous sepoys on the Parade, Peshawur', *Illustrated London News*, 3 Oct. 1857.

33. See also the brilliant article by Michael G. Vann, 'Of Pirates, Postcards, and Public Beheadings: The Pedagogic Execution in French Colonial Indochina, *Historical Reflections/Réflexions Historiques*, 36, 2 (2010), pp. 39–58.

34. 'Blown Away!', *Household Words*, 27 March 1858, p. 350.

35. Roberts, *Forty-One Years in India*, p. 69.

36. Wilberforce, *An Unrecorded Chapter*, p. 42.

37. Maude, *Memories of the Mutiny*, I, p. 277; and 'India', *The Preston Guardian*, 7 Nov. 1857.

38. 'India', *The Preston Guardian*, 7 Nov. 1857.

39. *Hansard*, 3rd ser. (Commons), cviii, cols. 146–60 (14 March 1859).

40. See also Diana Paton, 'Punishment, Crime, and the Bodies of Slaves in Eighteenth-Century Jamaica', *Journal of Social History*, 34, 4 (2001), pp. 923–54; and Taylor Sherman, 'Tensions of Colonial Punishment: Perspectives on Recent Developments in the Study of Coercive Networks in Asia, Africa and the Caribbean', *History Compass*, 7, 3 (2009), pp. 659–77.

41. Ball, *The History of the Indian Mutiny*, II, p. 394.

42. 'An Execution at Sealkote', *The Sheffield & Rotherham Independent*, 26 Sept. 1857.
43. 'Correspondence', *Dunstable Chronicle, and Advertiser for Beds, Bucks & Herts*, 30 Oct. 1858.
44. 'The Overland Mail', *The Morning Post*, 4 Sept. 1858.
45. Gordon, *Our India Mission*, pp. 157–8.
46. F.H. Cooper to A.A. Roberts, 5 Aug. 1857, Mutiny Records 7:1, p. 394.
47. Ball, *The History of the Indian Mutiny*, II, p. 145; and Gordon, *Our India Mission*, p. 158.
48. 'The Overland Mail', *The Morning Post*, 4 Sept. 1858.
49. Diary of John Murray, 18 Jan. 1858, quoted in Sean Willcock, 'The Aesthetics of Imperial Crisis: Image Making and Intervention in British India, c. 1857–1919', unpublished PhD thesis, University of York, 2013, p. 120.
50. 'Correspondence', *Dunstable Chronicle, and Advertiser for Beds, Bucks & Herts*, 30 Oct. 1858.
51. Ibid.
52. Gordon, *Our Indian Mission*, p. 158.

11. BUT FROM THE SKULLS OF THE SLAIN

1. 'Queen's Troops', *Allen's India Mail*, 4 Oct. 1858, p. 808.
2. The scholarship that I have found most useful, and most inspiring, includes Simon Harrison, *Dark Trophies: Hunting and the Enemy Body in Modern War*, New York: Berghahn, 2012; Frances Larson, *Severed: A History of Heads Lost and Heads Found*, London: Granta, 2014; Edgar V. Winnans, 'The Head of the King: Museums and the Path to Resistance', *Comparative studies in Society and History*, 36, 2 (April 1994), pp. 221–41; Helen MacDonald, *Human Remains: Dissection and Its Histories*, New Haven: Yale University Press, 2006; Luise White, 'The Traffic in Heads: Bodies, Borders and the Articulation of Regional Histories', *Journal of Southern African Studies*, 23, 2 (1997), pp. 325–38; Cora Bender, '"Transgressive Objects" in America: Mimesis and Violence in the Collection of Trophies during the Nineteenth Century Indian Wars', *Civil Wars*, 11, 4 (Dec. 2009), pp. 502–13; Antonia Lovelace, 'War Booty: Changing Contexts, Changing Displays—Asante 'Relics' from Kumasi, Acquired by the Prince of Wales's Own Regiment of Yorkshire in 1896', *Journal of Museum Ethnography*, 12 (May 2000), pp. 147–60; Merrick Burrow, 'The Imperial Souvenir: Things and Masculinity in H. Rider Haggard's *King Solomon's Mines* and *Allan Quartermain*', *Journal of Victorian Culture*, 18, 1 (2013), pp. 72–92; and Ricardo Roque,

Headhunting and Colonialism: Anthropology and the Circulation of Human Skulls in the Portuguese Empire, 1870–1930, Cambridge Imperial and Post-Colonial Studies, Basingstoke: Palgrave Macmillan, 2010.

3. Court-house.

4. Tribal headman.

5. S.S. Thorburn, *Bannu: Our Afghan Frontier*, London: Trübner & Co., 1876, p. 54.

6. R. E. Cholmeley, *John Nicholson: The Lion of the Punjaub*, London: Andrew Melrose, 1908, chapter VI.

7. See Larson, *Severed*; Patricia Palmer, *The Severed Head and the Grafted Tongue: Literature, Translation, and Violence in Early Modern Ireland*, Cambridge: Cambridge University Press, 2013; and Paton, 'Punishment, Crime, and the Bodies of Slaves'. Richard Ward (ed.), *A Global History of Execution and the Criminal Corpse*, Basingstoke: Palgrave 2015.

8. R. H. W. Dunlop, *Service and Adventure with the Khakee Ressalah, or Meerut Volunteer Horse, during the Mutinies of 1857–58*, London: s.n., 1858, p. 110. There were later attempts by the local rebels to recover the head, ibid., 112. See also Gautam Bhadra' 'Four rebels of Eighteen-Fifty-Seven, Ranajit Guha (ed.), *Subaltern Studies 4*, Delhi: Oxford University Press, 1985, pp. 229–75, reprint: Guha, Ranajit and Spivak, G.C.(eds.), *Selected Subaltern Studies*, New York: 1988, pp. 129–75.

9. Michael Edwardes, *Red Year: The Indian Rebellion of 1857*, London: Cardinal, 1975, p. 220; Forrest, *Selections*, III, pp. ccvi and cccx; Rizvi, *Freedom Struggle*, II, pp. 651–2.

10. See Rizvi, *Freedom Struggle*, V, pp. 536, 538, 539, and 545.

11. H.H. Spry to P. Spry, 12 Oct. 1832, Letters of Henry Harpur Spry, vol. 4, Mss Eur Photo Eur 308, APAC.

12. See Roger Cooter, *The Cultural Meaning of Popular Science: Phrenology and the Organization of Consent in Nineteenth-Century Britain*, Cambridge: Cambridge University Press, 1984; and John van Wyhe, *Phrenology and the Origins of Victorian Scientific Naturalism*, Aldershot: Ashgate, 2004.

13. K.A. Wagner, 'Confessions of a Skull: Phrenology and Colonial Knowledge in early nineteenth-century India', *History Workshop Journal*, 69 (Spring, 2010), pp. 28–51. See also Shruti Kapila, 'Race Matters: Orientalism and Religion, India and Beyond c. 1770—1880' *Modern Asian Studies*, 41, 3 (2007), pp. 471–513.

14. Robert Cox, 'Remarks on the Skulls and Character of the Thugs' *Phrenological Journal and Miscellany*, 8 (1834), pp. 524–30.

15. Ibid. 530.

16. Andrew Bank, 'Of 'Native Skulls' and Noble Caucasians: Phrenology in Colonial South Africa', *Journal of Southern African Studies*, 22, 3 (Sept. 1996), pp. 387–403; and Saul Dubow, *A Commonwealth of*

Knowledge: Science, Sensibility, and White South Africa 1820–2000, Cambridge: Cambridge University Press, 2006.

17. Harrison, *Dark Trophies*.
18. Denver A. Webb, 'War, Racism, and the Taking of Heads: Revisiting Military Conflict in the Cape Colony and Western Xhosaland in the Nineteenth Century', *The Journal of African History*, 56, 1 (March 2015), pp. 37–55.
19. Ibid., p. 45. See also P. Lalu, *The Deaths of Hintsa: Postapartheid South Africa and the Shape of Recurring Pasts*, Cape Town: HSRC Press, 2009.
20. For the commodification of shrunken heads, or *tsantsas*, from South America, and Maori heads, or *mokomokai*, from New Zealand, see Larson, *Severed*, pp. 17–28, 40–3; and Harrison, *Dark Trophies*, p. 62.
21. Quoted in Webb, 'War, Racism, and the Taking of Heads', p. 47.
22. Ibid., p. 44.
23. Ibid., p. 47.
24. Isabel Burton, *The Life of Captain Sir Richard F. Burton*, London: Duckworth & Co., 1898, p. 211.
25. See also Richard F. Burton, *Zanzibar: City, Island, and Coast*, 2 vols, London: Tinsley Brothers, 1872, II, p. 346.
26. R.G. Woodthorpe, *The Lushai Expedition, 1871–1872*, London: Hurst and Blackett, 1873, pp. 282–283.
27. The National Army Museum, London, has several such souvenirs, including children's shoes and locks of hair: 'Child's shoe recovered from the well at Cawnpore, 1857', NAM 1963–10–237–1; and 'Lock of hair taken from Cawnpore and mounted on velvet board, 1857', NAM 1960–02–2–1. http://www.nam.ac.uk/online-collection/results.php?searchType=simple&simpleText=indian%20mutiny&them eID=&resultsDisplay=list&page=3
28. These were untouchable sweepers and scavengers often used to assist in executions.
29. Ball, *The History of the Indian Mutiny*, II, p. 602. A lock of Tantia Tope's hair was actually on display at the National Army Museum in London, when it re-opened in 2017: 'Snuff box containing a lock of Tatya Tope's hair, removed after his execution in 1859', NAM 1965–09–54–1.
30. See for instance Ruth Penfold-Mounce, 'Consuming Criminal Corpses: Fascination with the Dead Criminal Body', *Mortality*, 15, 3 (2010), pp. 250–65; and Sarah Tarlow, 'Curious Afterlives: The Enduring Appeal of the Criminal Corpse', *Mortality*, 21, 3 (2016), pp. 210–28.
31. Russell, *My Diary in India*, I, p. 202.
32. Butler, *Land of the Veda*, p. 417. The quote is from the *Illiad*.
33. Majendie, *Up Among the Pandies*, pp. 278–9.
34. 'Local News: Soldier from India', *Stirling Observer*, 12 Jan. 1860.

35. 'Tragedy of a Skull', *Eastbourne Gazette*, 18 Jan. 1911.
36. Harrison, *Dark Trophies*; and Larson, *Severed*.
37. Dunlop, *Service and Adventure*, p. 14.
38. See Burrow, 'The Imperial Souvenir'. We know that Costello, like most British officers at the time, was an avid hunter, see 'Diary of William B. Armstrong', entry for 11 Feb. 1858.
39. 'Diary of William B. Armstrong', entry for 9, 11 and 26 July 1858.
40. See Burrow, 'The Imperial Souvenir', p. 73.
41. Sharpe, *Allegories of Empire*; Paxton, *Writing under the Raj*; and Blunt, 'Embodying War'.
42. See also Anderson, *Subaltern Lives*, pp. 124–56.
43. R.W. Kostal, *A Jurisprudence of Power: Victorian Empire and the Rule of Law*, Oxford: Oxford University Press, 2008.
44. By 1872, the case was fresh in everyone's mind and in fact the cost of Eyre's legal defence was still being decided, 'Weekly Reviews', *The Pall Mall Gazette*, 13 July 1872.
45. Wagner, 'Calculated to Strike Terror'. This was the last time that cannon was used for executions in British India.
46. Henry M. Stanley, *How I Found Livingstone: Travels, Adventures, and Discoveries in Central Africa*, London: Sampson Low, Marston & Company, 1871, pp. 270–271.
47. Cornelius Vijn, *Cetshwayo's Dutchman, Being the Private Journals of a White Trader in Zululand during the British Invasion*, London: Longman's, Green, and Co., 1880, p. 38.
48. 'Zulu Skulls', *The Globe*, 12 March 1880.
49. For a description of the whole range of human and animal trophies and body parts sold in one shop, see 'Sporting Trophies', *The Sportsman*, 31 January 1883.
50. 'Skulls for Cigar-Holders', *Punch*, 77, December 1879, p. 268. Italics in original
51. 'Society Gossip', *Beverley and East Riding Recorder*, 10 July 1880.
52. Henry M. Stanley, *Coomassie and Magdala: The Story of Two British Campaigns in Africa*, New York: Harper & Brothers, 1874, p. 231.
53. Jameson's posthumously published account suggests that he actually skinned the head like that of an animal and that the skull itself was of no interest to him, see James S. Jameson, *The Story of the Rear Column of the Emin Pasha Relief Expedition*, London: R.H. Porter, 1890, p. 204.
54. 'Mr. Bonny and the cannibal story', *The Times*, 14 Nov. 1890.
55. Hedley A. Chilvers, *The Yellow Man Looks On: Being the Story of the Anglo-Dutch Conflict in Southern Africa and its Interest for the Peoples of Asia*, London: Cassell, 1933, p. 132.
56. 'The Mutilation of Luka Jantje—Treatment of Langeberg Rebels', *Glasgow Herald*, 22 Sept. 1897.

57. Ibid.

58. Ibid.

59. Chilvers, *The Yellow Man Looks On*, p. 133. For a very different version of the story, see: https://dustymuffin.wordpress.com/2007/07/01/luka-jantje-pieces-of-the-puzzle/—last accessed 24 June 2017.

60. Ernst N. Bennett, 'After Omdurman', *Contemporary Review*, January 1899, p. 29

61. Quoted in George H. Gilpin, *Art of Contemporary English Culture*, Basingstoke: Palgrave Macmillan, 1991, p. 6.

62. 'The Vote to Lord Kitchener', *Yorkshire Post and Leeds Intelligencer*, 6 June 1899.

63. 'Treatment of the Mahdi's body condemned', *Manchester Guardian*, 21 Feb. 1899.

64. Lord Kitchener to Queen Victoria, 7 March 1899, quoted in Philip Magnus, *Kitchener: Portrait of an Imperialist*, New York: E.P. Dutton & Co, 1968, p. 134.

65. Queen Victoria to Lord Kitchener, 24 March 1899, ibid.

66. Wilfred Scawen Blunt, *My Diaries: Being a Personal Narrative of Events 1888–1914*, New York: Alfred A. Knopf, 1922, diary entry for 27 April 1899, p. 320.

67. 'London Correspondence', *Freeman's Journal*, 24 Feb. 1899.

68. Winston S. Churchill, *The River War: An Historical Account of the Conquest of the Soudan*, 2 vols, London: Longmans, Green & Co., 1899, II, p. 196.

69. Official report cited in 'Bambaata's Head', *Dundee Courier*, 19 July 1906.

70. Ibid.

71. Ibid.

72. Harrison, *Dark Trophies*, pp. 71–2.

73. Hatch, D. Spencer, 'Beyond the End of the Road: Legs for knowledge', unpublished typescript, n. d. [c. 1962], University of Arizona, Tucson, Special Collections, Spencer Hatch Collection, Box 3. Thanks to Harald Fisher-Tiné for this reference.

74. Ibid.

75. Harrison, *Dark Trophies*, pp. 157–8.

76. Ibid., pp. 155–163

77. See for instance Jose E. Alvarez, *The Betrothed of Death: The Spanish Foreign Legion During the Rif Rebellion, 1920–1927*, Westport, Connecticut: Greenwood Press, 1995.

78. Harrison, *Dark Trophies*, pp. 129–53 and 165–85.

79. It should be noted, however, that the use of photography in either celebrating or documenting different forms of atrocities has a long his-

tory—in the American case dating back to lynching and colonial campaigns in the Philippines of the early twentieth century, see for instance Wood, *Lynching and Spectacle*. See also Vann, 'Of Pirates, Postcards, and Public Beheadings'.

80. William Morris, 'Notes on Passing Events', *The Commonweal*, 15 May 1886, p. 50.

EPILOGUE: THE DEAD BODIES OF THY SERVANTS

1. 'India: Arrival of refugees', *The Newcastle Courant*, 6 Nov. 1857.
2. George Smith, *Stephen Hislop: Pioneer Missionary & Naturalist in Central India from 1844 to 1863*, London, John Murray, 1888, pp. 185–186.
3. Letter from A. Gordon, 4 Aug. 1857, *Evangelical Repository*, p. 386.
4. J. Graham to S. Graham, 29 July 1857, *The Graham Indian Mutiny Papers*, p. 74.
5. Gordon, *Our India Mission*, p. 166.
6. J. Graham to A. Graham, 27 July 1857, *The Graham Indian Mutiny Papers*, p. 73; and W. Graham to D. Cullimore, 17 Nov. 1858, ibid., p. 88.
7. W. Graham to D. Cullimore, 27 Sept. 1857, *The Graham Indian Mutiny Papers*, p. 82.
8. 'The old imbecile King', as the historian John Kaye described Bahadur Shah, was found guilty of having conspired and waged war against the British and was exiled to Rangoon where he died in 1862, see Kaye, *A History of the Sepoy War*, III, p. 634. Most of Bahadur Shah's sons and male relatives had been summarily executed and the last surviving members of the Mughal dynasty reduced to abject poverty and consigned to oblivion, see Dalrymple, *The Last Mughal*.
9. Zahir Dehlavi, *Dastan i-Ghadr*, cited in Dalrymple, *The Last Mughal*, p. 387.
10. Kaye, *A History of the Sepoy War*, III, p. 638.
11. Kaye, *Lives of Indian Officers*, London: W.H. Allen, 1889, II, pp. 671–683.
12. Ibid., p. 688.
13. Rich, *The Mutiny in Sialkot*, p. 80.
14. Photographs currently in the possession of Catherine Nichol, the last remaining Scottish missionary in Sialkot.
15. Gordon, *Our India Mission*, pp. 163–4.
16. Ibid. See also 'Hormut Khan', *Allen's India Mail*, 8 Aug. 1862, p. 621. Interestingly, a shrine was later erected on the tomb of Hurmat Khan where apparently the prostitutes of Sialkot kept a light burning, see Gordon, *Our India Mission*, p. 164. See also Green, *Islam and the Army*, pp. 84–85.

17. http://www.dover-kent.com/lord-clyde-walmer.html—last accessed 28 July 2017.

18. The politics behind the lack of official interest are not entirely clear to me, but see for instance: http://indianexpress.com/article/india/india-others/the-black-hole/—last accessed 4 Aug. 2017.

BIBLIOGRAPHY

ARCHIVAL MATERIAL

National Archives of India (NAI), New Delhi:

Military Department
Thagi & Dakaiti
Political Department

British Library, Asian and African Studies Collections:

Kaye Papers, H/725(2),1057
Boards Collections
Home Miscellaneous

Royal Dragoon Guards Museum:

'Diary of William B. Armstrong 4th Dragoon Guards and 7th (Princess Royal) Dragoons'
'Diary of 7th Dragoon Guards 1851–1859'

University of Arizona

Hatch, D. Spencer, 'Beyond the End of the Road: Legs for knowledge', unpublished typescript, n. d. [c. 1962], University of Arizona, Tucson, Special Collections, Spencer Hatch Collection, Box 3.

PRIMARY MATERIAL PUBLISHED

Depositions taken at Cawnpore under the directions of Lieut-Colonel G. W. Williams (Allahabad, 1858).
Disorders Inquiry Committee, 1919–1920: Evidence, III: Amritsar (Calcutta, 1920), PP 1857–58 [2449]

BIBLIOGRAPHY

Forrest, George W. (ed.), *Selections from the Letters, Despatches and Other State Papers Preserved in the Military Department of the Government of India, 1857–58*, 4 vols, Calcutta Military Department Press, 1893.

Government Records,Vol. 7:1–2—Punjab: Mutiny Records (Correspondence), Lahore: Punjab Government Press, 1911.

Government Records, Vol. 8:1–2—Punjab: Mutiny Records (Reportse), Lahore: Punjab Government Press, 1911.

Harrison, A.T. (ed.) *The Graham Indian Mutiny Papers*, Belfast: Public Record Office of Northern Ireland, 1980.

Ibbetson, Denzil (ed.), *Gazetteer of the Sialkot District, 1883–4*, Lahore: Civil and Military Press, 1884

Metcalfe, C. T. (trans.), *Two Native Narratives of the Mutiny in Delhi*, Westminster: A. Constable and Co., 1898.

Nayar, P.K. (ed.), *The Trial of Bahadur Shah* (Hyderabad, Orient Longman, 2007)

Official Catalogue of the Royal United Service Museum, London: J.J. Keliher & Co., 1914.

The Letters of Indophilus to "The Times"—with additional notes, London: Longman, Brown, Green, Longman's, and Roberts [1858].

NEWSPAPERS & PERIODICALS

Allen's India Mail
Beverley and East Riding Recorder
Contemporary Review
Daily News
Dublin Daily Express
Dublin Evening Mail
Dublin Evening Post
Dundee Courier
Dunstable Chronicle, and Advertiser for Beds, Bucks & Herts
Eastbourne Gazette
Evangelical Repository
Freeman's Journal
Glasgow Herald
HouseholdWords
Illustrated London News
Isle ofWight Observer
Mayo Constitution
Stirling Observer
The Belfast Newsletter
The Commonweal

BIBLIOGRAPHY

The Delhi Gazette
The Derby Mercury
The Globe
The Homeward Mail
The London Gazette
The Manchester Times
The Morning Chronicle
The Morning Post
The Newcastle Courant
The Pall Mall Gazette
The Preston Guardian
The Sheffield & Rotherham Independent
The Sportsman
The Standard
The Times
Yorkshire Post and Leeds Intelligencer

WORKS PUBLISHED BEFORE 1947

Ball, Charles, *The History of the Indian Mutiny*, 2 vols, London: London Printing & Publishing Co., 1858.

Biographical and descriptive Sketches of the Distinguished Characters which compose the Unrivalled Exhibition and Historical gallery of Madame Tussaud and Sons, London: W.S. Johnson, 1866.

Blunt, Wilfred Scawen, *My Diaries: Being a Personal Narrative of Events 1888–1914*, New York: Alfred A. Knopf, 1922.

Bourchier, G., *Eight Month's Campaign Against the Bengal Sepoy Army, During the Mutiny of 1857*, London: Smith, Elder and Co., 1858.

Burton, Isabel, *The Life of Captain Sir Richard F. Burton*, London: Duckworth & Co., 1898.

Burton, Richard F., *Zanzibar: City, Island, and Coast*, 2 vols, London: Tinsley Brothers, 1872.

Butler, W., *Land of the Veda*, New York: Hunt & Eaton, 1895.

Cardew, F. G., *A Sketch of the Services of the Bengal Army*, Calcutta: Office of the Superintendent of Government Printing, 1909.

Cave-Browne, John, *The Punjab and Delhi in 1857: Being a Narrative of the Measures by which the Punjab was Saved and Delhi Recovered during the Indian Mutiny*, London: W. Blackwood and Sons, 1861.

Chilvers, Hedley A., *The Yellow Man Looks On: Being the Story of the Anglo-Dutch Conflict in Southern Africa and its Interest for the Peoples of Asia*, London: Cassell, 1933.

Cholmeley, R. E., *John Nicholson: The Lion of the Punjaub*, London: Andrew Melrose, 1908.

263

BIBLIOGRAPHY

Churchill, Winston S., *The River War: An Historical Account of the Conquest of the Soudan*, 2 vols, London: Longmans, Green & Co., 1899.

Conrad, Joseph, *Heart of Darkness*, orig. 1899, Norton Critical Edition, 3rd edition; New York: Norton, 1988.

Cooper, Frederic, *The Crisis in Punjab, from the 10th of May until the Fall of Delhi*, London: Smith, Elders and Co., 1858.

Cox, Robert, 'Remarks on the Skulls and Character of the Thugs' *Phrenological Journal and Miscellany*, 8 (1834), pp. 524–30.

Dodd, G., *The History of the Indian Revolt and of the Expeditions to Persia, China, and Japan, 1856–7–8*, London: W. and R. Chambers, 1859.

Duff, Alexander, *The Indian Rebellion: Its Causes and Results—In a Series of Letters*, London: s.n., 1858.

Dunlop, R.H.W., *Service and Adventure with the Khakee Ressalah, or Meerut Volunteer Horse, during the Mutinies of 1857–58*, London: s.n., 1858.

Fitzclarence, Lieutenant-Colonel [G.A.], *Journal of a Route across India, through Egypt, to England*, London: John Murray, 1819.

Gimlette, G.H.D., *A Postscript to the Records of the Indian Mutiny*, London: H.F. & G. Witherby, 1927.

Gordon, A., *Our India Mission: A Thirty Years' History of the India Mission of the United Presbyterian Church of North America*, Philadelphia: Andrew Gordon, 1886.

Hodson, G.H. (ed.), *Hodson of Hodson's Horse; or Twelve Years of a Soldier's Life in India*, London: Kegan Paul, Trench, & Co., 1883.

Jameson, James S., *The Story of the Rear Column of the Emin Pasha Relief Expedition*, London: R.H. Porter, 1890.

Kaye, J.W., *Lives of Indian Officers*, London: W.H. Allen, 1889.

———— *A History of the Sepoy War in India 1857–1858, 3 vols*, London: W.H. Allen & Co., 1876–80.

Kaye, John, and GB. Malleson (ed.), *Kaye's and Malleson's History of the Indian Mutiny, I-VI*, London: Allen, 1888–9.

Khan, Syud Ahmed, *The Causes of the Indian Revolt*, orig. 1858, Benares: Medical Hall Press, 1873.

Kipling, R., *Kim*, orig. 1901, Norton Critical Edition, New York: Norton, 2002.

———— 'The Lost Legion', *The Strand*, May, 1892.

Lancaster, Percival, *Chaloner of the Bengal Cavalry*, London: Blackie and sons Limited, 1915.

Leckey, Edward, *Fictions Connected with the Indian Outbreak of 1857 Exposed*, Bombay: Chesson and Woodhall, 1859.

Leeke, W., *The History of Lord Seaton's Regiment (The 52nd Light Infantry)*, London: Hatchard and Co., 1866.

Majendie, V.D., *Up Among the Pandies; or, A Year's Service in India*, London, 1859.

BIBLIOGRAPHY

Martin, R. Montgomery, *The Indian Empire: With a Full Account of the Mutiny of the Bengal Army*, London: London Printing and Publishing Co., 1861.

Maude, F.C., *Memories of the Mutiny*, London and Sydney: Remington and Company Limited, 1894.

Medley, J.G. Medley, *A Year's Campaigning in India, from March, 1857, to March, 1858*, London: W. Thacker and Co., 1858

Moorsom, W.S., *Historical Record of the Fifty-Second Regiment (Oxfordshire Light Infantry) from the year 1755 to the year 1858*, London: Richard Bentley, 1860.

Morris, William, 'Notes on Passing Events', *The Commonweal*, 15 May 1886, pp. 49–50.

Norman, H. W., *Delhi—1857: The Siege, Assault, and Capture*, London and Edinburgh: W. & R. Chambers, 1902.

Rich, Gregory, *The Mutiny in Sialkot—With a brief description of the Cantonment from 1852 to 1857*, Sialkot, 1924.

Roberts, Lord [F.S.], *Forty-One Years in India: From Subaltern to Commander-in-Chief*, London: Macmillan and Co., 1897.

Russell, W.H., *My Diary in India, in the year 1858–9*, 2 vols, London: Routledge, Warne, and Routledge, 1860.

Sherring, M.A., *The Indian Church During the Great Rebellion*, London: James Nisbet and Co., 1859.

Sleeman, W.H., *On the Spirit of Military Discipline in our Native Indian Army*, Calcutta: Bishop's College Press, 1841.

Smith, George, *Stephen Hislop: Pioneer Missionary & Naturalist in Central India from 1844 to 1863*, London, John Murray, 1888.

Spry, H.H., *Modern India: with Illustrations of the resources and Capabilities of Hindustan*, 2 vols, London: Whittaker & Co., 1837.

Stanley, Henry M., *How I Found Livingstone: Travels, Adventures, and Discoveries in Central Africa*, London: Sampson Low, Marston & Company, 1871.

———— *Coomassie and Magdala: The Story of Two British Campaigns in Africa*, New York: Harper & Brothers, 1874.

Stewart, C.E., *Through Persia in Disguise: With Reminiscences of the Indian Mutiny*, London: George Routledge & Sons, 1911.

Thompson, E.J., *The Other Side of the Medal*, London: The Hogarth Press, 1925.

Thorburn, S.S., *Bannu: Our Afghan Frontier*, London: Trübner & Co., 1876

———— *The Punjab in Peace and War*, Edinburgh: William Blackwood and Sons, 1904.

Verne, Jules, *The Steam House, part I: The Demon of Cawnpore & The Steam House, part II: Tigers and Traitors*, New York: Charles Scribner's Sons, 1881

Vibart, Edward, *The Sepoy Mutiny; as seen by a Subaltern from Delhi to Lucknow*, London: Smith Elder and Co., 1898.

Vijn, Cornelius, *Cetshwayo's Dutchman, Being the Private Journals of a White Trader*

BIBLIOGRAPHY

in Zululand during the British Invasion, London: Longman's, Green, and Co., 1880.

Wilberforce, R.G., *An Unrecorded Chapter of the Indian Mutiny*, London: John Murray, 1894.

Wilks, M., *Historical Sketches of the South of India, in an Attempt to Trace the History of Mysoor*, London: Longman, Hurst, Rees, Orme, and Brown, 1810.

Woodthorpe, R.G., *The Lushai Expedition, 1871–1872*, London: Hurst and Blackett, 1873.

Youngson, John F. W., *Forty Years of the Panjab Mission of the Church of Scotland, 1855–1895*, Edinburgh: R. & R. Clark, 1896.

WORKS PUBLISHED AFTER 1947

Alavi, Seema, *The Sepoys and the Company: Tradition and Transition in Northern India 1770–1830*, Delhi: Oxford University Press, 1995.

Alvarez, Jose E., *The Betrothed of Death: The Spanish Foreign Legion During the Rif Rebellion, 1920–1927*, Westport, Connecticut: Greenwood Press, 1995.

Anderson, Clare, *The Indian Uprising of 1857–8: Prisons, Prisoners and Rebellion*, London: Anthem, 2007.

Anderson, Clare, *Subaltern Lives: Biographies of Colonialism in the Indian Ocean World, 1790–1920*, Cambridge: Cambridge University Press, 2012.

Bandyopadhay, P., *Tulsi Leaves and the Ganges Water: The Slogan of the First Sepoy Mutiny at Barrackpore 1824*, Kolkata: K. P. Bagchi and Co., 2003.

Bank, Andrew, 'Of 'Native Skulls' and Noble Caucasians: Phrenology in Colonial South Africa', *Journal of Southern African Studies*, 22, 3 (Sept. 1996), pp. 387–403.

Bates, Crispin, 'Some Thoughts on the Representation and Misrepresentation of the Colonial South Asian Labour Diaspora', *South Asian Studies*, 33 (2017), pp. 7–22.

Bayly, C.A., *Empire & Information: Intelligence Gathering and Social Communication in India 1780–1870*, Cambridge: Cambridge University Press, 1996.

Bender, Cora, '"Transgressive Objects" in America: Mimesis and Violence in the Collection of Trophies during the Nineteenth Century Indian Wars', *Civil Wars*, 11, 4 (Dec. 2009), pp. 502–13.

Bhadra, Gautam, 'Four rebels of Eighteen-Fifty-Seven, Ranajit Guha (ed.), *Subaltern Studies 4*, Delhi: Oxford University Press, 1985, pp. 229–75, reprint: Guha, Ranajit and Spivak, G.C.(eds.), *Selected Subaltern Studies*, New York: 1988, pp. 129–75.

Blunt, Alison, 'Embodying war: British women and domestic defilement in the Indian 'Mutiny', 1857–8', *Journal of Historical Geography*, 26, 3 (2000), pp. 403–28.

Burrow, Merrick, 'The Imperial Souvenir: Things and Masculinity in H. Rider

BIBLIOGRAPHY

Haggard's *King Solomon's Mines* and *Allan Quartermain'*, *Journal of Victorian Culture*, 18, 1 (2013), pp. 72–92.

Chaudhuri, Nupur and Rajat Kanta Ray, '1857: Historical Works and Proclamations', in Crispin Bates (ed.), *Mutiny at the Margins: New Perspectives on the Indian Uprising of 1857 Volume VI: Perception, Narration and Reinvention: The Pedagogy and Historiography of the Indian Uprising*, London and New Delhi: Sage, 2014, pp. 19–30.

Choudhury, D.K.L., 'Sinews of Panic and the Nerves of Empire: The Imagined State's Entanglement with Information Panic, India 1880–1912', *Modern Asian Studies*, 38, 4 (Oct. 2004), pp. 965–1002.

Condos, Mark, *The Insecurity State: Punjab and the Making of Colonial Power in British India*, Cambridge: Cambridge University Press, 2017.

Cooter, Roger, *The Cultural Meaning of Popular Science: Phrenology and the Organization of Consent in Nineteenth-Century Britain*, Cambridge: Cambridge University Press, 1984.

Copland, Ian, 'Christianity as an Arm of Empire: The Ambiguous Case of India under the Company, c. 1813–1858', *The Historical Journal* (2006), pp. 1025–54.

Dalrymple, William, *The Last Mughal: The Fall of Delhi 1857*, London: Bloomsbury, 2006.

Darnton, Robert, *The Great Cat Massacre and Other Episodes in French Cultural History*, New York: Basic Books, 1984.

Dasgupta, Sabyasachi, *In Defence of Honour and Justice: Sepoy Rebellions in the Nineteenth Century*, New Delhi: Primus Books, 2015.

David, Saul, *The Indian Mutiny*, London: Viking, 2002.

Davis, Natalie Zemon, *The Return of Martin Guerre*, Cambridge, Mass.: Harvard University Press, 1983.

Devji, Faisal, 'The Mutiny to Come', *New Literary History*, 40, 2, India and the West (Spring 2009), pp. 411–430.

Dixon, Thomas, *Weeping Britannia: Portrait of a Nation in Tears*, Oxford: Oxford University Press, 2015.

Dubow, Saul, *A Commonwealth of Knowledge: Science, Sensibility, and White South Africa 1820–2000*, Cambridge: Cambridge University Press, 2006.

Edwardes, Michael, *Red Year: The Indian Rebellion of 1857*, London: Cardinal, 1975

Ferguson, Niall, *Empire: How Britain Made the Modern World*, London: Penguin, 2003.

Fischer-Tiné, Harald (ed.), *Anxieties, Fear and Panic in Colonial Settings: Empires on the Verge of a Nervous Breakdown*, Cham, Switzerland: Palgrave Macmillan, 2016.

Foucault, M., *Discipline and Punish: The Birth of the Prison*, London: Allen Lane, 1977.

BIBLIOGRAPHY

Fraser, George Macdonald, *Flashman and the Great Game*, London: Barrie and Jenkins, 1975.

Gilpin, George H., *Art of Contemporary English Culture*, Basingstoke: Palgrave Macmillan, 1991

Ginzburg, Carlo, *The Cheese and the Worms*, Baltimore: Johns Hopkins University Press, 1980.

Gott, R., *Britain's Empire: Resistance, Repression and Revolt*, London: Verso, 2011.

Green, N., *Islam and the Army in Colonial India: Sepoy Religion in the Service of Empire*, Cambridge: Cambridge University Press, 2009.

Guha, R., *Elementary Aspects of Peasant Insurgency in Colonial India*, Delhi: Oxford University Press, 1983.

———— 'The Prose of Counterinsurgency', *Subaltern Studies II*. Delhi, 1983, pp. 1–42. Reprint: Guha, Ranajit and Spivak, G.C.(eds.), *Selected Subaltern Studies*, New York: 1988, pp. 45–88.

Guha, Sumit, 'An Indian Penal Regime: Maharashtra in the Eighteenth Century', *Past & Present*, 147 (May 1995), pp. 101–26.

Harrison, Simon, *Dark Trophies: Hunting and the Enemy Body in Modern War*, New York: Berghahn, 2012.

Herbert, Christopher, *War of No Pity: The Indian Mutiny and Victorian Trauma*, Princeton, NJ: Princeton University Press, 2008.

Hoover, James W., *Men Without Hats: Dialogue, Discipline, and Discontent in the Madras Army 1806–1807*, Delhi: Manohar, 2007.

Hussain, Naser, *The Jurisprudence of Emergency: Colonialism and the Rule of Law*, Ann Arbor, MI: University of Michigan Press, 2003.

Hynd, Stacey, *Imperial Gallows: Capital Punishment, Violence and Colonial Rule in Britain's African Territories c. 1903–1968*, Oxford: Oxford University Press, 2007.

Kapila, Shruti, 'Race Matters: Orientalism and Religion, India and Beyond c. 1770—1880', *Modern Asian Studies*, 41, 3 (2007), pp. 471–513.

Kolff, Dirk H. A., *Naukar, Rajput and Sepoy: The Ethno-history of the Military Labour Market in Hindustan, 1450–1850*, Cambridge: Cambridge University Press, 1990.

Kostal, R.W., *A Jurisprudence of Power: Victorian Empire and the Rule of Law*, Oxford: Oxford University Press, 2008

Lalu, P., *The Deaths of Hintsa: Postapartheid South Africa and the Shape of Recurring Pasts*, Cape Town: HSRC Press, 2009.

Larson, Frances, *Severed: A History of Heads Lost and Found*, London: Granta, 2015.

Lovelace, Antonia, 'War Booty: Changing Contexts, Changing Displays— Asante 'Relics' from Kumasi, Acquired by the Prince of Wales's Own Regiment of Yorkshire in 1896', *Journal of Museum Ethnography*, 12 (May 2000), pp. 147–60

BIBLIOGRAPHY

MacDonald, Helen, *Human Remains: Dissection and Its Histories*, New Haven: Yale University Press, 2006.

Magnus, Philip, *Kitchener: Portrait of an Imperialist*, New York: E.P. Dutton & Co, 1968

Major, Andrea, *Sovereignty and Social Reform in India: British Colonialism and the Campaign Against Sati, 1830–60*, Abingdon: Routledge, 2010.

Metcalf, Thomas, *The Aftermath of the Revolt: India 1857–1870*, London: Oxford University Press, 1965.

Mukherjee, Rudrangshu, *Awadh in Revolt 1857–1858: A Study of popular Resistance*, 1st ed. 1983, New Delhi: Permanent Black, 2001.

———— *Mangal Pandey: Brave Martyr or Accidental Hero?*, New Delhi: Penguin Books India, 2005.

———— '"Satan let loose upon the earth": The Kanpur Massacres in India in the revolt of 1857' *Past and Present*, 128 (Aug. 1990), pp. 92–116.

———— 'The Kanpur Massacres in India in the Revolt of 1857: Reply', *Past & Present*, 142 (Feb. 1994) pp. 178–189.

Palmer, Patricia, *The Severed Head and the Grafted Tongue: Literature, Translation, and Violence in Early Modern Ireland*, Cambridge: Cambridge University Press, 2013

Paton, Diana, 'Punishment, Crime, and the Bodies of Slaves in Eighteenth-Century Jamaica', *Journal of Social History*, 34, 4 (2001), pp. 923–54.

Paxton, Nancy L., *Writing Under the Raj: Gender, Race and Rape in the British Colonial Imagination, 1830–1947*, New Brunswick: Rutgers U.P., 1999.

Peckham, R. (ed.), *Empires of Panic: Epidemics and Colonial Anxieties*, Hong Kong: Hong Kong University Press, 2015.

Peers, Douglas M., '"The Habitual Nobility of Being": British Officers and the Social Construction of the Bengal Army in the Early Nineteenth Century', *Modern Asian Studies*, 25, 3 (Jul., 1991), pp. 545–569.

Penfold-Mounce, Ruth, 'Consuming Criminal Corpses: Fascination with the Dead Criminal Body', *Mortality*, 15, 3 (2010), pp. 250–65.

Ray, Rajat Kanta Ray, *The Felt Community: Commonality and mentality before the emergence of Indian Nationalism*, Oxford, Oxford University Press, 2003.

Rizvi, S. A. A. and M. L. Bhargava (eds.), *Freedom Struggle in Uttar Pradesh*, Lucknow: Publications Bureau, 1957–61.

Roberts, Andrew, *A History of the English-Speaking Peoples since 1900*, London: Weidenfeld & Nicolson, 2006.

Robinson, Frances, *Angels of Albion: Women of the Indian Mutiny*, London: Viking, 1996.

Roque, Ricardo, *Headhunting and Colonialism: Anthropology and the Circulation of Human Skulls in the Portuguese Empire, 1870–1930*, Cambridge Imperial and Post-Colonial Studies, Basingstoke: Palgrave Macmillan, 2010.

———— 'Stories, Skulls, and Colonial Collections, *Configurations*, 19, 1 (Winter 2011), pp. 1–23.

BIBLIOGRAPHY

———— 'Mimesis and Colonialism: Emerging Perspectives on a Shared History', *History Compass*, 13,4 (April 2015), pp. 201–211.

Roy, Kaushik (ed.), *1857 Uprising: A Tale of an Indian Warrior (Translated from Durgadas Bandopadhyay's Amar Jivancharit)*, Delhi: Anthem Press, 2008.

Roy, Tapti, 'Visions of the Rebels: A study of 1857 in Bundelkhand', *Modern Asian Studies*, 27, 1, (Feb. 1993), pp. 205–228.

———— *The Politics of a Popular Uprising: Bundelkhand in 1857*, Delhi: Oxford University Press, 1994.

———— 'Rereading the Texts: Rebel Writings in 1857–58', in Sabyasachi Bhattacharya (ed.), *Rethinking 1857*, New Delhi: Orient Longman, 2007, pp. 221–36;

Safadi, Alison, '*From Sepoy to Subadar/Khvab-o-Khayal* and Douglas Craven Phillott', *The Annual of Urdu Studies*, 25 (2010), pp. 42–65.

Sharpe, Jenny, *Allegories of Empire: The Figure of Woman in the Colonial Text*, Minneapolis: University of Minneapolis Press, 1993.

Sherman, Taylor, 'Tensions of Colonial Punishment: Perspectives on Recent Developments in the Study of Coercive Networks in Asia, Africa and the Caribbean', *History Compass*, 7, 3 (2009), pp. 659–77.

Singh, Gajendra, 'Finding Those Men with Guts: The Ascription and Re-Ascription of Martial Identities in India after the Uprising', in Crispin Bates and Gavin Rand (eds.), *Mutiny at the Margins: New Perspectives on the Indian Uprising of 1857, Vol. 4: Military Aspects of the Indian Uprising*, London and New Delhi: Sage, 2013, pp. 113–34.

———— *The Testimonies of Indian Soldiers and the Two World Wars: Between Self and Sepoy*, London and New York: Bloomsbury, 2014.

Singha, Radhika, *A Despotism of Law: Crime and Justice in Early Colonial India*, New Delhi: Oxford University Press, 1998.

Stokes, Eric (C. A. Bayly ed.), *The Peasant Armed: The Indian Rebellion of 1857*, Oxford: Clarendon Press, 1986.

Stoler, Ann Laura, *Along the Archival Grain: Epistemic Anxieties and Colonial Common Sense*, Princeton; Oxford: Princeton University Press, 2009.

Tarlow, Sarah, 'Curious Afterlives: The Enduring Appeal of the Criminal Corpse', *Mortality*, 21, 3 (2016), pp. 210–28.

Taussig, Michael, *Shamanism, Colonialism, and the Wild Man: A Study in Terror and Healing*, Chicago, IL: University of Chicago Press, 1987.

Tharoor, Shashi, *Inglorious Empire: What the British Did to India*, London: Hurst, 2017.

Vann, Michael G., 'Of Pirates, Postcards, and Public Beheadings: The Pedagogic Execution in French Colonial Indochina, Historical Reflections/Reflexions Historiques, 36, 2 (2010), pp. 39–58.

Wagner, Kim A., *Thuggee—Banditry and the British in Early Nineteenth-Century India*, Cambridge Imperial and Post-Colonial Studies, Basingstoke: Palgrave, 2007.

BIBLIOGRAPHY

————— *The Great Fear of 1857: Rumours, Conspiracies and the Making of the Indian Uprising*, Oxford: Peter Lang Oxford, 2010.

————— 'Calculated to Strike Terror: The Amritsar Massacre and the Spectacle of Colonial Violence', *Past & Present*, 233, 1 (November, 2016), pp. 185–225.

————— 'Treading Upon Fires': The 'Mutiny'-Motif and Colonial Anxieties in British India', *Past & Present*, 218, 1 (February, 2013), pp. 159–97.

————— 'The Marginal Mutiny: The New Historiography of the Indian Uprising of 1857', *History Compass*, 9, 10 (Oct. 2011), pp. 760–66.

————— 'Confessions of a Skull: Phrenology and Colonial Knowledge in early nineteenth-century India', *History Workshop Journal*, 69 (Spring, 2010), pp. 28–51.

————— '"In Unrestrained Conversation": Approvers and the Colonial Ethnography of Crime in nineteenth-century India', in Roque, Ricardo and Kim A. Wagner (eds.) *Engaging Colonial Knowledge: Reading European Archives in World History*, Cambridge Imperial and Post-Colonial Studies Series, Basingstoke: Palgrave, 2011), pp. 135–62.

————— (co-written with Gavin Rand), 'Recruiting the 'Martial Races': Identities and Military Service in Colonial India', *Patterns of Prejudice*, 46, 3–4 (2012), pp. 232–54.

————— 'Seeing Like a Soldier: The Amritsar Massacre and the Politics of Military History', in Martin Thomas and Gareth Curless (ed.), *Decolonization and Conflict: Colonial Comparisons and Legacies*, London: Bloomsbury, 2017, pp. 23–37.

Ward, Andrew, *Our Bones are Scattered: the Cawnpore Massacre and the Mutiny of 1857*, London: John Murray, 1996.

Ward, Richard (ed.), *A Global History of Execution and the Criminal Corpse*, Basingstoke: Palgrave 2015.

Webb, Denver A., 'War, Racism, and the Taking of Heads: Revisiting Military Conflict in the Cape Colony and Western Xhosaland in the Nineteenth Century', *The Journal of African History*, 56, 1 (March 2015), pp. 37–55.

White, Luise, 'The Traffic in Heads: Bodies, Borders and the Articulation of Regional Histories', *Journal of Southern African Studies*, 23, 2 (1997), pp. 325–38.

Winnans, Edgar V., 'The Head of the King: Museums and the Path to Resistance', *Comparative studies in Society and History*, 36, 2 (April 1994), pp. 221–41.

Wood, Amy Louise, *Lynching and Spectacle: Witnessing Racial Violence in America, 1890–1940*, Chapel Hill: The University of North Carolina Press, 2009.

van Wyhe, John, *Phrenology and the Origins of Victorian Scientific Naturalism*, Aldershot: Ashgate, 2004.

Yang, Anand A., 'Disciplining "Natives": Prisons and Prisoners in Early Nineteenth Century India, *South Asia*, 10, 2 (1987), 29–46.

BIBLIOGRAPHY

UNPUBLISHED

Smith, Jacob Ramsay, 'Imperial Retribution: The hunt for Nana Sahib and rebel leaders in the aftermath of the Indian "Mutiny" of 1857', unpublished PhD thesis, Queen Mary, University of London, 2017.

Willcock, Sean, 'The Aesthetics of Imperial Crisis: Image Making and Intervention in British India, c. 1857–1919', unpublished PhD thesis, University of York, 2013.

INDEX

INDEX

INDEX

INDEX

278

INDEX

Enfield rifles, 15, 37–50, 58–63, 74, 75, 79, 139
Eurasians, 125, 126, 167
Evangelicalism, 90
executions, 152–60, 175–89
  of 26th BNI (Ajnala), 157–8, 159
  of 35th BNI (Lahore), 89–90
  of 55th BNI (Peshawar), 90, 178, 180, 181, 183
  by cannon, xix, xx, 3, 5–6, 89–90, 175–89, 204, 253
  and caste, 177, 252
  and divine powers, 178
  of *Rissaldar* and jail guards, 151–2, 154
  of servants, 152–3
  and Sikh levies, 152, 157
  of Thugs, 177–8, 179, 194, 195
  at Trimmu Ghat, 145, 147–8
Eyre, Edward John, 203–4, 215

fakirs, 76, 165, 166
Fan people, 205
Farquharson, Colonel G., 15, 105, 106–7, 124, 128
Fashoda Incident (1898), 210
Fatehgarh, Punjab, 48
Ferguson, Niall, 8
firman, 82
Fitzgerald, C. M., 85
floggings, 56–7, 101, 152–3, 165
foodstuff, pollution of, 48, 59–60, 74, 78
Fraser, Simon, 31
French nuns, 13, 29, 95, 98, 120–21, 125, 126
Friend of India, 168
From Sepoy to Subedar, 7
Frontier Wars (1779–1879), 196
fugitives, 161–73
funeral rites, 20, 57, 147, 176, 178–9

furlough, 17–18, 42

gallows, 151, 156
Ganges river, 16, 20–21, 22
Ganges, ship, 4
Gangetic Plain, 13, 16
ganja, 141
Garrard, Mr, 112, 113
General Enlistment Order (1856), 22–3, 26
Gholab Singh, Raja of Jammu, 148
'going native', 121
Golgotha, 206
Gordon, Andrew, 6–7, 29, 30–34, 35, 70–74, 218
  on Abdul Razak, 114
  on Bishop, death of, 123
  church, building of, 219
  and climate, 30, 72
  on communications cut off, 65
  on destruction of Sialkot, 150, 151
  execution of Alum Bheg, 186–7, 188–9
  funds, loss of, 72, 85
  on Graham, death of, 110, 120, 243
  on Hurmat Khan, 101
  on Hunters, death of, 119–20
  Hunters, relations with, 29, 86, 91
  on killings, 128
  Lahore, evacuation to, 72, 85–7, 91, 94
  on Plassey conspiracy, 73–4
  on plundering, 151
  preaching, 51–2, 53, 69
  on *sepoys*, 71
  servants, suspicion of, 32
  Silas, illness and death of, 31, 72, 85, 149
  on stiff upper lip, 68

279

INDEX

INDEX

INDEX